Vicki Audette's BARGAIN HUNTER'S GUIDE

You may order single copies from the publisher. Send the cover price plus $1.00 for postage and handling to:

Waldman House Press
525 North Third Street
Minneapolis, Minnesota 55401

Library of Congress Cataloging in Publication Data

Audette, Vicki.
Vicki Audette's Bargain hunter's guide to the Twin Cities.

Includes index.
1. Shopping—Minnesota—Saint Paul—Directories.
2. Shopping—Minnesota—Minneapolis—Directories.
3. Saint Paul (Minn.)—Stores, shopping centers, etc.—Directories. 4. Minneapolis (Minn.)—Stores, shopping centers, etc.—Directories. I. Title. II. Title: Bargain hunter's guide to the Twin Cities.
TX335.A93 1984 380.1'45'0009776579 84-19577

ISBN 0-931674-06-9

Editor: Kathe Grooms
Cover and text design: Nancy MacLean
Cover art and production: Mike Tuminelly

First Printing October 1984
Printed in the United States of America

Contents

What These Tags Mean . . .

 = THINGS TO WATCH FOR

= BEST DAYS, MONTHS, SEASONS

 = EARLY BIRD GETS YOU-KNOW-WHAT

 = TIPS WORTH REMEMBERING

 = CALL FOR INFORMATION

= MAILING LISTS

 = EXTRA SAVINGS AND SPECIAL DEALS

 = BRIGHT IDEA

ABOUT THE AUTHOR

In the *Minneapolis Tribune,* Vicki Audette was dubbed a "professional cheapskate." In *Twin Cities Magazine,* Margaret Morris called her "an intrepid bargain hunter." According to Vicki, she's both—and more. Her love for bargain hunting started with her pre-teen addiction to Nancy Drew mysteries, which founded her sleuth's interest in hunting up facts. She later parlayed this skill into a writing and television reporting career. She loves nothing more than relentlessly pursuing the stories behind the bargain, then playing back her moneysaving discoveries to her hometown viewers.

The author of *Dress Better for Less,* she's also the producer and talent of "The Bargain Hunter" feature on KSTP TV's Good Company Show and a public speaker on the subject of bargain hunting. Currently living in St. Paul, she shares space with two sons, a visiting dog and a cache of bargains.

INTRODUCTION

*Discovery consists of seeing what everybody has seen
and thinking what nobody has thought.*

—Albert Szent-Gyorgyi

Notes of a Bargain Hunter

I know the heart of the hunter. Whether you have a million or just loose change, you can't escape the rush that comes from finding a good deal. Even the shopping sage, Stanley Marcus, former owner of the fancy Nieman Marcus stores, commented to me, "The days of the mass consumer paying full retail price are over."

Happily, the Twin Cities are fast becoming a prime bargain-hunting ground. Off-price stores and malls are finally gaining a strong foothold in Minnesota. With the off-pricers' influx and consumers' consistent demands to buy at prices below retail, regular retailers have been forced to offer better markdowns, earlier in each season. This retail revolution means good news for shoppers: there are more bargains to choose from! It also means you need all the information you can get in order to find good deals and not miss the best discount prices and values in town.

That is where this guide book comes in. It is designed to keep you moneysaving miles ahead in the bargain hunting game. With it, you won't experience "shopper's guilt" when you find out the identical item was selling somewhere else for less. You will be the most well-informed comparison shopper in town, and nobody will get better bargains.

I you've seen me on KSTP TV's Good Company show, you know that I share all my inside shopping tips—and have I got tips to share! I've gleaned many from the best hunters among you. My background as a television producer gives me an edge in asking the tough questions and really researching a bargain source. My dream was to work for the 60 Minutes Show, on national TV. But instead, I've put my snooping talents to work for you.

With this book, you're going to discover places you never even knew existed, from fancy to funky. You'll save more money than you ever imagined possible. Since I've tried to respect the interests of all types of bargain hunters, there isn't one among you that isn't going to find places that fit your personality or budget. So, no matter what you're searching for—clothes, food, jewelry, furniture, toys, services, even toilet tank tops—you can find what you want quickly (and cheaply) with this book. Take it along and let me be your shopping guide.

Best of Bargains,

Vicki

P.S.: I have no affiliation with any of the stores I reviewed. No one paid to be in this book, nor were my comments subject to store approval.

ACKNOWLEDGEMENTS

I would like to thank all the Twin Cities bargain hunters who were instrumental in urging me to write this book. Special thanks are due to my researchers, Dave Rarick, Chris Drees, Nancy Stesin, Annette Wuertz, Dawn La Favor, and loving acknowledgment to my sons, Jim and Dave Audette.

PART I

CLOTHES AND ACCESSORIES

CHAPTER 1

WOMEN'S CLOTHES

Working as a bargain bloodhound on the wardrobe shopping trail, I've run the gamut of off-price rag merchants. I've found there are *plenty* of places to save money on clothes for men, women, and children. In the chapters of this section, you'll travel from stores located in Outlet Malls to obscure, tucked-away shops. The atmosphere varies from elegant to frankly shabby, and the price ranges vary accordingly.

No matter what clothing you need, you're going to find it here at a reduced price. In researching these chapters, I approached all stores expecting the usual retail bargains, but digging for more. Yes, you're going to buy at "below retail prices" right in the beginning of a season...but I wanted to give you the insider's tips, too. Whenever I could, I included information about the store's clearance months, the seasonal markdown times, the best days to shop, and the sources of the off-price goods. I tried to spare you any unpleasant surprises: be sure to check the policies listed for each store. Being prepared leaves you ready for the fun of the hunt.

Off-Price Clothes Shopping Strategies

- Phone stores first when you're looking for a specific item. Use this chapter to help you comparison shop between the off-price retailers and the regular retailers.
- Sharpen your sense of current clothing styles. Flip through fashion magazines to save yourself time, because often you will find discontinued styles hanging among the current ones. You should expect to save more on last year's styles.
- Be sure to check the merchandise carefully before you buy. If an item is marked irregular, don't automatically shy away. The savings may justify a minor flaw—just know what you're buying.
- Shop stores frequently in the beginning of each buying season (March and April for spring fashions; August and September for fall and holiday wear; October and November for cruisewear). You'll find the best selection of off-price merchandise at these times.
- Check stores for coat bargains in July at "pre-season discounts" and for kids' back to school clothing in August.

Women's Clothes

LOEHMANN'S

5141 W. 98th St.
Loehmann's Plaza
Bloomington
PHONE: 835-2510
HOURS: Mon.-Sat., 10 a.m.-5:30 p.m.; Wed.-Fri., 10 a.m.-9 p.m.; Sun., noon-5 p.m.
POLICIES: No credit cards; checks accepted; no returns; lay-by: 1/3 down, 1 week to pick up.

In the Twenties, New Yorker Frieda Loehmann, the store's founder, began her Seventh Avenue forays in designer workrooms. Coming in with ready cash to buy designers' samples and overruns, she was soon labeled "the undertaker." She stocked her famous Brooklyn store with her finds and sold them at 50% off retail. Today, Loehmann's has 69 stores in 25 states and still buys up women's size 4 to 16 designer samples and overstocks. Except now, buyers fill out their stock with many off-price name brands. The store is packed with suits, dresses, blouses, slacks, coats and accessories, all discounted 30% to 50% (often a lot more).

To some shoppers, Loehmann's designer bargains seem expensive, but for those who peruse the pages of *Vogue* and *Glamour*, they are exciting treasures. Anne Kleins and Calvins appear regularly, particularly in the Back Room. But beware...this place can be addictive. One shopper reported, "My husband thinks it is our favorite charity."

Don't bring your credit cards; it's cash or check only. There's a communal dressing room, so don your best underwear. Some busy shoppers go right to the dressing room and check the discards rack, believing the best selection winds up there. Examine everything carefully and be sure to try on items before you buy, because there are no returns and some items are irregular.

There are more secrets hidden in a Loehmann's price tag than even this bargain hunter can reveal—honest. Although this store still cuts out the clothing labels, you can recognize many brands just from the corners that are left. But you'll find letters on the price tag that can tip you off. Look for these (they do change periodically):

ADOLPHO	AD	PAULINE TRIGERE	IX
HALSTON	HAL	ABE SCHRADER	SCH
ALBERT NIPON	PON	HARVE BERNARD	FEB
ADRI	ADR	ALBERT CAPRARO	JET
BONNIE CASHIN	HYD	PERRI ELLIS	PER
RALPH LAUREN	RL	CALVIN KLEIN	GJG
ANNE KLEIN	AK	OSCAR DE LA RENTA	ORC

Since shipments arrive daily, there's really no best time to shop. If merchandise hangs on the racks for six weeks, it's reviewed for a markdown. After the first markdown there are additional reductions about every two weeks. Ultra suede, however, seldom passes the markdown review.

The successful Loehmann's shopper stops by frequently (even three times a week). This keeps her up to the minute with the latest arrivals. She has a sharp eye for current styles, but most of all, she has a sense of adventure. She never knows when a pass through the racks will uncover a winner.

When you see a long narrow blue ticket hanging separately, it means there is a companion item somewhere in the store. This matching piece could be in a different size, but you may want to check it out.

In August each year, Loehmann's has a fall preview day. Women line up for hours before the doors open. If you can handle the crowds, you may want to go just for the excitement...but nothing is marked down more than usual. Furs come into the store for about two or three weeks after the fall preview.

LE SHOP

926 Nicollet Mall
Downtown Minneapolis
PHONE: 332-5700
HOURS: Mon.-Sat., 9 a.m.-5:30 p.m.
POLICIES: Credit cards—VISA, Master, Shoppers, American Express; checks accepted; returns: within 3 days; lay-by: 30 days.

Le Shop takes the bite off women's couture fashions by offering a 20% to 60% savings on high-ticket designer items (the actual outlay may thus be higher than some bargain hunters would expect). In passing this sumptuous downtown Minneapolis location, you wouldn't suspect it houses an off-price retailer. On entering, you're still not sure. The surroundings contradict all your "no frills" conditioning. Italian and French imports hang discreetly. The discount percentage and names on labels vary, since much is dependent on how "right" owner Hannah Levine can buy each season. Sizes range from 4 to 16, and the selection may be limited, so if you find it, buy it. You probably won't see it in the store again.

There are two clearance sales each year, right after Christmas and right after the 4th of July.

When you're buying women's clothes made in Europe, sometimes it really throws you off when you see an unfamiliar size number. This chart will save you the guessing time.

WOMEN'S EUROPEAN SIZES EQUAL THESE AMERICAN SIZES

1 or 36	=	4 or 6
2 or 38	=	8
3 or 40	=	10
4 or 42	=	12
5 or 44	=	14
6 or 46	=	16

THE SIDE DOOR

539 E. Lake St.
Wayzata
PHONE: 473-1937
HOURS: Mon.-Sat. 10 a.m.-5 p.m.
POLICIES: Credit cards—VISA, Master; checks accepted; no lay-by; returns: exchange only.

The Side Door is cautiously tucked away in downtown Wayzata. The store has high style women's designer fashions (size 4-14). The savings are always 20% below retail—sometimes more. At the beginning of each season, shipments arrive weekly. Everything is bought directly from designer's manufacturers. *No* closeouts, irregulars, or last year's styles here!

Here's a list of labels that will help you recognize a designer's *lower-priced collection.* Many have some of the familiar touches that add big money to their more expensive designs.

- ANNE KLEIN II
- ACTIVEWEAR *from Calvin Klein*
- BEENE BAG *from Geoffrey Beene*
- ROUGHWEAR *from Ralph Lauren*
- BODY RAPPINGS *from Adri*
- BLASSPORT *from Bill Blass*
- EXECUTIVE DRESS *from Albert Nipon*
- TYGER-TYGER *from Ron Leal*
- MISS O *from Oscar De La Renta*

THE WOOL-N-SHOP

101-27th Ave. S.E.
Minneapolis
PHONE: 331-1813
HOURS: Mon.-Fri., 9:30 a.m. to 5:30 p.m.; Sat., 10 a.m.-4 p.m.
POLICIES: Credit cards—VISA, Master, Shoppers; checks accepted; 45-day lay-by if purchase over $45; returns: cash or credit.

Manager David Becker runs this shop for a wool cooperative, and prices are always 20% off regular retail. The quality is excellent, with no irregulars or seconds. The shop carries Pendleton, Austin Hill, Villager, Crazy Horse sweaters (lots of them), John Henry and more. There really is a mix of merchandise here. John Henry blouses range $24 to $30; women's suits average $149; men's Pendleton sportscoats average $110; Crazy Horse sweaters range from $21 to $30. They also have women's Pendleton coats, wool socks, mittens and scarves.

There are also good buys for home sewers. Look for 15 to 20 different 100% wool color choices, all first quality. You can usually find 8 to 15 yards in each style. Pendleton woolens, 60" wide are $18.89/yard.

The second week of September and the third week in March you will get an additional 20% to 25% off on the current season's merchandise. These two sales are great and clearance sales are held in July and January.

HIT OR MISS

Southdale Square
2928 W. 66th St.
Richfield
PHONE: 869-9957

Crystal Shopping Center
133 Willow Bend Road
Crystal
PHONE: 537-9785

Burnsville Shopping Center
2182 Burnsville Center
Burnsville
PHONE: 435-9906

HOURS: Mon-Fri., 10 a.m.-9 p.m.; Sat., 10 a.m.-6 p.m.; Sun., noon-5 p.m.

Har Mar Mall
2100 N. Snelling
Roseville
HOURS: Mon.-Fri., 10 a.m.-9 p.m.; Sat., 9:30 a.m.-5:30 p.m.; Sun., noon-6 p.m.

Ridgehaven Mall
13107 Ridgedale Rd.
Minnetonka
PHONE: 545-9880
HOURS: Mon.-Fri., 10 a.m.-9 p.m.; Sat., 9:30 a.m.-6 p.m.; Sun., noon-6 p.m.

Downtown Minneapolis
900 Nicollet Mall
PHONE: 332-2003
HOURS: Mon.-Fri., 9 a.m.-6 p.m.; Sat., 9:30 a.m.-6 p.m.; CLOSED SUNDAY.

POLICIES: Credit cards—Master, VISA, Shoppers and American Express; lay-by: 30 days; returns: cash or credit.

Hit or Miss marks down 20% to 50% below regular retail prices. They carry first quality in-season goods and specialize in women's career fashions, sportswear, and evening wear, with sizes ranging from 3 to 14. The name brands are Calvin Klein, Kathy Hardwick, Albert Nipon, Harve Benard, Evan Picone, and more. As part of a national chain, stores get their shipments weekly. In July, they have their pre-season Winter Coat sale with markdowns of 40% to 60%; and at the end of July and beginning of August, they have an all-season consolidation sale with some very good buys. Watch for winter clearance in January and February.

The best day to shop for new merchandise and markdown changes is Wednesday.

CONNIE'S

3133 S. Hennepin
Minneapolis
PHONE: 827-5609
HOURS: Mon. & Thurs., 9 a.m.-8 p.m.; Tues.-Wed., Fri.-Sat., 9 a.m.-5 p.m.
POLICIES: Credit cards—Master and VISA; checks accepted; lay-by: 30 days; returns in 5 days, cash; 10 days, store credit only.

Connie's is unique and fun. Some of the stock is priced at regular retail prices, but the majority is marked 30% to 60% below regular retail. Sometimes I've run into one exciting designer piece that is discounted well and other times only the items priced at regular retail interest me. That's the temptation you face here.

The shop is located in a large, quaint house with easy parking in the back. Service is the specialty—Connie even offers special treats from 11:30 a.m. to 1:00 p.m., in case you're missing lunch. You'll always notice a major European brand name in samples here, sized 6 to 10. The other designer brands are women's sizes 4 to 14. For the working woman, they carry a private label tropical wool worsted suit that is good quality and competitively priced at $155 with other suit discounters. But you don't want to miss the Bargain Room on the second floor. If anything is slightly damaged or a separates collection gets broken up, it gets marked down and moved there.

Connie's puts on two rock-bottom clearance sales each year, in June and January. Everything is marked *an additional* 40% off, no matter what it was selling for before.

WINDFALL

Knollwood Mall
8332 Hwy. 7
St. Louis Park
PHONE: 933-1651
HOURS: Mon.-Fri., 10 a.m.-9 p.m.; Sat., 10 a.m.-5:30 p.m.; Sun., noon-5 p.m.

POLICIES: Credit cards—VISA, Master, Shoppers and American Express; checks accepted; lay-by: 30 days; returns: cash or credit in 10 days.

Windfall is a pleasant place to shop; the name brands are very good (Liz Claiborne, Prestige, Country Suburban); but the discount in season is only 15% below regular retail. The designer items vary, depending on what the owner can buy "right" for spring or fall. Markdowns are made as a season progresses, however. The emphasis here is on service, with clothes geared for the working woman's wardrobe, as well as casual weekend and evening wear.

CLASSIC FASHION

Ridgehaven Mall
(Across from Ridgedale Center)
Minnetonka
PHONE: 544-0666
HOURS: Mon.-Fri., 10 a.m.-9 p.m.; Sat., 9:30 a.m.-6 p.m.; Sun., noon-5 p.m.

Har Mar Mall
Roseville
PHONE: 631-1631
HOURS: Mon.-Fri., 10 a.m.-9 p.m.; Sat., 9:30 a.m.-5:30 p.m.; Sun., noon-5 p.m.

POLICIES: Credit cards—VISA, Master and Shoppers; checks accepted; no lay-by; returns: within one week, cash or exchange.

Classic Fashion carries women's size 4 to 16 in coats, blouses, skirts, sweaters, suits, dresses—a nice selection of merchandise. All the clothes are first quality, in season, moderate to better quality priced fashion. The average off-price savings in the beginning of a season is 25% to 30%. Designer names will vary, depending on what the owner can stock.

Buy what you like, because you probably won't find it here again. Fall merchandise gets into the store in July and August, and spring and summer fashions in March, cruisewear in November and December. Shop early during these times for the best selection. The Ridgehaven store has the largest array of clothes.

Watch for a good coat sale in October, when you'll get an additional 20% off.

HUNT & PECK

932 Nicollet Ave.
Downtown Minneapolis
PHONE: 339-7969
HOURS: Mon. & Thurs., 9:30 a.m.-7 p.m.; Tues.-Wed., Fri.-Sat., 9:30 a.m.-5:30 p.m.

Highland Village Shopping Center
2040 Ford Parkway
St. Paul
PHONE: 690-3069
HOURS: Mon.-Fri., 10 a.m.-9 p.m.; Sat., 9:30 a.m.-5:30 p.m.; Sun., noon-5 p.m.

309 Southdale Center
Edina
PHONE: 920-1662
HOURS: Mon.-Fri., 10 a.m.-9:30 p.m.; Sat., 9:30-6 p.m.; Sun., noon-5 p.m.

Knollwood Mall
8332 Hwy. 7
St. Louis Park
PHONE: 938-7317
HOURS: Mon.-Fri., 10 a.m.-9 p.m.; Sat., 10 a.m.-5:30 p.m.; Sun., noon-5 p.m.

POLICIES: Credit cards—Master, VISA, Shoppers and American Express; checks accepted; lay-by: 90 days; returns: cash or credit.

Hunt & Peck runs clearances for the Peck & Peck stores. Stock includes blazers, skirts, suits, sweaters and blouses—any upbeat item that just didn't strike the fancy of the Peck & Peck woman at its full retail price. Some of the merchandise may be manufacturers' overstocks; you will find some clothes out of season. But the longer something has been around, the more money you're going to save (up to 85% off retail). Most of the stock is reduced at least 20% to 25%. Women's sizes range from 4 to 14. Look for good name brands: Prophecy, John Meyer, Donna Morgan Dresses, Regatta Sportswear, and Gentry. If you're lucky, you'll find something on the first pass through

through here. More than likely, though, you will have to hit this place several times.

The largest store is the one at Southdale Center in Edina.

BRAUN'S OUTLET STORES

Coon Rapids Family Mall
2899 Coon Rapids Boulevard
Coon Rapids
PHONE: 421-6294
HOURS: Mon.-Fri., 10 a.m.-9 p.m.; Sat., 10 a.m.-5:30 p.m.; CLOSED SUNDAY.

Eden Prairie Center
1224 Eden Prairie Center
Eden Prairie
PHONE: 944-6747
HOURS Mon.-Fri., 10 a.m.-9 p.m.; Sat., 10 a.m.-6 p.m.; Sun., noon-5 p.m.

Wards Terrace Mall
Robbinsdale
529-9164
HOURS: Mon.-Fri., 10 a.m.-6 p.m.; Sat., 9:30 a.m.-5:30 p.m.; Sun., noon-5 p.m.

POLICIES: Credit cards—Braun's, Master, VISA, Shoppers and American Express; lay-by: 90 days; returns: cash or credit.

Braun's outlets carry clearance items from their regular stores, some of it out of season. The current style goods are special purchase buys—they're marked with a yellow ticket. And then there's what is called the "special value" merchandise, which is what you'll find at any of their retail stores (turtlenecks for $8.99-$9.99). It's all women's (sizes 6-14) and junior's (sizes 5-13) clothes. You can find some great buys here for teens. Braun's Ardee Simpson jeans are usually available. The markdowns at the outlets always range from 20% to 50%.

Sometime around Christmas they have a sale that is wild but good, so get on the mailing list.

If you can't make it to one of these three main outlets, check out the smaller outlet back rooms in most of the stores.

LANCER STORE'S OUTLET CENTERS

Eden Prairie Center
8251 Flying Cloud Drive
Eden Prairie
PHONE: 944-6766
HOURS: Mon.-Fri., 10 a.m.-9 p.m.; Sat., 10 a.m.-6 p.m.; Sun., noon-5 p.m.

Loehmann's Plaza
98th and Normandale
Bloomington
PHONE: 831-0114
HOURS Mon.-Tues., Fri., 10 a.m.-8 p.m.; Wed.-Thurs., 9:30 a.m.-5:30 p.m.; Sun., noon-5 p.m.

Phalen Shopping Center
Johnson Parkway and Magnolia
St. Paul
PHONE: 774-0182
HOURS: Mon.-Fri., 9:30 a.m.-9:00 p.m.; Sat., 9:30 a.m.-5:30 p.m.; Sun., 1:00-5:00 p.m.

Wards Terrace Mall
35th and West Broadway
Robbinsdale
PHONE: 588-3883
HOURS: Mon.-Fri., 10 a.m.-9 p.m.; Sat., 9:30 a.m.-5:30 p.m.; Sun., noon-5 p.m.

L. A. Clothing
Southtown Shopping Center
I494 and Penn Ave.
Bloomington
PHONE: 881-6364
HOURS: Mon.-Fri., 10 a.m.-9 p.m.; Sat., 9:30 a.m.-5:30 p.m.; Sun., 1-5 p.m.

POLICIES: Credit cards—Master, VISA and Shoppers; checks accepted; lay-by available; returns: cash or credit.

Lancer's clears out men's, women's, and junior's clothing at these outlets. (L.A. Clothing is actually another Lancer's outlet, despite its name.) The markdown is 20-50% below retail and sometimes even higher. Often you'll find winter clothes in the summer and summer clothes in the winter. But if you don't mind buying off-season, you're going to get some good savings here. You *can* hit on a woman's suit right in season or a man's sportcoat, too. It just depends on what sizes are available that day. There are also basement clearance rooms available in the Hub Shopping Center and Downtown Hopkins stores.

WOMEN'S SAMPLES

The influx of all the off-price discounters in the Twin Cities has overshadowed some of the good bargains to be found in sample shops. Clothing salesmen have to buy their samples and when they're finished, they turn a profit by selling their line to sample shops. Often these samples are made better than the product that eventually goes to the retailer. Some fashion lemons and leftovers will turn up, and on occasion you'll run across a sample that was made in haste. The real advantage, however, is that buying samples gets you a price break and a jump on each season's merchandise. Most sample shops will have spring and summer clothes in their stores by January and February, fall clothes in June and July, and cruisewear in October. The only problem is that not all of us wear the popular women's sample size—8 or 10.

Each store listed below has some ranges in size and may be worth checking out for the automatic *early* savings, but bear in mind that selection can be very limited.

RECIE'S

1975 Seneca Rd., Hwy. 13
Eagan
PHONE: 454-7720
HOURS: Mon. & Thurs., 10 a.m.-9 p.m.; Tues.-Wed., Fri.-Sat., 10 a.m.-5:30 p.m.
POLICIES: Credit cards—Master, VISA and Shoppers; lay-by: 6 weeks; returns: exchange for store merchandise in 7 days.

Recie's has been known in the Twin Cities for women's samples, supplied by over 100 salesmen, but Recie Holland also buys from some very good manufacturers. You'll find Howard Wolf, John Meyer, Jones of New York, Izod, Joyce, Junior House, Gloria Vanderbilt, and more. The discount is 30% to 50% below retail, with the best markdown on the samples in sizes 5 to 12. Her fall line comes into the store in May and June and her spring items in October and November. Most will be kept in the back room until the buying season gets closer. But if you want a preview, Recie is more than willing to oblige.

Get on Recie's mailing list for sale notices. She has two big ones each year, after Christmas and after July 4th.

CAROLE'S SAMPLE HUTCH

2726 E. 50th St.
Minneapolis
PHONE: 721-1500
HOURS: Mon.-Fri., 10 a.m.-5:30 p.m.; Sat., 10 a.m.-5 p.m.
POLICIES: Credit cards—Master, VISA and Shoppers; lay-by 30 days; refunds: exchange only.

Carole's has been open for 10 years and carries women's and juniors' sizes 5 to 16 (best selection is sizes 5-10). Children's sizes are infant, 9 to 24 months (except no 18 months), 2 to 6X, 7 to 14, and a good selection of pre-teen sizes. You'll find lots of sportswear in good name brands: Calvin Klein, Russ, Jordache, Pandora, Polly Flinders, Buster Brown—all at 33% to 60% below retail.

Be sure to get on Carole Bloom's mailing list for special sales where you will save an *additional* 30% to 50%.

SAMPLE RACK

4313 Upton Ave. S.
Minneapolis
PHONE: 922-3828
HOURS: Tues.-Sat.. 10 a.m.-5 p.m.
POLICIES: Credit cards—Master, VISA and Shoppers; checks accepted; 25% down and will lay by for 12 months; returns: exchange only (but you can take items home on approval).

This store is another old-timer in the sample scene. It's been around for 12 years. Usually the longer someone's been in this business, the better they've established themselves with certain salesmen's clothing lines. So each season they can get an exclusive on clothes...or at least get the best items. That's the case with owner Doris Herman.

The discount here is 33% to 50% below retail. You'll find women's and juniors' sportswear, dresses, blazers, and sleepwear, in brand names such as Country Suburban, Russ, Point of View, and Kate Kenny Classics. The selection is best in sizes 8-10.

SAMPLE MART

5406 Florida Ave. N.
Minneapolis
PHONE: 533-0077
HOURS: Mon.-Fri., 10 a.m.-6 p.m.; Sat., 9:30 a.m.-5:30 p.m.
POLICIES: No credit cards; lay-by: 30 days; returns: exchange only.

Women's, but largely junior's, clothing in sizes 7 to 10. Look for Breckenridge, Intuition, Modern Jr., Cambridge sweaters, Genesis, Collage, Zena Jeans—all discounted 33% below retail. Sample Mart has been in business 15 years and specializes in moderately priced sportswear...no high fashion designer labels here. The best size selection is 7, 9 & 10, but as always in a sample shop, the assortment really depends on what's available.

Watch for clearance sales in July and January.

YOUR FAVORITE THINGS

4345 France Ave. S.
Minneapolis
PHONE: 929-1691
HOURS: Mon.-Sat., 10 a.m.-5:30 p.m.
POLICIES: Credit cards—Master, VISA and Shoppers; checks accepted; lay-by: 30 days; return: exchange or store credit only.

Patty Dreis gets in new stock weekly for women size 8 to 12 at this store. The clothes are very career-oriented in brand names like Joanie Char, Schroeder, Austin Hill, Prophecy. You'll find lots of blazers, skirts, slacks, and blouses. The discount is 33% below retail; clearance sales are in January and July. This shop is very much like shopping in a regular specialty store, with the bonus that it's conveniently connected to The Lacy Touch (below).

THE LACY TOUCH

4345 France Ave. S.
Minneapolis
PHONE: 929-7020
HOURS: Mon.-Sat., 10 a.m.-5:30 p.m.
POLICIES: Credit cards—Master, VISA and Shoppers; checks accepted; returns: exchange or store credit only.

The lacy touch here is in the lingerie, beachwear—and even gifts. Women's sizes are predominantly small and medium. In the beachwear, it's 8 to 12. There are great brand names to look for, including Christian Dior, Oscar de Larenta, Royal Robes, Formfit, Bill Theis and more. Some of the medium-sized lingerie will actually fit a size 14 (just so you don't feel left out).

PATTY'S OF STILLWATER

324 S. Main
(in the Grand Garage Building)
Stillwater
PHONE: 430-2957
HOURS: Mon.-Wed., Sat., 10 a.m.-5:30 p.m.; Thurs.-Fri., 10 a.m.-9 p.m.; Sun., noon-5 p.m.
POLICIES: Credit cards—Master, VISA and Shoppers; checks accepted; lay-by: 30 days; returns: exchange or store credit only.

Patty's is also owned by Patty Dreis, so in Stillwater, the stock combines what you'll find at her other stores, Your Favorite Things and The Lacy Touch (above).

CLASSIC COLLECTIONS

975 Grand Ave.
St. Paul
PHONE: 227-4092
HOURS: Mon., noon-8 p.m.; Tues.-Fri., 10 a.m.-5:30 p.m.; Sat., 10 a.m.-5 p.m.
POLICIES: Credit cards—VISA, Master and Shoppers; checks accepted; lay-by 30: days; returns: exchange only.

If preppy is your style of dressing, you've got to shop this store. Samples and some off-price merchandise range from women's 8 to 14, though you will occasionally find 6's and 16's. When you walk in, you feel as though you're entering the pages of a Talbot or Carroll Reed catalog. The brands are David Brooks,

Lanz, Robert Scott...very traditional. There's everything from golf skirts to blazers. Trendy types will definitely feel excluded. The discount is 30% to 50% below retail.

Get on the mailing list for the big January and July clearance sales.

D'ARCY SAMPLE SHOP

2525 Nevada Ave. N., Suite 101
Golden Valley
PHONE: 546-2448
HOURS: Mon.-Wed., 10 a.m.-5 p.m.; Thurs.-Fri., 10 a.m.-8 p.m.; Sat., 10 a.m.-4 p.m. Note: The store is often closed during the first week of the month. Call ahead.
POLICIES: No credit cards; checks accepted; lay-by: 2 weeks; returns: credit only.

At one time this store carried only samples. Today there are samples, closeouts, overstocks—you name it, all for women and juniors size 4 to 18. Ann Denzin, the owner, buys from 70 different name brands (White Stag, Catalina, Wrangler, Fritzi, Stuffed Jeans, Koret). Most of the clothes are in the moderate quality and price range. The discount savings at the store is 35% to 75% below retail. Note that not all the goods are first quality; you'll find irregulars, and some last year's fashions.

The first weekend of every month, Ann closes the store for a week and holds special sales, usually at the Marriot near the airport. Call to get on her sale mailing list. Many bargain hunters, though, wait until the week *after* she has her sales to look for the leftover merchandise at the shop. Then it's reduced even further.

WOMEN'S LARGE SIZES

The Big Beautiful Woman has a tough time getting a good-sized bargain. The quality of clothes manufactured for size 20 and above is improving each season, but the chances of the fine designer items filtering into off-price levels are slim, and polyesters are still abundant. Looking for natural fabrics and blends at good prices can add to your hunting time.

Large Size Fashions at Major Retailers

- **J.C. PENNEY:** Large Size Department, sizes 38 to 44 in tops, slacks 32 to 38. Brands: Lady Queen, Lady Devon, B.B.W., Par Four (Penney's label).

- **DAYTONS:** Women's World Department (a nice selection), sizes 38 to 44 in tops, skirts and pants 30 to 38, dresses 36 to 44. Brands: Amy Adams, Lesley Palmer, Chaus, Koret, Personal II, and many more.

- **DONALDSONS:** Women's World Department, sizes 32 to 44 in tops and pants. Brands: Koret, Russ, Miss Dream.

- **POWERS:** Women's World Department, sizes 38 to 44 in tops, pants and skirts 30 to 38. Brands: Punchline, Barry Ashley, Chaus, Tomorrow's Dream.

- **MARSHALL'S:** Marshall's does carry some sportswear in women's large sizes, but the selection and range of sizes can be very limited. In the future, however, if more designers continue to manufacture for the big beautiful woman, you're bound to see more items showing up here and at the other large off-price retailers.

NOTE: Also check out *The Weight Loss Closet* (p. 72) for large size second-hand clothing bargains, and United Stores in this chapter for women's size 32-44 jeans.

SCHLAMPP'S SALON MEGALO

2919 Hennepin Ave.
Minneapolis
PHONE: 823-7272
HOURS: Mon., 9:30 a.m.-9 p.m.; Tues.-Sat. 9:30 a.m.-5:30 p.m.
POLICIES: Credit cards—Master, VISA, Shoppers and American Express; no lay-by; refunds: cash or credit.

You must browse this salon even if it's just to see the current designer names now available in large sizes (16 to 46). There's Evan Picone, Givenchy En Plus, Pendelton, Harve Benard Woman, Schroeder, Pierre Cardin and more. Pauline Dell Brooks, manager of this salon, is a big beautiful woman herself and says the large size clothing market is changing. "Today this woman has a choice. She can buy an ultra suede suit, or find a silk blouse. In the past, it didn't matter how much money she had—she just couldn't find high quality fashions."

To save money buying the "good stuff" here, concentrate on special markdown times: for spring and summer clothes you'll get at least 20% discount from mid-June to July 4th (and the selection will be best). After July 4th, the selection gets spotty but markdowns are deeper. If you can hold off your fall buying until right after Christmas, you can pick up some good designer bargains here. Then, in February, Schlampp's has its huge storewide clearance sale. Whatever is left gets slashed considerably (30% to 50%).

Here's a shoe buying tip gleaned from the Salon: if you wear a wide width shoe and have a difficult time finding good quality fashionable shoes, go to Naturalizer Shoes at 918 Nicollet Mall in downtown Minneapolis. Although you may not find discounts, they have the largest selection of women's shoes in wide sizes in town.

NANCY LAWRENCE

3922 W. 50th St.
Edina
PHONE: 925-9305
HOURS: Mon.-Fri., 10 a.m.-5:30 p.m.; except Thurs., until 8 p.m.; Sat., 10 a.m.-5 p.m.

POLICIES: Credit cards—VISA, Master, Shoppers and American Express; no lay-by; returns: within 7 days for cash or credit; sale items are final.

Nancy Lawrence is an exclusive large size designer women's store with sizes 16 to 26 in dresses (half-sizes from 14 1/2 to 24 1/2), 30 to 40 in pants, and 36 to 46 in tops. Again, this is not an off-price store, but during the year Nancy has two very good clearance sales that you might want to know about if you're into the very best labels. The fall and winter sale is in January; the spring and summer sale is in July. Look for savings during these sales from 33% to 50% below retail.

LANE BRYANT

Rosedale Shopping Center
Hwy. 36 and Snelling Ave.
Roseville
PHONE: 636-0615
HOURS: Mon.-Fri., 10 a.m.-9 p.m.; Sat., 9:30 a.m.-6 p.m.; Sun., noon-5 p.m.

Northtown Shopping Center
Hwy. 10 and University Ave.
Blaine
PHONE: 784-8549
HOURS: Mon.-Fri., 10 a.m.-9 p.m.; Sat., 10 a.m.-6 p.m.; Sun., noon-5 p.m.

Ridgedale Shopping Center
12707 Wayzata Blvd.
Minnetonka
PHONE: 544-3500
HOURS: Mon.-Fri., 10 a.m.-9:30 p.m.; Sat., 9:30 a.m.-6 p.m.; Sun., noon-5 p.m.

POLICIES: Credit cards—Master, VISA and Lane Bryant; checks accepted; lay-by: 30 days, returns: cash or credit.

Here's the skinny on Lane Bryant sales...and I do mean skinny. The sales at the Twin Cities Lane Bryant stores at Rosedale Shopping Center, Northtown Shopping Center and Ridgedale Shopping Center are completely controlled by a New York office. They never advertise sales, and they have no sales mailing list for preferred customers. In fact, the store managers here don't even know when clothes will be marked down until the go-ahead comes across their computer monitor! But they do regularly have items marked down. You just have to be there at the right time. All the clothes are the Lane Bryant private label. Dresses go from 16 1/2 to 26 1/2, pants from 32 to 42, and blouses from 38 to 46.

HOUSE OF LARGE SIZES OUTLET STORES

1117 Excelsior Ave. E.
Hopkins
PHONE: 935-8214

Phalen Shopping Center
1369 E. Magnolia
St. Paul
PHONE: 771-4097

Midway Shopping Center
Snelling & University Ave.
St. Paul
PHONE: 642-9347

HOURS: Mon.-Fri., 9:30 a.m.-9 p.m.; Sat., 9:30 a.m.-5:30 p.m.; Sun., noon-5 p.m.

POLICIES: Credit cards—VISA, Master and Shoppers; no lay-by; returns: exchange only or gift certificates (these can be used in the regular retail stores).

The House of Large Sizes retail store chain has about 14 locations in the Twin Cities. Most of the merchandise is in the moderate quality and price range, though some of the goods fall well below. Yet avid shoppers of this retail chain claim that the Edina store stocks better quality clothes. But no matter what they have in their regular retail stores, some of it eventually ends up in their *outlets*.

You'll find all women's clothing ranging from sizes 14 1/2 to 32 1/2, blouses size 36 to 52, and pants size 30 to 46. Selection in each size may be limited. The clothes are a hodgepodge of all seasons; it is very typical to find winter clothes from the previous year along with a few summer items from the current season. Generally, the outlets average a half a season behind in getting their regular retail store merchandise. Years ago, polyester was the only fabric visible; now there are more blends and some natural fabrics. Shop these outlets when you've got some time.

If you're really a serious hunter, you can hit the "House of Large Sizes Auditorium Sales" held every two months. To find out about these sales, you can sign up on the sale mailing list at any of the store locations.

EXTRA SPECIAL

Knollwood Mall
8332 Hwy. 7
St. Louis Park
PHONE: 933-7551

Hub Shopping Center
22 W. 66th St.
Richfield
PHONE: 861-6610

Wards Terrace Mall
3501 W. Broadway
Robbinsdale
PHONE: 529-4878

Har Mar Mall
Co. Rd. B & N. Snelling
Roseville
PHONE: 633-8918

HOURS: Mon.-Fri., 10 a.m.-9 p.m.; Sat., 10 a.m.-5:30 p.m.; Sun., noon-5 p.m.
POLICIES: Credit cards—Shoppers, Master and VISA; checks accepted; lay-by: 21 days; returns: credit or exchange.

These stores specialize in women's casual to evening wear. The sizes are not always that large (they range from 14 to 20, plus tops from 32 to 46) yet occasionally some larger sizes are available. The managers are very tight-lipped about the discount markdown percentage, but I'd say they tend to range from 20% to 33% off retail. The merchandise is fashionable, mostly moderately priced name brands.

Maternity Fashions

OVER THE RAINBOW MATERNITY OUTLET

25 N. Fourth St., Third Fl.
Minneapolis
PHONE: 332-0446
HOURS: Mon.-Fri., 9 a.m.-5 p.m.; Sat., 10 a.m.-5 p.m.
POLICIES: Credit cards—Master, VISA and Shoppers; lay-by: 30 days; returns: exchange only.

This is a true factory outlet store in the warehouse district just north of downtown Minneapolis. In the factory, they manufacture Over the Rainbow maternity clothes sizes 4-16 (petite, small and large). Up front, Janet Daverne manages an outlet open to the public where they sell their overruns (these are always marked down 20% off the *wholesale* price) and their seconds (these are always marked down 50% below wholesale). You'll find dresses, workout suits, cruisewear, a special holiday line, slacks, and tops, but no bathing suits or lingerie. The staff love giving good deals here and want you to get those bargains...their prices really reflect this attitude.

Four special sales give you an additional 50% off: spring and summer clothes in May-June, fall clothes in August-September, and holiday and cruisewear in January-February.

DAN HOWARD MATERNITY FACTORY OUTLETS

Brooklyn Center
5900 Shingle Creek Pkwy
Brooklyn Park
PHONE: 566-6200

7931 1/2 Southtown Center
Bloomington
PHONE: 881-1734

HOURS: Mon.-Fri., 10 a.m.-9 p.m.; Sat., 10 a.m.-6 p.m.; Sun., noon-5 p.m.
POLICIES: Credit cards—VISA, Master and American Express; checks accepted; no lay-by; refunds: exchange only.

Dan Howard's outlets are large and carry their own brand of maternity clothes at 25% below the regular retail price. All the clothes are first quality goods here. New merchandise arrives weekly. Four times a year, watch for special 50% off sales advertised in the *Minneapolis Tribune* (twice a year you can get their lingerie at half price). They carry sizes 4 to 24, and the selection is good.

BABY SPECIALTIES

P.O. Box 4043
St. Paul, MN 55104
POLICIES: Credit cards—VISA and Master; checks accepted; no lay-by; returns: cash or credit. Manufacturers' warranties apply. Shipping extra. Orders take 3 weeks.

If you're expecting a baby and you hate shopping, Baby Specialties will make life easy for you. You can order Snugli soft baby carriers, matching diaper bags, and Cosco/Peterson car carriers at discount prices. The Snugli II carrier is $31, the Snugli Deluxe is $45. Just send a postcard to the address above and ask for information on the item you're interested in. The Snugli carriers come in a nice selection of fabrics. You'll receive a Snugli brochure with price list, fabric colors and pattern choices.

Women's Coats

THE COAT COMPANY

1/2 mile south of Hwy. 7 on
Shady Oak Rd.
Hopkins
PHONE: 933-4335

Midway Shopping Center
University & Snelling Ave.
St. Paul
PHONE: 644-6366

HOURS: Mon.-Fri., 10 a.m.-9 p.m.; Sat., 10 a.m.-5 p.m.; Sun., noon-5 p.m. (hours change in the summer).
POLICIES: Credit cards—Master and VISA; no lay-by; refunds: cash or exchange.

The longer a coat hangs around in these stores, the less money you're going to pay for it. So if you're into instant gratification, you won't save as much. There's a huge selection of women's coats (and some sportswear and suits), all good name brands...Harve Benard, Luba, Drizzle, and some top designer coats...Perry Ellis, Bonnie Cashin, Searle, and sometimes Albert Nipon and Trigere. There are *no* closeouts, overruns or irregulars here. Everything is first runs and bought for the current season. You'll probably run across the styles you see here in major stores. Now, maybe you won't see as many different styles from each designer, but you will have several variations to choose from in each designer's line. The sizes range from 4 to 20, and in half-sizes from 16 1/2 to 26 1/2.

Here's the Coat Company's schedule for discounting each season. For fall, the coats start coming in during July and are automatically priced at 25% off retail. For spring, the coats will come in during February. If a style is not moving in the first six weeks, it will be marked down to 40% off retail. Then if it's still around a few weeks later, it is dropped to 50% off retail. In December and January, a winter coat may be as much as 75% below retail. All the merchandise is high ticket to begin with, so 25% off may not hit your bargain fancy.

THE FACTORY STORE

Sharpe Manufacturing Co.
1015 S. Sixth St.
Minneapolis
PHONE: 332-2724
HOURS: Mon.-Fri., 9:30 a.m.-4:30 p.m.; Sat., 9 a.m.-2 p.m.
POLICIES: No credit; checks accepted; no lay-by; refunds: exchange only.

The Factory Store really is a factory outlet where Sharpe manufactures a nationally distributed line of women's and children's clothing. At this store they sell their seconds, irregulars and overstocks. Here you shop in a warehouse atmosphere that helps create that feeling that you're hot on the bargain trail—and you are.

You'll find some good deals on coats here. The least you'll save is 40% below retail...sometimes a whole lot more, especially if you shop the way one bargain hunter I know does, from Sharpe's testing rack. All the garments on that rack are tested for durability. They are stained, then spotted, and put under stress tests. When they are finished they go on the test rack at a big markdown. Check these items carefully before you buy. Down coats, wool coats, raincoats, women's blazers, and men's trench coats may turn up. If you're a home sewer, look for their outerwear fabric bargains and their good heavy coat zippers.

THE COAT STORE

M. Liman Co.
230 E. Fifth St., 4th Floor
St. Paul
PHONE: 222-0579
HOURS: Mon.-Fri., 9 a.m.-4 p.m.; Sat., 9 a.m.-11 a.m.
POLICIES: No credit; checks accepted; no lay-by; no returns.

Liman's manufactures a national line of women's coats, labeled Penguin. You have a choice of a basic wool dress coat or a car coat style in sizes 6 to 26 1/2, quite conservative, with not a trendy thread stitched anywhere. The Coat Store is where Liman's hangs its surplus, overruns, samples, seconds, and irregulars. You'll save 50% on the samples and overruns, and as much as 66% off retail on the seconds. Now the problem is finding what you need...selection and sizes can be very uneven.

WINONA KNITTING MILLS

609 E. Lake St.
Wayzata
PHONE: 476-1798
HOURS: Mon.-Sat., 9 a.m.-6 p.m.; except Thurs., until 8 p.m.

215 S. Main St.
Stillwater
PHONE: 430-1711
HOURS: Mon.-Sat., 10 a.m.-8 p.m.; Sun., noon-5 p.m.

Eden Prairie Factory Outlet Center
12475 Plaza Dr.
Eden Prairie
PHONE: 944-5190
HOURS: Mon.-Fri., 9:30 a.m.-9 p.m.; Sat., 9 a.m.-6 p.m.; Sun., 11 a.m.-5:30 p.m.

POLICIES: Credit cards—Master and VISA; checks accepted; no lay-by; returns; cash or credit.

Winona Knitting Mills is probably best known for its sweaters, hats, scarves, and mittens, but they also have casual outerwear (parkas, jackets, vests). Most are bought from select manufacturers around the country. The savings here range 33% to 50% below retail. These mill stores act as factory outlets.

You'll see some irregulars and seconds but most of the stock is first quality. Expect chamois shirts for $15.00, ragg wool sweaters for $18.00, and of course, their famous $3.00 reversible mittens made from thick sweater scraps. This is not just a winter store: they are adding more sportswear all the time. Winona Knitting Mills has shops in Red Wing, Duluth, Winona; and two more will be opening in the Twin Cities soon.

You can tell if an item was made by Winona Knitting Mills by the 'made in Minnesota' label (these items are discounted most heavily). All well-known name brand labels are removed from their off-price merchandise and tagged "Made in U.S.A."

RIBNICK FURS

224 N. First St.
Minneapolis
PHONE: 332-4321
HOURS: Mon.-Fri., 9:30 a.m.-6 p.m.; except Mon. & Thurs., until 8 p.m.; Sat., 9:30 a.m.-5 p.m.; Sun., noon-5 p.m. (call for summer hours)
POLICIES: Credit cards—Master, VISA, Shoppers and American Express; lay-by: flexible; no returns, but can take furs home on approval.

Ribnick's has new and used furs for men and women. The new furs are usually 40% below regular retail. Racoon and mink coats start at $1750. Burt Ribnick claims that they won't be undersold...so if you're able to come up with a price somewhere cheaper (perhaps an ad in the newspaper), Ribnick will match it. You'll find designer labels here—Anne Klein, Bob Mackie, Pauline Trigere—all in current season. But if you're really into a fashion cut fur without the designer label, maybe the best deal for you will be a designer look-alike. The real thing in an Anne Klein sells for $4,000 to $6,000...the copy will cost you half that. In the second-hand fur room everything is repaired and reconditioned. There are very few men's furs. Incidentally, don't expect to find anything under $100.

MEN'S AND WOMEN'S CAREER CLOTHES

When you're shopping discount sources for a good suit, you're going to find that many stores have their own private labels—and no matter where you go, you'll be told the store carries only the best quality. Well, there's an old Russian proverb that says, "Believe not your own brother, believe instead your own crooked eye." I would like to pass on some quality-spotting tips to help you develop your own eye, crooked or otherwise.

Quality Tipoffs in Suits

- Get beyond the 100% wool or Harris tweed label and hold the fabric up toward a light to see how tight the weave is...the less light you see, the better the weave.
- Look at the buttons. A good sign of quality is the hand-sewn type with a stem wrapped in heavy thread, leaving some space between the jacket and the button.
- Check to see if the sleeve has an open vent at the cuff, rather than no vent at all. The open vent allows comfort and movement at the wrist. (This is more applicable to men's than women's suits.)
- Inspect the stitching. Don't buy a suit that has plastic thread or glue at the seams.
- Watch out for isolated quality details. Flipping the jacket collar up and looking for a felt liner underneath used to be a good tipoff to quality. Now the cheap manufacturers are all putting this feature in.
- Know what's what with fabrics. The key trade-off involves durability vs. softness. *Worsted wools,* woven from twisted fibers, are rich-looking and durable, because they have a harder finish. Look for them if you're in and out of a car a lot, but be prepared for a bit of wrinkling. The best of these wools is *merino wool.*
- As a compromise, look for *wool-dacron worsteds* — softer, cheaper, but still durable, with a little less richness in the finish. At the extreme end of the softness scale (and practically unwrinkable, but least durable) are *cashmere* and *camelhair.*

SHOPPER'S FACTORY OUTLET

912 Currie Ave.
(Right across from Greyhound
Bus Depot)
Downtown Minneapolis
PHONE: 332-9090
HOURS: Mon. & Thurs., 10 a.m.-7 p.m.; Tues.-Wed., Fri., 10 a.m.-5 p.m.; Sat., 10 a.m.-5 p.m.; Sun., noon-5 p.m.
POLICIES: Credit cards—Master and VISA; checks accepted; no lay-by; returns: for exchange; alterations extra.

This factory outlet store is located in front of its manufacturing plant, where they make classic suits and sportswear with the Scotland Yard label for men, and the Justin Ltd. label for women. Customers are "dress for success" types and the merchandise reflects the image. Besides suits, women will find blazers, silk and oxford blouses, and sweaters. Men can look for suits, sportcoats, shirts and ties. Harris Tweed jackets range from $99 to $189, men's suits will range from $99 to $189, and women's suits from $99 to $169.

Shopper's Factory Outlet always has a special sale in November and one in April. Some of their best bargains here are the seconds, which are drastically reduced. Savvy home sewers head for the back of the store and stock up on the silks selling for $6 a yard or the Harris Tweed for about $9 a yard. Manager Jan McCann and the salespeople are very helpful, hunting up fabric from the plant if you have trouble finding what you need.

THE FACTORY RACK

6105 42nd Ave. N.
Minneapolis
PHONE: 535-6523
HOURS: Mon.-Sat., 9 a.m.-5 p.m.; Thurs., 9 a.m.-8 p.m.
POLICIES: Credit cards—VISA and Master; checks accepted; no lay-by; returns accepted; alterations extra.

The Factory Rack manufactures most of the suits you'll find in this outlet and you'll save 50% to 60% on them, compared to regular retail prices. They have suits, sportcoats, slacks, sweaters, shirts. The men's sizes go up to a 48 but the staff claims "there's no one we can't fit." Talls, portlies and sizes for athletic builds help salespeople prove their claim. Women's sizes are 4 to 16, and suits for her average $110. Men's suits range from $110 to $150. A camelhair sportcoat is $140.

MILBERN CLOTHING CO.

1685 University Ave.
St. Paul
PHONE: 645-2922
HOURS: Mon., 9 a.m.-9 p.m.; Tues.-Wed., 9 a.m.-5 p.m.; Thurs., 9 a.m.-9 p.m.; Fri.-Sat., 9 a.m.-5 p.m.
POLICIES: Credit cards—VISA and Master; checks accepted; lay-by: flexible; refunds: cash or credit; alterations extra.

Milbern's is a very dependable family-owned business. All the men's and women's suits here carry the Milbern label, but the owner, Herb Bernack, buys direct from several name brand manufacturers. All the merchandise is in style, and there are no factory seconds or irregulars. The discount averages about 40% below regular retail prices. Inventory is geared to fit the professional image (suits, shirts, rain and shine coats, sportcoats). The size range is good and a real bonus is their special orders for men's small or portly sizes.

MILTON CLOTHING COMPANY

242 E. Fifth St.
St. Paul
PHONE: 224-6443
HOURS: Mon.-Sat., 9 a.m.-5 p.m.
POLICIES: Credit cards—VISA and Master; checks accepted; lay-by available; returns: cash or credit.

Many St. Paulites are familiar with Milton Bernack, who manufactured menswear for over 20 years and heads Milton Clothing Company himself. You'll find a discount operation similar to Milbern's, above.

TITUS MACDUFF

2323 Wayzata Blvd., Highway 12 & Penn Ave.
Minneapolis
PHONE: 374-9176

276 E. Lafayette Frontage Rd.
(Watch for the signs)
St. Paul
PHONE: 227-4947

HOURS: Fri., 5 p.m.-9 p.m.; Sat., 9 a.m.-5 p.m.; Sun., noon-5 p.m. (closed on other days).

POLICIES: Credit cards—VISA, Master and American Express; no lay-by; returns: satisfaction guaranteed; alterations extra and take two weeks.

Titus MacDuff has created a mysterious image among discount stores in town, probably to get you out to investigate his operation. At his freeway-fronting locations, the exterior is clearly "no frills." But step inside, and the intrigue dissipates. The atmosphere is extremely casual, with people shopping in shorts and jeans. This casual atmosphere works well with the corporate male and female customer who wears the formal image all week and on weekends likes to dress down (the stores are only open Friday nights and weekends).

Although there are nice discounts, there are no factory seconds here, and no designer fashion suits. The cut is traditional, sporting the Titus MacDuff label, but the colors and fabric are more upbeat than has been traditional for the boardroom. The day I shopped, I saw a *takeoff* of a Burberry man's trench coat selling for $86.00. Men's 100% wool suits ranged from $168 to $178, and a wool blend was $151.97. A man's 100% wool navy blazer was priced $89.00, and a woman's silk suit was $119. Women's sizes range from 4 to 16; men's from size 36 to 46. You'll find accessories (Oxford shirts, sweaters, silk ties) stocked here too, but you won't get your best savings on those items. Anyone suiting up for the 9 to 5 routine should check out the goods here. But don't look for Titus MacDuff...he doesn't exist. Actually, rumor has it this store is run by a national company that has a regular retail store in town.

NATES OF ST. PAUL

Corner of Eighth & Wabasha
Downtown St. Paul
PHONE: 224-2026
HOURS: Mon.-Sat., 10 a.m.-5:30 p.m.; except Thurs., until 7 p.m.
POLICIES: Credit cards—Master, VISA and Shoppers; checks accepted; lay-by: flexible; returns: cash or credit; alterations extra.

The St. Paul Nate's, owned by Tim Bloom, has both men's and women's clothing. The women's department, though very small, has plans to expand. Prices are dependable and good here, since discounts average 20% to 35% below regular retail. A man's shetland wool grey herringbone sportcoat sells for $99.90; 100% wool topcoats, single-breasted, $119.90; and the double-breasted for $10 more. A better quality 3-piece wool flannel man's suit is $209.00. You'll have a real range of prices and quality to work with here. One style woman's suit is as low as $38.90, and a man's navy poly/wool hopsack blazer is $89.90 all the time.

Nate's is not big on designer labels, but they do carry some Calvin Klein and Nicola Mancini. Updated traditional cuts are their specialty. They buy some off-price goods and some right from the manufacturer. Their alterations prices are unbelievably cheap: a pair of slacks hemmed is $1.00 (that's *both* legs)! The wait is normally two days, OR, if you're just getting the pants hemmed, you can wait. They don't discriminate against the women on the alteration prices...that's nice.

CHAPTER 2

MEN'S CLOTHES

Men have the reputation of hating to shop for clothes, but now that fashions for men are beginning to get more lively (and are letting men express their taste and personality a little more), that reputation seems to be fading a bit. Come to think of it, most of the men I know who get a kick out of finding a good deal on clothes are the best-dressed guys I know, too. At any rate, whether you're a male bargain hunter—or a female who's shopping for one—I know you'll appreciate the leads I've got for you in this chapter. (Don't overlook the stores in Chapter 1 that carry men's and women's career clothes, as well.)

FOREMAN & CLARK

Town Square Shopping Center
Downtown St. Paul
PHONE: 224-2196
HOURS: Mon.-Sat., 9 a.m.-6 p.m.; except Mon. & Thurs., until 9 p.m.

Northtown Store
194 N.E. Northtown Dr.
Minneapolis
PHONE: 786-1631
HOURS: Mon.-Fri., 10 a.m.-9 p.m.; Sat., 9:30 a.m.-6 p.m.; Sun., noon-5 p.m.

Ridgedale Center
Minnetonka
PHONE: 546-1113

HOURS: Mon.-Fri., 10 a.m.-9:30 p.m.; Sat., 9:30 a.m.-6 p.m.; Sun., noon-5 p.m.

Burnsville Store
1136 Burnsville Shopping Center
Burnsville
PHONE: 435-8791
HOURS: Mon.-Fri., 10 a.m.-9 p.m.; Sat., 9:30 a.m.-6 p.m.; Sun., noon-5 p.m.

POLICIES: No credit cards; checks accepted; lay-by: 60 days with a $5.00 minimum payment; returns: cash (items must not be altered); alterations are *free*.

Foreman & Clark has been offering savings on menswear for so many years that, frankly, we take them for granted. And yet this family-owned business pioneered the idea of "direct from factory to you savings" 75 years ago. Foreman & Clark has a huge selection of suits, sportcoats, and slacks at each location. Suits range from $65 to $175, sportcoats $50 to $175, pants $15 to $35, dress outercoats $50 to $175. This company manufactures goods for their stores...there are no closeouts or overrun buys here. The sizes range from 34 and up (portlies, extra longs, short stouts—you name it, they have it). They offer continental to traditional styles, but the young preppy or high style designer look is not their market.

Here's a shopper's comments: "I've shopped Foreman & Clark for nine years. Last fall I thought I would check out a few others. Believe me, I ran back when I saw the prices. At Foreman & Clark I walked into a pair of 100% wool pants for $30 and a Harris Tweed sportcoat for $60. The salesman even suggested that I go elsewhere to buy the shirt for less. I appreciate the fact that there's no pressure and the alterations are free. It's nothing fancy here, but it is dependable."

NATE'S CLOTHING CO.

25 N. Fourth St.
Downtown Minneapolis
PHONE: 333-1401
HOURS: Mon. & Thurs., 8:15 a.m.-8:45 p.m.; Tues.-Wed., Fri.-Sat., 8:15 a.m.-5:45 p.m.

POLICIES: Credit cards—Master, VISA and Shoppers; lay-by: flexible with payments; returns: cash or credit; alterations extra.

If you're trying to hunt down a good deal on a man's suit, put Nate's on your list. Shopping is fun here, reminiscent of the Manhattan Garment District. In fact, the price tags are still coded as in the old days, when regular retailers would try to find out how much Nate's was discounting. You can crack the code by looking at the middle three numbers and then dividing them by two—that's the price of the suit. Actually, all you have to do is ask. And if you're into designer labels, be sure to ask about the back room, where all the Givenchys, Daniel Hechters, YSL, and Evan Picone goods are stored.

The savings here will be 30% to 35% off the regular retail price. Part of the inventory is overstock and closeout, but most of the stock is ordered in season, just like the major retailers. There is a good selection of classic traditional suits—none of which are recognizable because they are manufactured for stores that stick their own private labels inside. Sizes range from 36 to 56.

KUPPENHEIMER FACTORY STORES

3650 Hazelden Rd.
Edina
PHONE: 927-6100
HOURS: Mon.-Fri., 10 a.m.-9 p.m.; Sat., 9 a.m.-6 p.m.; Sun., noon-5 p.m.

7700 42nd Ave. N.
New Hope
PHONE: 533-3077
HOURS: Mon.-Fri., 10 a.m.-9 p.m.; Sat., 9 a.m.-6 p.m.; Sun., noon-5 p.m.

12475 Plaza Dr.
Eden Prairie
PHONE: 944-5622
HOURS: Mon.-Fri., 9:30 a.m.-9 p.m.; Sat., 9:30 a.m.-6 p.m.; Sun., 11 a.m.-5 p.m.

Signal Hills Shopping Center
S. Robert & Butler Ave.
West St. Paul
PHONE: 450-0421
HOURS: Mon.-Fri., 10 a.m.-9 p.m.; Sat., 9:30 a.m.-5:30 p.m.; Sun., noon-5 p.m.

POLICIES: Credit cards—VISA and Master; checks accepted; no lay-by, but will hold for 3 days; returns: cash or credit; alterations extra.

You'll find the Kuppenheimer label on all the suits, sportcoats and slacks here, since this is a factory store that carries its own manufactured goods (though the factory is not on the premises). Expect a large selection of wools, wool blends, and some polyesters. The discount averages 30% to 45% below regular retail. They also carry accessories, but again, the savings on ties, shirts and belts are not as great as you can get elsewhere. However, it's nice to be able to complete an outfit in one place when you're short on time.

Incidentally, women will find some blazers here. There are no seconds, irregulars, sales, or promotions, which is too bad for the hard-core bargain hunter who likes to sift through to get a great markdown.

HEIMIE'S MEN'S STORE

1510 S. Robert
West St. Paul
PHONE: 457-0001
HOURS: Mon.-Fri., 9 a.m.-9 p.m.; except Tues.-Wed. 9 a.m.-6 p.m.; Sat., 9 a.m.-5:30 p.m.
POLICIES: Credit cards—VISA, Master, Shoppers and American Express; checks accepted; lay-by: flexible; returns: exchange only; alterations *free*.

Believe it or not, Heimie's has been off-pricing in St. Paul for 53 years. They always offer a 20% to 25% savings. Most of the suits sport the store's label. That is because Heimie's buys first runs from the manufacturer, just like any other regular retailer. They do carry a few designer labels...Oleg Cassini, Stanley Blacker, Phoenix, Groshire. The merchandise is a mix of traditional and upbeat menswear fashions ranging in sizes 36 short to 54 long. You can custom order Big and Tall sizes. Suits average $125 to $250.

An interesting feature of this store is their Freeman shoes, discounted 15% to 20% (sizes 8 to 13, but they'll special order larger sizes). When shoe sizes get broken, the remaining sizes are marked down even more. So give them a call when you're shoe shopping to see if your size is on sale.

Speaking of sales, they have two clearance times, July-August for spring and summer suits, and January-February for fall and winter.

GOLD'S CLOTHING

4818 Excelsior Blvd.
St. Louis Park
PHONE: 927-8585
HOURS: Mon., Thurs.-Fri., 9:30 a.m.-8:30 p.m.; Tues.-Wed., Sat., 9:30 a.m.-6 p.m.
POLICIES: Credit cards—VISA, Master and Shoppers; checks accepted; lay-by: 30 days; refunds: cash or exchange; alterations extra.

Gold's has been offering menswear discounts for many years in the Twin Cities. It is family-owned and operated and has been promoted by word of mouth for ages. You'll benefit from Max Gold's low-profile advertising. The discounts start at 40% below retail and go down even more on some items. A large selection of men's sportcoats, suits, outerwear and accessories (even hats) range in size from 38 to 50.

CLOTHING DISTRIBUTION CENTERS

5808 W. 36th St.
St. Louis Park
PHONE: 926-9663
HOURS: Mon.-Fri., 10 a.m.-9 p.m.; Sat., 10 a.m.-5:30 p.m.; Sun., 11 a.m.-5 p.m.
POLICIES: Credit cards—VISA, Master, Shoppers and American Express; lay-by: flexible; returns: refund if not worn or altered; alterations extra.

This store carries over 44 different name brands of menswear. Some are familiar, some not. It's a mix of traditional and trendy. There are wools, blends, and polyester in suits, sportcoats, slacks, outerwear, ties, shirts and sweaters. The familiar name brands are Nino Cerutti, Hardy Amies, Pierre Cardin. In men's longs, the sizes range from 38 to 56, regulars 36 to 56, and short 36 to 46. They also carry some portly. But even with all the stock here, shopping can be hit or miss. It pays to check in often.

GENTLEMAN'S WEARHOUSE

Crystal Shopping Center
107 Willow Bend Rd.
Crystal
PHONE: 535-8246

5803 W. 36th St.
St. Louis Park
PHONE: 925-1405

6601 Nicollet Ave. S.
Richfield
PHONE: 869-2394

HOURS: Mon.-Fri., 10 a.m.-9 p.m.; Sat., 10 a.m.-6 p.m.; Sun., noon-5 p.m.
POLICIES: Credit cards—VISA and Master; checks accepted; returns: cash or credit.

Gentleman's Wearhouse has a factory in Massachusetts that makes all their suits, slacks and sportcoats, but this manufacturer also sells to regular retailers. The stock is discounted 30% to 50% below retail. A Harris Tweed coat sells for $85. The suits and sportcoats range from 36 short to 48 long. Accessories are reasonable...a dress shirt sells for $10 to $13.99. The quality of the suits falls in the moderate price range originally, so the discount makes them affordable for the man who's just beginning the corporate climb.

CHAPTER 3

CHILDREN'S CLOTHES

Keeping growing kids' ankles and wrists covered is hard enough—doing it without running your budget to ruin is an art all its own. Fortunately for parents, though, there are many good alternatives to paying full retail prices on kids' clothes. Some of them are listed in this chapter; others are in the next one, as well as in some of the other bargain sources listed for second-hand clothes (see pp. 68).

Here are some ideas for best buys when you're weighing new versus second-hand choices for children's clothes. Incidentally, if you do go the second-hand route, garage sales are gold mines.

BEST TO BUY NEW	BEST TO BUY SECOND-HAND
Babies' rubber pants	Dressy clothes, shoes, and coats
Winter coats and snowsuits, including down-filled items	Jeans, shorts, and overalls
Rugged clothes and play shoes	Boots, skates, and skis
T-shirts	
Nightgowns, sleepers, and pajamas (old ones may not be flame retardant)	

PRAIRIE KIDS

7406 Mitchell Rd.
Eden Prairie
PHONE: 934-6302
HOURS: Mon.-Sat., 10 a.m.-5 p.m.; except Thurs., until 8 p.m.; Sun., noon-5 p.m.
POLICIES: Credit cards—VISA, Master and Shoppers; checks accepted; lay-by: 60 days; refunds: cash or credit.

Even though Prairie Kids doesn't have a lot of room, owner Colleen Cavara has managed to squeeze in a playroom anyway. The discount starts at 20% early in the season and can go to 40% or more below retail. I've talked to lots of parents who love this store. One reported, "The prices are very good. They usually have print Oshkosh overalls. I've paid as little as $6.00 for the short style and $9.00 for the long. The stock is the best variety I've seen anywhere in town." The clothes are geared for back to school and casual wear, with lots of name brands...Carters, Lee, Jet Set, Healthtex, Weather Tamer. Sizes range from newborn to size 14 for boys and girls. There's always a clearance rack to rustle through.

KIDSMART

Crystal Shopping Center
325 Willow Bend
Crystal
PHONE: 537-7060
HOURS: Mon.-Fri., 9:30 a.m.-9 p.m.; Sat., 9 a.m.-6 p.m.; Sun., noon-5 p.m.

Sun Ray Shopping Center
2137 Hudson Rd.
St. Paul
PHONE: 735-4900
HOURS: Mon.-Fri., 9:30 a.m.-9 p.m.; Sat., 9 a.m.-5:30 p.m.; Sun., noon-5 p.m.

Southtown Shopping Center
7965 Southtown Center
Minneapolis
PHONE: 888-3777
HOURS: Mon.-Fri., 10 a.m.-9 p.m.; Sat., 9:30 a.m.-5:30 p.m.; Sun., noon-5 p.m.

7-Hi Shopping Center
4830 State Hwy. 101
Minnetonka
PHONE: 474-6624
HOURS: Mon.-Fri., 9:30 a.m.-9 p.m.; Sat., 9:30 a.m.-6 p.m.; CLOSED SUN.

Eden Prairie Factory Outlet Centre
12475 Plaza Dr.
Eden Prairie
PHONE: 944-5264
HOURS: Mon.-Fri., 9:30 a.m.-9 p.m.; Sat., 9:30 a.m.-6 p.m.; Sun., 11 a.m.-5 p.m.

POLICIES: Credit cards—Master and VISA; checks accepted; lay-by: 90 days; returns: cash or credit.

Kidsmart carries a wide variety of children's clothes, ranging from newborn to size 14, for both boys and girls. The name brands include Levi, Lee, Carter, Healthtex, Little Topsy, Polly Flinder, and more. The discount is automatically 20% below retail at the beginning of the season. For bigger savings, watch for the pre-season outerwear sale in July (20%-33% off), the back to school promotions in August (20%-33% off), the summer clearance (50% off) in mid-June, and the winter clearance (50% off) in January.

MCKIDS

5425 Xerxes Ave. N.
Brooklyn Center
PHONE: 560-0200
HOURS: Mon.-Fri., 10 a.m.-9 p.m.; Sat., 10 a.m.-6 p.m.; Sun., noon-5 p.m.
POLICIES: Credit cards—Master, VISA and Shoppers; checks accepted.

McKids is a kids' department store. Sizes range from infant to boys' and girls' size 14. All name brands are sold in outerwear, sportswear, dressy items and—what a bonus—even *shoes* (Nike, Adidas, Buster Brown). The merchandise is mostly first quality, with some closeouts and irregulars. Not everything is discounted, but only a very small percentage is sold at regular retail prices. The rest averages 20% off, with special promotions throughout the year cutting as much as 50% off retail.

You should be able to completely clothe your children here from head to toe.

CHILDREN'S OUTLET

1047 Grand Ave.
St. Paul
PHONE: 224-3777
HOURS: Mon.-Sat., 10 a.m.-5:30 p.m.
POLICIES: Credit cards—Master and VISA; checks accepted; lay-by: flexible; returns: credit only.

Here's a cute shop. It's small and has a limited selection, but the kid clothes make it worth frequent visits. They regularly carry Oshkosh, Calabush, Doespun, and Billy the Kid. Expect infant to size 14 girls, and up to size 8 in boys—some samples, but also closeouts. Most items are reduced 20%. You can save up to 50% when the store owners have made a good closeout buy, but such finds will be hit or miss. Some items are seasonal, such as snowsuits and Christmas holiday clothes.

CHILDREN'S SAMPLE SHOP

4064 Lakeland Ave. N.
Robin Center
Robbinsdale
PHONE: 537-3330
HOURS: Mon.-Fri., 10 a.m.-9 p.m.; Sat., 10 a.m.-5 p.m.; Sun., noon-5 p.m.
POLICIES: Credit cards—VISA, Master and Shoppers; checks accepted; lay-by: 25% down, with three payments to pay; refunds: cash or credit.

This is a family-run store that's been open for 13 years under the ownership of the mother-daughter team of Edie Jackson and Carol Leiner. Children's sizes are newborn to size 10. The discount is 20% to 30% below retail. The stock includes many items in play, back to school and dress clothes for kids. Some of the brand names are popular...Weather Tamer, Sweet 'n Sassy, Gunne Sax, Halo, Joni J.

KELLY'S TOTS TO TEENS

Midway Center
University & Snelling Ave.
St. Paul
PHONE: 646-5737

St. Anthony Village Shopping Center
2933 Pentagon Dr.
Minneapolis
PHONE: 781-4616

HOURS: Mon.-Fri., 9:30 a.m.-6 p.m.; Sat., 9:30 a.m.-9 p.m.
POLICIES: Credit cards—Master, VISA and Shoppers; checks accepted; lay-by: on outerwear only; returns: exchange or store credit.

Owner Molly Kelly carries the basics for kids at her stores. Let me share one shopper's story. "This is smaller than some stores, but they have their shelves jammed. The best buy is Carter's and Healthtex. I paid $5.00 for footed Carter's pajamas. When they have sales, they are better than any hotel salesman's sample sale advertised. Their kids' coats are reasonable, too. I found a coat for $22 here and later saw the same coat selling for $50 at a ritzy kids' store." Carter's closeouts are always marked down at 33% below retail, outerwear is always 33% off, and everything else is at least a 20% savings. In the Midway Center store, watch for the big sales in May, July and September. Sizes range from infants to boys' and girls' size 14.

CHAPTER 4

CLOTHES — AND LOTS MORE

Most of the bargain spots I've shared with you up to now stock merchandise that's geared toward specific shoppers, but there are lots of places that carry something for everyone, and even merchandise besides clothes. At a place like Bank's, you may find frozen fish selling at the same time as snowmobile suits. Or at Marshall's, you can pick up a wedding gift while you shop for your outfit for the occasion.

This chapter will also help you complete your wardrobe of new clothes and accessories and outfit you from head to foot. You'll find everything from gold chains to eelskin briefcases—a real potpourri of bargains.

MONTGOMERY WARDS CLEARANCE OUTLETS

Phalen Shopping Center
1441 E. Magnolia
St. Paul
PHONE: 647-3177
HOURS: Mon.-Fri., 9:30 a.m.-9 p.m.; Sat., 9:30 a.m.-5:30 p.m.; Sun., 11 a.m.-5 p.m.

1425 S. Robert St.
West St. Paul
PHONE: 647-2595
HOURS: Mon.-Fri., 9:30 a.m.-9 p.m.; Sat., 9:30 a.m.-5:30 p.m.; Sun., noon-5 p.m.

POLICIES: Credit cards—Wards, VISA and Master; no lay-by; returns: exchange or refund.

Wards outlets carry both their retail store and catalog overstocks. The Phalen Shopping Center location has clothes for the entire family, furniture, electronics, appliances, housewares. Everything is 30% to 50% off the original price. If it hangs around for a while it goes even lower. One smart shopper says, "I look for their catalog overstock items for really super deals. These are marked on the signs over the merchandise."

Shopping here is strictly catch as catch can. Merchandise is constantly changing, so if you see something you like, buy it. All the appliances and other hard merchandise are warrantied.

Truckloads arrive daily, so hardcore hunters shop here twice a week. At the West St. Paul store, the bulk of the merchandise is clothing, with some furniture and appliances.

Their shipments arrive on Tuesday and Friday. The new week's goods are put out on those days.

MONTGOMERY WARDS

Midway Store,
2nd and 3rd floor
1400 University Ave.
St. Paul
PHONE: 647-2100
HOURS: Mon.-Fri., 9:30 a.m.-9 p.m.; Sat., 9:30 a.m.-5:30 p.m.; Sun., 11 a.m.-5 p.m.
POLICIES: Credit cards—Wards, VISA and Master; no lay-by; returns: exchange or refund.

The same deals described above in the other Wards outlets are available here, too.

SEARS SURPLUS STORES

1907 Suburban Ave.
St. Paul
PHONE: 739-4330

6199 N.E. Hwy. 65
Fridley
PHONE: 571-8010

9056 Penn Ave. S.
Bloomington
PHONE: 884-5317
HOURS: Mon.-Fri., 9 a.m.-9 p.m.; Sat., 9 a.m.-6 p.m. (except the St. Paul store, Sat., 10 a.m.-6 p.m.); Sun., noon-5 p.m.
POLICIES Credit cards—Sears only; checks accepted; no lay-by; refunds: refund or exchange...satisfaction guaranteed.

Seventy-five percent of the merchandise at Sears Surplus Stores is overstocks from their catalog. The rest is from Sears' other sources. You'll find clothes for men, women and children, but also housewares, furniture and electronics. There are very few irregulars, but some of the furniture and small appliances may be reconditioned or just sold "as is." The markdown averages 40% to 60% below the catalog price on clothing, and 30% to 50% off on everything else.

Shipments arrive almost daily, and the aisles beckon with the promise of a bargain. Maybe not one you came in for...but you'll find some use for whatever you do buy. Many shoppers rave about the great deals on kids' clothes, and their "Circus Days" Toy Sale is just that—a circus. For one reason, it's wild. People line up hours before it starts. They bring big plastic garbage bags (carts go fast) and once they're let in, it's a mad scramble.

Here's one toy hunter's story. "I just went crazy at this sale. I bought a 15-inch Effanbee collector's doll for $19.99 (they're normally $49.99) and I grabbed a Barbie doll for $2.50. A lot of toys come from the Christmas catalog of the year before." Traditionally this sale is held at all three outlets in September. The only way to keep posted is to call the store.

Depending on the Christmas overstock, another toy sale is held in July. And a popular all-around sale is held the day after Thanksgiving.

BANK'S

Main Store
615 First Ave. N.E.
Minneapolis
PHONE: 379-1222

Burnside Plaza
14314 Burnside Dr.
Burnsville
PHONE: 435-3338

Warehouse Store
1551 Vernon Ave.
St. Louis Park
PHONE: 544-5394

New Hope Outlet Mall
42nd & Winnetka
New Hope
PHONE: 533-4248

Eden Prairie Shopping Center
1018 Eden Prairie Center
Eden Prairie
PHONE: 941-2180

HOURS: Mon.-Fri., 8:30 a.m.-9 p.m.; Sat., 8:30 a.m.-6 p.m.; Sun., noon-5 p.m.

POLICIES: No credit cards; checks accepted; no lay-by; returns: currently for exchange only.

Bank's is an unbeatable store for bargain hunting adventure. All the elements of intrigue are there, in their main store especially. You'll discover goods you never would expect to find at bargain prices. The reason: Bank's is a liquidator for large insurance companies. So, if a store has a fire, or any other unforeseen disaster, chances are the merchandise will travel across the country and into a Bank's store. Here's just a sample of goods that showed up in the last few years: Ethan Allen furniture; musical instruments; a complete Denver department store (this store had a whole section just for Ralph Lauren Polo shirts); and for a while, handmade craftsman quality rocking horses (these were similar to the type you would see at the children's fantasy store, F. A. O. Schwartz, in Manhattan). These are not sales you can plan most major purchases around, and what's worse, they will actually spark the idea that maybe you need something you never even thought of before.

Bank's is now buying off-price merchandise to fill out their regular liquidated goods. When they get a huge amount of merchandise in to liquidate, prices will be reduced 40-60% (sometimes even more), and can be a real bargain, if you can tolerate the crowds. If you are a frequent Bank's shopper, you'll hit a clearance item marked down *another* 50%.

You can always count on finding men's, women's and children's clothes at Bank's stores. You can't always count on finding your size. Shoes, considered by many bargain hunters to be Bank's best buy, are always stacked up at the Main Store. In general, it is the smart shopper who knows how to spot a good deal at Bank's. This shopper is more energetic, can take some time for digging, knows other prices around town, has sharply honed quality spotting skills and probably can successfully shop any bargain haunt in town.

Get familiar with Bank's coding system: When you spot an 0 on a tag, you know the item was damaged and the price will be cheaper. A clerk can point one out.

SALES HOTLINE—379-4321. Call this phone number and you'll find out what the current sales are for that week at all the Bank's stores.

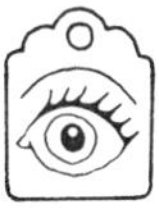

NEWSPAPER CALENDAR OF SALES. Each month, usually on the first Sunday, Bank's will print a "calendar of sales" for the entire month in the *Minneapolis Tribune* and the *St. Paul Pioneer Press*. You can get one at the stores, too.

MAILING LIST—379-2803. Call this number and get on the Bank's mailing list. You'll get their Calendar of Sales each month.

WEEKLY SALES. New merchandise goes on sale every Wednesday and Friday at one or more of Bank's stores. Check the classified ad section of the *Minneapolis Tribune* or the *St. Paul Pioneer Press* in Tuesday and Thursday papers.

MARSHALL'S

Har Mar Mall
2100 N. Snelling Ave.
Roseville
PHONE: 636-6688

Hub Shopping Center
36 W. 66th St.
Richfield
PHONE: 866-4200

Crystal Shopping Center
201 Willow Lane
Crystal
PHONE: 533-8383

Columbia Heights Mall
4001 Central Ave.
Columbia Heights
PHONE: 781-2677

Valley West Shopping Center
France Ave. S.
Bloomington
PHONE: 881-2433

HOURS: Mon.-Sat., 9:30 a.m.-9:30 p.m.; Sun., 11 a.m.-5 p.m.
POLICIES: Credit cards—VISA, Master and American Express; checks accepted; lay-by: 30 days; returns: cash or credit.

Marshall's advertises that you can save 20% to 60% on brand name and designer fashions for the whole family—and you can. Now, this doesn't mean you can go to a designer trunk showing at a major department store and stop at Marshall's on the way home to pick up what you saw. But you will find very fashionable clothes with good labels (none cut out) and you can often uncover good designer names in your size. New merchandise arrives weekly and stock is put out every day. So if you see something you like, buy it. The good stuff doesn't hang around for long. Marshall's carries menswear; women's and junior sportswear; dresses; suits; women's large-size sportswear; lingerie; shoes; accessories; infants', toddlers', and children's wear; maternity fashions; luggage; linens; drapes; home fashions (a friend just got a great deal on a Dhurie rug). At the Har Mar store you'll find the best selection of home fashions, giftware, gold and silver jewelry, and you may find some petite fashions here. Some of the merchandise will be last year's styles, but if they are, the tag will say so. There are also some irregulars. These are clearly marked, but many shoppers search for these because the savings are even greater.

I personally love Marshall's shoe department and clearance racks. Sports enthusiasts tell me the athletic wear is a super buy.

During the year, watch for the following special sales and best selection times: spring and summer fashions in March and April; fall fashions during August, September, October; and back to school items during August. Each week watch the *Minneapolis Tribune* and *St. Paul Dispatch* Sunday and Thursday papers for specials.

Allow yourself some time to shop. The selection is so large that it can take a while, but you can count on Marshall's as a mainstay for your bargain wardrobe.

T. J. MAXX

Wards Southtown Shopping Center
Penn Ave. S. just off I-494
Bloomington
PHONE: 881-2211

Knollwood Mall
Hwy. 7 at Texas Ave.
St. Louis Park
PHONE: 938-3335

HOURS: Mon.-Sat., 10 a.m.-10 p.m.; Sun., noon-6 p.m.
POLICIES: Credit cards—all majors; checks accepted; lay-by: 30 days; returns: "hassle-free" refunds.

The T. J. Maxx stores are similar to Marshall's. In fact, the person who helped create this off-price retailer was formerly a V.P. for Marshall's corporation. Again, you'll save 20% to 60% on name brands and designer fashions for the whole family. You'll always find many name brands here (many are closeouts or overruns), but when you hit the top of the line designer labels, you feel great. One activewear shopper commented she found Harlequin sweats, the stylish kind that are showstoppers even out of the sports arena, selling for less than half the suggested retail price. Another reported seeing designer Italian mohair sweaters for only $12.00, compared to $60.00 at regular department stores. This is no-frills shopping but the stores are organized in such a way that a frequent shopper can quickly scan the stock.

You'll find all types of clothing for men, women, and children (they don't carry shoes). At the Bloomington store, you'll also find giftware and housewares. Serious bargain hunters putting together a seasonal wardrobe usually hit both T. J. Maxx and Marshall's to increase their shopping success rate.

Shipments arrive twice a week. The best days to shop for the latest merchandise are Tuesdays or Fridays.

BURLINGTON COAT FACTORY

Hwy. 100 & W. 36th St.
St. Louis Park

2021 S. Robert St.
West St. Paul

HOURS: Mon.-Sat., 10 a.m.-9 p.m.; Sun. noon-5 p.m.
POLICIES: Credit Cards—Master, VISA; checks accepted; returns: exchange only.

The Burlington Coat Factory is a national off-price chain that sells a whole lot more than coats. You'll find designer and name brand men's, women's and children's clothing discounted 30%

to 60% below regular retail prices. These large stores, which opened in September 1984, are a welcome addition to the Twin Cities off-price retail shopping market.

Activewear and Rugged Clothes

PAPILLON

7 E. 70th St.
Richfield
PHONE: 866-2141
HOURS: Tues.-Wed., 10 a.m.-8 p.m.; Sat., 10 a.m.-4 p.m. (3 days only).

4308 Excelsior Blvd.
St. Louis Park
PHONE: 927-9133
HOURS: Tues.-Sat., 10 a.m.-5 p.m.
POLICIES: No credit cards; checks accepted; no lay-by; returns: exchange only.

Quite a mix of sizes and activewear for the whole family here! Girl's sizes 8 and 10; junior's sizes 7 and 9; women's sizes small and medium; boy's sizes 12 and 14; and men's sizes small, medium and large. The brand names include: OP, Levi, London Fog, Duffel, Alps, Michael Jordan. Styles and sizes are always limited, so if you find something you like, but don't have the ready cash, put it on hold for a week. New shipments are put out weekly. All the merchandise is marked at 40% to 60% below regular retail prices.

KAPLAN BROTHERS DEPARTMENT STORE

1435 E. Franklin Ave.
Minneapolis
PHONE: 871-1233
HOURS: Mon.-Fri., 9 a.m.-9 p.m.; Sat., 9 a.m.-6 p.m.
POLICIES: No credit cards; checks accepted; no lay-by; returns accepted.

When you first walk into Kaplan's you're positive this is where Guindon found his inspiration. The merchandise is perfect for hanging out on cold bus stops or casting for carp. Every fall, I make my annual trek there for wool socks, long underwear and gloves. (Have you ever lost yours in February? If so, you know how hard it is to find a pair. Well, Kaplan's always stocks them.) Leather dress gloves sell for $9.99 to $14.99.

The real lifeblood of a Minnesotan existence rests in this store. You'll find flannel shirts, turtlenecks, boots, outerwear, underwear and jeans ($10.99 to $14.99) packed on shelves that stretch to the ceiling. Some of the goods are closeouts or overstocks; most are special purchases. The savings average about 25% below moderately priced regular retail stores. Last year a hiking boot lined with Thinsulate sold for $49 at Kaplan's, while at a major discount chain, the price was $79.99. Down coats range from $69.99 to $89. They specialize in men's outdoor, casual and work clothes, but some of the stock is sized for women and children.

SYLVESTER SALES

30 miles north of Minneapolis
on Hwy. 65 at 219th Ave.
Soderville
PHONE: 434-9571
HOURS: Mon.-Sat., 9 a.m.-5:30 p.m.; except Wed., until 9 p.m.; Sun., noon-5:30 p.m.
POLICIES: Credit cards—VISA, Master and Shoppers; no lay-by; returns: everything is sold as is—no refunds.

Sylvester Sales is a liquidation and surplus store that always has a large supply of men's, women's and children's Oshkosh brand clothes. Some are first quality but most are irregulars (clearly marked). The clothing section of this rambling building is a real treasure chest for parents who must dress several youngsters. As one shopper put it, "You have to be a serious bargain hunter to take this long ride, but Sylvester's has everything you want in Oshkosh clothes for kids...and there is so much of it compared to other stores. The best deal is on their irregulars."

If you've got any energy left after the drive, you may want to check out their household goods. Owner Wayne Sylvester always has paint and stains at markdown prices, some furniture, and occasionally groceries. But the fun of it is that you never know what you'll uncover.

The time to plan a trip here is in August during their back to school sale. If you want information about their sales, just call them and get on their mailing list.

UNITED STORES

Har Mar Mall
2100 N. Snelling Ave.
Roseville
PHONE: 631-0260
HOURS: Mon.-Fri., 9 a.m.-9 p.m.; Sat., 9 a.m.-5:30 p.m.; Sun., 11:30 a.m.-5 p.m.
POLICIES: Credit cards—VISA, Master, Shoppers and American Express; returns accepted (even on special sales).

At the Har Mar store, ask about the back room, full of irregular winter jackets at 30% to 50% below retail. Most of the irregular jackets that United carries come from the Woolrich Company, though occasionally you'll find a Field and Stream or an Adventure Gear jacket. But you can shop here early in the season and if you're lucky (sizes and selection can be limited), you'll save a bundle.

UNITED STORES WAREHOUSE

785 53rd Ave. N.E.
Fridley
PHONE: 572-8818
HOURS: Mon.-Fri., 9:30 a.m.-9 p.m.; Sat., 9 a.m.-5:30 p.m.; Sun., noon-5:30 p.m.
POLICIES: Credit cards—VISA, Master, Shoppers and American Express; returns accepted (even on special sales).

All the United Stores have a 10% to 20% automatic markdown over regular retail stores. But there are *special* United Stores where you can get even better deals. At the warehouse, United liquidates odds and ends in camping equipment. They have a lot of irregular jeans and a back room with irregular winter jackets...all 30% to 50% below retail. Twice a year there are two big camping equipment sales, during the third weeks in May and in June. Then everything is marked down another 20%. It's the best time of year to get a good deal on hiking boots.

UNITED STORES/THE SURPRISE STORE

1084 University Ave.
St. Paul
PHONE: 646-3544
HOURS: Mon.-Fri., 9 a.m.-9 p.m.; Sat., 9 a.m.-5:30 p.m.; Sun., noon-5 p.m.
POLICIES: Credit cards—VISA, Master, Shoppers and American Express; returns accepted (even on special sales.)

This is a new concept for the United Stores, converting a regular store into a "Surprise Store." It's a real mishmash of goods here. You've got to take some time for digging, but the discount is 50% to 60% on almost everything. You'll always find some styles in jeans here selling for $5.00. Rumor is that the regular downtown Hopkins United Store will also be converted to a "Surprise Store."

Shoes

FASHION FOOTWEAR

Cedarvale Mall
Eagan
PHONE: 452-3633

Apple Valley Shopping Center
Apple Valley
PHONE: 432-1144

Valley Creek Mall
1750-16 Weir Dr.
Woodbury
PHONE: 739-2666

HOURS: Mon.-Fri., 9:30 a.m.-9 p.m.; Sat., 9:30 a.m.-5:30 p.m.; Sun., noon-5 p.m.
POLICIES: Credit cards—all major credit cards; checks accepted; lay-by: 30 days; returns: cash or credit.

Fashion Footwear is a high quality off-price shoe retailer. That means you're going to find the "good stuff," but not at rock bottom discounts. There's a large inventory of women's name brands: Nickles, Nina, Candies, Bass, Dexter; in children's shoes it's Miss Capezio, Stride Right, Jumping Jacks, Sperry Topsiders, and Buster Brown, just to mention a few. They don't carry men's shoes.

These stores offer two different discount options. The first is their 'Salon' shoes (here you get all the service). These are discounted about 15% below retail. So, if one of the large department stores has a woman's shoe for $69.00, Fashion Footwear will have it for $57.99. Stride Rites are priced at $17.99 and $18.99. All the shoes in the Salon are "full runs," meaning they have all sizes in each style, not just one or two pairs, and all are this season's styles. Women's sizes range from 5 to 10, and children's from infant to youth sizes.

The second discount option is their self-service shoe area, where all the shoes are on racks. This section is discounted 20% to 60%. The "rack shoes" are bought differently than the "salon shoes." The stock is manufacturer's overruns and closeouts (all name brands, however).

Here's a schedule of their special sales to get you some big savings on the "salon shoes." Winter markdowns (including boots) begin right before and after Christmas. The full winter clearance is in January. The summer clearance begins right before and after July 4th. Back to school specials start in August. Children's shoes are available in all the stores *except* the Woodbury location.

FAMOUS FOOTWEAR

7581 Brooklyn Blvd.
Brooklyn Park
PHONE: 560-1585

2950 White Bear Ave.
Maplewood
PHONE: 777-7600

13153 Ridgedale Dr.
Minnetonka
PHONE: 544-4212

Har Mar Mall
Roseville
PHONE: 636-3398

Loehmann's Plaza
West 98th St. & Hwy 100
Bloomington
PHONE: 835-9676

Burnhaven Mall
850 W. Co. Rd. 42
Burnsville
PHONE: 435-2488

Highland Center
2022 Ford Pkwy
St. Paul
PHONE: 698-3144

Columbia Heights Mall
4037 Central Ave. N.E.
Columbia Heights
PHONE: 788-9415

Hub Shopping Center
32 W. 66th St.
Richfield
PHONE: 866-5700

Southview Square Shopping Center
1867 S. Robert
West St. Paul
PHONE: 450-0688
HOURS: Mon.-Fri., 10 a.m.-9 p.m.; Sat., 10 a.m.-6 p.m.; Sun., noon-5 p.m.
POLICIES: Credit cards—all major credit cards; checks accepted; will hold shoes for 3 days; lay-by: 30 days; returns: cash or exchange.

Famous Footwear carries its own brands in most shoes, but also name brands such as Bass, Nike, Florsheim and Adidas in athletic shoes. Men's shoes range $3 to $10 below regular retail; women's and children's shoes are usually $2 to $5 below regular retail. The big winter clearance sale is in January; the summer in July; and back to school specials run weekly in August and September. Shipments are brought in weekly and the best time to shop is Thursday and Friday. All the merchandise is well displayed on the sales floor. If you don't see it in your size, they don't have it.

To spot the "tucked-away leathers" at discount shoe stores, read the writing inside the shoes or on the sole. When you see "all parts are man-made," that means none of it is leather. If it reads "leather uppers," then just the outside is leather while the sole and inside are man-made. In a very expensive shoe, even the sole is made of leather. You can test this by wetting your finger and touching the sole. If it leaves an imprint...you've found a shoe with a leather sole. So if the shoe fits (and you like it!), buy it. It was probably selling for a whole lot more before it got to the shoe discounter.

CONN-CO SHOES

201 N. Second St.
Stillwater
PHONE: 439-5415

8200 Hadley Dr.
Cottage Grove
PHONE: 459-9471

3180 Country Drive
Little Canada
PHONE: 483-0670

Apache Plaza
37th & Silver Lake Rd.
Minneapolis
PHONE: 781-8611

3250 Excelsior Blvd.
St. Louis Park
PHONE: 927-5090

7500 Hudson Blvd.
Lake Elmo
PHONE: 731-1045

7316 Lakeland Ave. N.
Brooklyn Park
PHONE: 425-5696

3150 W. Hwy. 13
Burnsville
PHONE: 890-4611

8949 University Ave.
Blaine
PHONE: 784-9006

7820 Olson Memorial Hwy.
Golden Valley
PHONE: 544-0766

13601 Ridgedale Dr.
Minnetonka
PHONE: 546-8111

8098 Morgan Circle
Bloomington
PHONE: 881-1090

HOURS: Mon.-Fri. 9 a.m.-9 p.m.; Sat. 9 a.m.-6 p.m.; Sun., noon-5 p.m.
POLICIES: No credit cards; no lay-by; will hold shoes 3 days; returns: cash or exchange.

Sixteen years ago, Conn-Co was the hot shoe outlet out in Stillwater. Today, with multiple locations, they are a big off-price retailer selling men's, women's and children's shoes. The average discount here is 20%. You can't come here shopping with an exact style in mind, since this is hit or miss shopping. What you see on the floor that day is what you get. Most of the shoes are factory overruns, closeouts, and some irregulars (these are clearly marked), and not all the shoes are from the current season. You'll find a variety of brand names at various times: Bass, Dexter, Air Step, Nike, Puma, Adidas.

GUSSINI'S

Midway Shopping Center
1558 University Ave.
St. Paul
PHONE: 646-9343
HOURS: Mon.-Fri., 10 a.m.-9 p.m.; Sat., 10 a.m.-6 p.m.; Sun., noon-5 p.m.
POLICIES: No credit cards; checks accepted; hold shoes for one week; returns: exchange only.

In Chicago this discount store is highly visible in its Michigan Avenue location, but in the Twin Cities, Gussini's is tucked away in the Midway Center in St. Paul. All their shoes are always priced at $13.88. They carry women's sizes 5 to 11 in shoes and boots.

The majority of the shoes are vinyl, not leather. These vinyl "make ups" of current shoe styles are not that great in quality, but the colors and styles are fashionable. Occasionally you'll find leather shoes in your size by Nickles, Hippopotamus—and once I even found Andrew Geller black pumps for, of course, $13.88 (regular retail would have been at least $90). Now, granted they were not this season's Andrew Geller shoes, but the style was classic so they were still in fashion. Incidentally, this is not the shopping spot for a very narrow shoe size.

The best days to shop are Thursday or Friday, since that's when their weekly shoe shipment is put out.

At the beginning of each season (spring and fall), it's best to hunt through here once a week (on Thursday) until you find what you need. Winter shoes and boots are marked down to $8.88 or less on February 1st. Summer shoes are marked down on June 1st.

SHOE KICKS

3493 W. Broadway
Robbinsdale
PHONE: 588-8343
HOURS: Mon.-Fri., 10 a.m.-9 p.m.; Sat., 9:30 a.m.-5:30 p.m.; Sun., noon-5 p.m.
POLICIES: Credit cards—Master and VISA; checks accepted; hold shoes for 24 hours; returns: cash or credit.

Shoe Kicks is a lot like Gussini's and also sells women's size 5 to 11 shoes and boots for $13.88. Again, style, color and price are better than the quality. But you might find name brands like Naturalizers, Bass, 9 West or Espadrilles in your size. So the search could turn over a treasure. When there is a sale, everything gets marked down to $7.88.

New shoe shipments arrive weekly, and the best day to shop is Thursday.

PAYLESS SHOE STORES

7815 Portland Ave.
Bloomington
PHONE: 881-1200

1603 S. Robert St.
West St. Paul
PHONE: 455-4113

Grove Plaza Shopping Center
7280 Point Douglas Rd.
Cottage Grove
PHONE: 458-0017

Burnhill Plaza
1286 W. Co. Rd. 42
Burnsville
PHONE: 435-7515

Maplewood Square
3035 White Bear Ave.
Maplewood
PHONE: 777-4367

HOURS: Mon.-Sat., 9 a.m.-9 p.m.; Sun., 11 a.m.-5 p.m.

1472 University Ave.
St. Paul
PHONE: 644-7755

Broadway Center
615 W. Broadway
Minneapolis
PHONE: 521-5696

HOURS: Mon.-Fri., 9 a.m.-9 p.m.; Sat., 9 a.m.-7 p.m.; Sun., 11 a.m.-5 p.m.

3600 Nicollet Ave.
Minneapolis
PHONE: 822-6013
HOURS: Mon.-Sat., 9 a.m.-7 p.m.; Sun., 11 a.m.-5 p.m.

415 Wabasha St.
St. Paul
PHONE: 227-6725
HOURS: Mon. & Thurs. 9 a.m.-9 p.m.; Tues.-Wed., Fri.-Sat., 9 a.m.-6 p.m.; Sun., noon-5 p.m.

Franklin Circle Center
1213 E. Franklin Ave.
Minneapolis
PHONE: 872-8303
HOURS: Mon.-Fri., 9 a.m.-9 p.m.; Sat. 9 a.m.-7 p.m.; Sun., 11 a.m.-5 p.m.

Minnehaha Mall
2510 E. Lake St.
Minneapolis
PHONE: 722-6304
HOURS: Mon.-Fri., 9 a.m.-9 p.m.; Sat., 9 a.m.-6 p.m.; Sun., 11 a.m.-5 p.m.

POLICIES: Credit cards—Master, VISA and Shoppers; lay-by: 30 days; will hold shoes for 10 days; returns: cash or exchange.

If your budget is tight, this is a good store to buy men's, women's and children's casual shoes. Some of the quality is only so-so. You won't find any name brands, but sometimes you'll see a tennis shoe that looks familiar. That's because Payless does buy from famous manufacturers and puts a house label on instead. The bulk of the stock is displayed on racks and you serve yourself. Sizes in particular styles may be very limited. Children's athletic shoes range from $8.99 to $13.99. Women's casual shoes go from $12.99 to $14.99, and men's athletic shoes from $14.99 to $24.99.

New shipments arrive on Fridays and they are put on the shelves on Saturday.

SVEN'S FACTORY OUTLET

40 Hwy. 10
Blaine
PHONE: 780-2130
HOURS: Mon.-Fri., 10 a.m.-9 p.m.; Sat., 10 a.m.-5 p.m.; Sun., noon-5 p.m.
POLICIES: Credit cards—VISA, Master and Shoppers; lay-by considered; returns: exchange only.

This is a true factory outlet. Sven's manufactures Swedish clogs, clog boots, sheepskin boots and slippers, leather boots, and beaded and unbeaded Indian style mocassins for men, women and children. Manager Anders Skogland keeps prices extremely low, but I can't quote a figure, as he sells to major retailers in the Twin Cities. There's a wide selection of sizes. It's an interesting place to shop for anyone who loves clogs.

Accessories

COLLECTION'S BOUTIQUE

2312 Louisiana Ave. S.
St. Louis Park
PHONE: 542-8336
HOURS: Mon.-Fri., 10 a.m.-6 p.m.; Sat., 10 a.m.-5:30 p.m.
POLICIES: Credit cards—Master and VISA (but not on sale merchandise or purchases under $20); checks accepted; lay-by: 90 days; returns: exchange only.

Right at the beginning of each season, you can get a 20% discount on purses, belts, wallets and sportswear at Collection's Boutique. The name brands and quality are great here (Anne Klein, Meyers, Stone Mountain, Viva, copies of Coach handbags under the Dorcelle label, and snakeskin bags),and so is the selection. The prices on purses ranges from $12 to $300, but watch for 50% markdowns in July and January. (Owners Bobbie Fishbein and Sandy Shirling also carry better women's sportswear here at a savings.)

THE PICKPOCKET AND ETC. ETC. ETC.

6542 W. Lake St.
St. Louis Park
PHONE: 922-4426
HOURS: Mon.-Sat., 10 a.m.-5 p.m.
POLICIES: Credit cards—VISA, Master and Shoppers; lay-by: 30 days; returns: exchange only.

At Pickpocket you'll get a 20% to 30% discount on a variety of name brand and designer purses carrying the Anne Klein, Dorcelle, Jordache, and other well known brand names. Selection can sometimes be limited. Also in this location is Etc. Etc. Etc., and they fill out the stock with belts, wallets, gloves and even lucite giftware, all at 20% off. They have many fashion belts, some designer brands, but most are made just for this store. Leather belts range from $10 to $20. To pocket your savings, check out their wallets. Anne Kleins cost $18 to $40, and imported eelskin is $30 to $40.

Doody Imports

PHONE: 772-1600 or 457-7339 (anytime Mon.-Fri.)
Call for appointment and address.
POLICIES: No credit cards; checks accepted.

Doody Imports sells eelskin purses and accessories at a 50% discount. All you have to do is call one of the phone numbers above and set up an appointment with Mary or Chris Doody to see their wares. You'll find a large inventory; they also can special order items (eelskin briefcases). Once a month one of the partners flies to the Orient to make special buys. Checkbook covers sell for $17.00, men's two-fold wallets are $14.00, and purses average $40.90. They also sell silk beaded necklaces for $4.00. There are some real savings here and the quality is good.

Pedro's Luggage

510 N. Robert St.
(10th & Robert) FREE PARKING
Downtown St. Paul
PHONE: 224-2388
HOURS: Mon. & Thurs., 9:30 a.m.-8 p.m.; Tues.-Wed., Fri., 9:30 a.m.-5:30 p.m.; Sat., 9 a.m.-4:30 p.m.
POLICIES: Credit cards—all major credit cards, Master, VISA, Shoppers and American Express; checks accepted; lay-by: 30 days; returns: cash or credit.

At Pedro's they have a nice variety of name brand purses discounted 15% to 30%. Pedro's also manufactures its own brand luggage, business cases and briefcases, and sells them at factory outlet prices. Plus they have name brand luggage (American Tourister, Samsonite, Hartman, Ventura) for 30% to 50% less. If you need any type of purse or luggage repair, Pedro's can handle it though not at bargain rates.

Luggage World

1538 W. Larpenteur
St. Paul
PHONE: 644-1915

5807 W. 36th St.
St. Louis Park
PHONE: 929-7888

HOURS: Mon.-Fri., 10 a.m.-8:30 p.m.; Sat., 10 a.m.-5 p.m.; Sun.. noon-5:30 p.m.

POLICIES: Credit cards—VISA and Master; checks accepted; lay-by: 30 days; returns: cash or credit.

Leonard Ribnick carries over 100 different luggage brand names (though no purses) at his store. You'll find Samsonite, Tourister, Oleg Cassini, Ventura, and many more, all at 20%-50% off. Garment bags range from $29.95 to $350. Watch for their many sales promotions throughout the year.

In August they have a pre-fall inventory sale, plus half-price sales in January, February, June, and July. Also watch for the annual warehouse sale in February or March, when luggage will be selling for less than 50% off. With all these luggage savings, maybe you can budget more fun in your trip!

HAGEN IMPORTS

The Hayes Bldg., 2nd Fl.
1010 Currie Ave.
Minneapolis
PHONE: 333-4257
HOURS: Mon.-Fri., 10 a.m.-4 p.m.
POLICIES: Checks accepted; no lay-by; no returns.

Hagen's imports gloves. All kinds of hand warmers, ski gloves, snowmobile gloves, mittens—everything is 30% to 40% below retail prices. A really elegant bargain is the long sleek leather women's Italian dress gloves. Hagen's price is $19.95; normally they retail for $39 to $50.

Hagen's is located right next door to A. M. Martin, a purse importer. They are open to the public at various times. When you make the trip, check them out too.

JEWELRY

If you grew up in New York, you'll think nothing of going off the beaten track to uncover a jewelry discount. But in the Midwest it just hasn't been our style. We tend to be suspicious about diamond or gold discounts, figuring lowball prices may actually be tagged on "hot" goods. Personally, I'm leery of 50% to 80% discounts at jewelry store sale prices, when I know the markup can range from 100% to 300%. I'm not suggesting you throw caution to the wind—in fact, all the discount sources below suggest that you shop around before you even see their wares.

When you're buying diamonds it is the three Cs that count: cut, clarity and color. If your knowledge of diamonds is limited, rely on the Gemological Institute of America's (GIA) grading system. It is easier to really detect what you're buying if you buy the diamond loose. A mounted ring may have the flaw in the bottom of the stone where it cannot be easily seen. Always ask to examine a loose diamond under a jeweler's loop or a high-powered diamond scope (preferably the latter). A flawed diamond is fine...just know what it looks like yourself.

When you're buying gold chains, figuring the percentage discount is not as fair as buying by the gram weight. Your true savings is determined by weighing the chain on an electronic gram/pennyweight scale, then measuring the price against the going rate of gold that day...and of course, the seller has to make some money, so he or she will add 15% to 30% above that cost. So ask to have the chain weighed.

All gold is marked with a number and a Karat stamp, like 14K or 18K. A real peach will be marked with a KP, 14KP or 18KP...this means it is a Karat Plum, pure gold. Items with KP marks will be more expensive, of course. For the hunter who is still suspicious: many stores will encourage you to get a second opinion. I believe this shopping trip will open your eyes and gild your senses.

CONTINENTAL DIAMOND/ CERTIFIED GOLD, INC.

2736 Hennepin Ave. S.
Minneapolis
PHONE: 872-8302
HOURS: Mon.-Fri., 10 a.m.-5 p.m.; except Mon. & Thurs., until 7:30 p.m.; Sat., 10 a.m.-2 p.m.
POLICIES: Credit cards—VISA and Master; checks accepted; 15-day money-back unconditional guarantee.

Continental specializes in selling loose diamonds. You can select a GIA certified diamond or a non-certified diamond. But whatever you buy, you're going to save money. They encourage you to inspect all their stones under the Diamond-Scope. There are no fancy jewelry cases here, but 14K and 18K gold chains are regularly sold by the gram weighing system. You can rest assured that you will get a discount that is at least another 50% below any regular jewelry store's 50% off sale, and the quality will be the same. Continental encourages you to get a second appraisal on their diamonds. They also sell colored stones.

WILLIAM STUART JEWELRY CO.

24 Hamm Bldg (Skyway Level)
Downtown St. Paul
PHONE: 222-4887
HOURS: Mon.-Fri., 9:30 a.m.-5:30 p.m.; Sat., 9:30 a.m.-3 p.m.
POLICIES: Credit cards—American Express, VISA and Master; lay-by: 4 month plan; returns: cash or credit in 30 days.

Since Stuart's has been selling discount jewelry for 28 years, most of their business is by referral. When you get here, you'll ring a buzzer. For security reasons, if they don't recognize you or you look unpresentable, "like you just got off a freight train," you simply aren't let in.

William Stuart sells 14K and 18K gold jewelry, semi-precious stones, and loose or mounted diamonds, and also custom designs jewelry. The markup here averages 20% above what they paid for the item. Generally, 14K gold chains are sold for $13.00 a gram weighed by an electron gram/pennyweight scale. Diamonds are graded by the GIA system, and you can inspect your own with their high powered Diamond-Scope. At the time of sale, you'll get a written appraisal by a gemologist including a picture of the diamond and the mounting. You'll find good name brand watches (Seiko, Omega) discounted here, too. There's not much mystery about this place...just some legitimate savings.

What's nice is that you can get a price quote over the phone.

WHOLESALE GOLD & DIAMOND DISTRIBUTORS

Plymouth Bldg.
12 S. Sixth St., #328
Minneapolis
PHONE: 332-7117 or 332-0635
HOURS: Mon.-Fri., 10 a.m.-4:30 p.m.; Sat., 10 a.m.-1 p.m.

POLICIES: Credit cards—VISA and Master; checks accepted; satisfaction guaranteed; returns: cash or credit.

This company sells pearls, gold chains, engagement rings, precious and semi-precious gems and loose or mounted diamonds. Again, you won't find a huge inventory sitting in cases, but you can flip through jewelry catalogs and make a selection. It is best to come here with some idea of what you want. The savings is below anything you'll get at any regular jewelry store sale. Owner Ron Silver urges customers to get a second appraisal on any diamond. Jewelry repairs are available, too, and are very reasonable.

LA PETITE JEWELRY GALLERY

PHONE: 432-6278 (Showings by appointment only.)
HOURS TO CALL: Mon.-Fri., 6 p.m.-9 p.m.; Sat.-Sun., 1 p.m.-5 p.m.
POLICIES: No credit cards; must pay 75% at time of ordering; all sales are final but quality guaranteed; delivery takes one to eight weeks.

La Petite is a home buying service for better quality jewelry. Browsers beware—this is not your style of shopping. You set up an appointment and then go and page through catalogs to select from a wide variety of items, including 14K gold necklaces, bracelets, rings, diamonds, pearls and other gemstones. You can see a few samples, but there's really no jewelry inventory. Go with some idea of what you're looking for.

Here are some samples of the type of quality and savings you'll find. An 18-inch 14K gold necklace in a wide herringbone style retails regularly at $238. The retail *sale* price was $106—La Petite's price $65. A gold bracelet, 14K with a basket weave style *5 links wide*, is $250 at La Petite. A similar bracelet, but only *3 links* wide, is selling in a major jewelry store for $400. A 1/2 Carat, total weight pair of diamond stud earrings with 14K gold studs will sell for the regular retail price range of $900-$1200. La Petite's will range from $450-$600. But as with any great deal, you'll have to put up with some hassles, waiting for your item for anywhere from one week to two months, and paying a great deal upfront at the time of ordering.

CHAPTER 5

SECOND-HAND CLOTHES AND ACCESSORIES

Musty polyester double knits and leftover mini-skirts—is that what you picture when you think about second-hand shopping? Well, if the answer is yes, you're in for some surprises. The consumer push for quality and classic styles that has prevailed for the last five years has changed the look of recycled clothing. Consignment and thrift stores in the Twin Cities drape many well-heeled regular customers. I'll admit that it can still require persistence (and plowing through polyesters) to unearth the best buys. But this chapter uncovers every second-hand shopping corner, making "fashion on the cheap" easier than it's ever been.

Resale Know-How

- To find the best merchandise selection, shop in April for spring and summer clothes and late August through September for fall and winter wardrobes.
- If you are hunting later in the season, always ask whether the item you find is ready for a markdown. Most stores have a 30- to 60-day markdown policy.
- Unless a garment displays a fiber content tag inside, refuse to pay silk (or wool) prices just on the store owner's word that it is a pure fabric. If the tag is gone, the price should reflect the real uncertainty of the fiber.
- If you're looking for a particular item, ask the store owner if there's a special customer list. If so, ask if the owner will call you when the garment comes in. Also, ask if stores have anything interesting stored away; clerks will pull things out for you if they know you're a potential buyer.
- Do some comparison pricing, pitting the consignment cost against an off-price retailer. If the second-hand saving is only $10.00, why buy used? Marginal differences occur sometimes in resale shops, especially on higher-priced items like blazers.
- If you find an outfit or shoes that you really like and the fit is great, inquire about the person who brought the item in on consignment. Chances are there's more merchandise of his or hers tucked on the racks. Or maybe he or she is scheduled to bring in more items.
- The no-return policy is pretty consistent at the resale shops. Make sure you're certain before you buy. Many stores have a lay-by policy, so if you're short on cash and you find something great, consider that option.

RESALE AND CONSIGNMENT STORES

Most resale shops pride themselves on taking only "gently used" items; many are now filling their racks with new sample merchandise. The shopping atmosphere is like that of a boutique or specialty store, easing the first time second-hand shopper into this arena of previously owned bargains.

In the last three years, resale shops have opened all over the Twin Cities. Some offer unique specialties. The latest entry, Rodeo Drive, caters to the elegant, stocking international labels similar to those found in Beverly Hills. To keep you abreast of all your shopping options, I've compiled a Consignment Store Directory.

Consignment Store Directory

For Women

RODEO DRIVE

53 S. 9th St.
Minneapolis
332-4979

Mon.-Fri., 10 a.m.-6 p.m.; Sat., 10 a.m.-5 p.m. VISA, Master; checks accepted; no returns.

Designer women's clothes and accessories size 4 to 14. Very posh store. High class merchandise. Expensive price range. New items from local designers.

THE CLOTHES HORSE

1614 W. Lake St.
Minneapolis
822-6600

Mon.-Sat., 10 a.m.-5 p.m.; except Mon. & Fri., until 7 p.m. VISA, Master; checks accepted; no returns.

Women's designer clothes and accessories, size 4 to 14. Very good quality. Prices moderate to expensive. New samples.

FOXY LADY

6429 Lyndale Ave. S.
Minneapolis
861-4054

Tues.-Wed. & Fri.-Sat., 10 a.m.-4 p.m.; Thurs., 10 a.m.-8 p.m. VISA, Master; checks accepted; no returns.

Women's designer clothing, sizes 4 to 22. Very good quality. Prices moderate to expensive. Furs and accessories.

ROSIE'S CLOSET

3539 W. 44th St.
(near Reindeer Square)
Minneapolis
922-7363

Tues.-Sat., 10 a.m.-4 p.m. No credit cards; checks accepted; no returns.

Women's new brand name clothing, size 4 to 18. Some designer items. Quality is good. Prices moderate to expensive. New samples.

CLOTHES DEN

2550 Central Ave. N.E.
Minneapolis
789-4900

Tues., Wed., Fri., 10 a.m.-4 p.m.; Thurs., 10 a.m.-8 p.m.; Sat., 10 a.m.-3 p.m. No credit cards; checks accepted; no returns.

Women's name brand clothing, size 3 to 22 1/2 and 46 to 48. Quality is good. Moderate prices. New samples.

GENEVIEVE OF EDINA

4506 Valley View Rd.
Edina
925-5696

Tues.-Wed., 10 a.m.-5:30 p.m.; Thurs., 10 a.m.-7 p.m.; Fri.-Sat., 10 a.m.-5 p.m.; Sun., noon-5 p.m. VISA, Master; checks accepted; no returns

Designer women's clothing, size 2 to 48. Very good quality. Prices moderate to expensive. New samples and local designer items.

SECOND TIME AROUND

1122 Lowry Ave. N.
Minneapolis
522-1333

Mon.-Fri., 10:30 a.m.-6 p.m.; Sat., 10:30 a.m.-5 p.m. No credit cards; checks accepted; no returns.

Name brand women's clothing, size 3 to 40. Good quality. Prices moderate.

THE ELEGANTE CLOSET

1919 2nd Ave.
Anoka
421-6860

Mon.-Sat., 10 a.m.-5 p.m.; except Thurs., until 8 p.m. No credit cards; checks accepted; no returns.

Name brand women's size 5 to 22. Limited amount of maternity items. Good quality, moderate prices.

WEIGHT LOSS CLOSET

454 Snelling Ave. S.
St. Paul
690-0028

Tues.-Sat., 10 a.m.-5 p.m.; except Thurs., until 8 p.m. VISA, Master, Shoppers; checks accepted; no returns.

Large size women's shop. Sizes range from 16 to 52. Good quality. Prices moderate. New samples.

For Bridal Parties

ABBEY WEDDING STORE

2310 W. 50th St.
Minneapolis
920-7792

Mon.-Thurs., 10 a.m.-8 p.m.; Fri., 10 a.m.-6 p.m.; Sat., 10 a.m.-4 p.m. No credit cards; checks accepted; no returns.

Current fashion brides', bridesmaids', and flower girls' dresses. Some Forties vintage items. New veils and hats available. Brides' dresses range from $90 to $300. Good quality.

ALL OCCASION & BRIDAL CONSIGNMENT

7651 Old Central
Fridley
786-3738

Mon.-Sat., 10 a.m.-5 p.m. No credit cards; checks accepted; no returns.

Brides' dresses, bridesmaids', mother of the bride outfits, and all-occasion dressy garb. Special wedding accessories available. Good quality. Prices $50 to $295. Rentals available.

I DO—I DO

2118 1/2 Silver Lake Rd.
New Brighton
633-8227

Mon., Tues., Fri., 10 a.m.-5:30 p.m.; Wed.-Thurs., noon-8 p.m.; Sat., 10 a.m.-3 p.m. No credit cards; checks accepted; no returns.

Brides' gowns, bridesmaids' dresses, mother of the bride outfits. Good quality. Bridal gowns range from $100 to $300. Accessories, too.

For Expectant Mothers

THE STORK CLUB

6423 Lyndale Ave.
Richfield
869-0385

Tues.-Sat., 10 a.m.-4:30 p.m. No credit cards; checks accepted; no returns.

Maternity clothes, sizes 4 to 16. Good quality. Reasonable to moderate prices. Real bonus: clothing pick-up service.

For Expectant Mothers and Children

LITTLE RERUNS

Northbrook Center
Hwy. 100 & 57th Ave. N.
Brooklyn Center
566-2886

Mon.-Fri., 10 a.m.-5 p.m.; except Thurs., until 7 p.m.; Sat., 11 a.m.-5 p.m. VISA, Master; checks accepted; no returns.

Children's, infants' to size 20. Maternity, size 6 to 20. Good quality. Moderate to expensive prices. Toys and furniture.

KID STUFF CONSIGNMENT

5631 Manitou Rd.
Excelsior
474-1770

Mon.-Sat., 10 a.m.-6 p.m. VISA, Master, Shoppers; checks accepted; no returns.

Children's, infants' to size 14. Maternity, various sizes. Good quality and name brands. Moderate prices. New samples. Toys and furniture.

KIDS' COVE

3018 11th Ave. N.W.
Coon Rapids
427-0525

Mon. & Thurs., 9:30 a.m.-8 p.m.; Tues., Wed., Fri., 9:30 a.m.-6 p.m.; Sat., 9:30 a.m.-5 p.m. VISA, Master; checks accepted; returns for merchandise exchange.

Children's, infants' to size 14. Maternity clothes, mix of sizes. Good quality. Moderate prices.

YANKEE KIDS

8940 Lyndale Ave. S.
Bloomington
884-2116

Wed.-Fri., 10 a.m.-4 p.m.; except Thurs., until 8 p.m.; Sat., 10:30 a.m.-5 p.m. No credit cards; checks accepted; no returns.

Children's, infants' to size 12. Maternity various sizes. Good quality. Moderate prices.

TWICE BUT NICE

4209 E. 54th St.
Minneapolis
726-9309

Tues.-Sat., 10 a.m.-5 p.m. No credit cards; checks accepted; no returns.

Children's, infants' to size 14. Some maternity. Average quality, some designer items. Toys and books also.

PLAY IT AGAIN

Har Mar Mall
Roseville
636-6666

Mon.-Fri., 10 a.m.-9 p.m.; Sat., 9:30 a.m.-5:30 p.m.; Sun., noon-5 p.m. No credit cards; checks accepted; returns for store credit.

Infants and toddlers, children's size 7 to 14. Maternity in various sizes. Very nice quality. Moderate to expensive prices. New samples. Great furniture.

THE HOBO KIDS

708 Southview Blvd.
South St. Paul
450-0791

Tues.-Fri., 10 a.m.-5 p.m.; Sat., 10 a.m.-4 p.m. No credit cards; checks accepted; no returns.

Children's, infants' to size 14. Maternity clothes various sizes. Nice quality. Moderate prices. New samples. Toys and furniture.

For Children

TWO TIMERS

3735 W. Co. Rd. 42
Burnsville
890-1250

Wed.-Sat., 10 a.m.-4:30 p.m. No credit cards; checks accepted; no returns.

Boys' and girls', infant to junior high. Good quality. Moderately priced.

KID STOP

2316 W. 66th St.
Richfield
869-5156

Tues.-Sat., 10 a.m.-4 p.m. No credit cards; checks accepted; no returns.

Boys' and girls', infant to 14 years. Good quality. Moderately priced.

UPTON ALLEY

4303 Upton Ave. S.
Minneapolis
926-1446

Tues.-Sat., 10 a.m.-5 p.m.; except Thurs., until 8 p.m. VISA, Master; checks aced; no returns.

Boys', infant to size 20, girls', infant to size 14. No designer labels. Moderately priced. Toys and baby furniture.

BANANAS

North of Co. Rd. 6 on
Hwy. 101
Plymouth
473-3383

Tues.-Sat., 9 a.m.-5 p.m. VISA, Master; checks accepted; returns accepted.

Boys' and girls', infant to size 14. Moderate to expensive. Also new samples, toys and children's gifts.

MERRY-GO-ROUND

3511 W. 44th St.
Minneapolis
926-4437

Tues.-Sat., 10 a.m.-5 p.m. VISA, Master; checks accepted.

Children's, infant to 14. Good quality. Moderate prices. Special feature is the toy lending library. New hand-sewn clothes available.

LITTLE SPROUTS

6528 W. Lake St.
St. Louis Park
929-6221

Mon.-Sat., 10 a.m.-5 p.m.; except Thurs., until 8 p.m. VISA, Master; checks accepted; no returns on 2nd-hand items.

Children's, infants' to size 14. Good quality. Moderate prices. New samples available.

PASS IT ON

Rice Creek Center
2120 Silver Lake Rd.
New Brighton
633-6783

Mon.-Sat., 10 a.m.-5 p.m.; except Wed.-Thurs. until 8 p.m. No credit cards; checks accepted; no returns.

Children's, infants' to size 14. Good name brands and quality. Moderate prices. Cabbage Patch look-alike dolls and clothes.

ANOTHER GENERATION

1344 Thomas Ave.
St. Paul
644-9645

Mon.-Fri., 10 a.m.-5:30 p.m.; Sat., 10 a.m.-4 p.m. No credit cards; checks accepted; no returns.

Children's, infants' to size 14. Average quality, prices reasonable. Toys and children's furniture.

THE CHILDREN'S ATTIC

2216 3rd St.
White Bear Lake
426-5756

Mon.-Sat., 10 a.m.-5 p.m.; except Thurs., until 9 p.m. No credit cards; checks accepted; to return, call within 24 hours.

Children's, infant to size 16. Moderate to expensive. Good quality. Toys and furniture.

For Women and Children

FRIDAY'S CHILD

1206 W. Excelsior Ave.
Hopkins
938-0298

Tues.-Fri., 11 a.m.-5 p.m.; Sat., 10 a.m.-3:30 p.m. No credit cards; checks accepted; no returns.

Women's, children's, teen's, maternity. The majority of clothes are children's. Good quality kids' clothes, moderate prices. Some baby furniture.

SCARLET TRUNK

922 Excelsior Ave. E.
Hopkins
933-2776

Tues.-Sat., 10 a.m.-4 p.m.; except Thurs., 6:30-8:30 p.m.; closed Sat. in summer. No credit cards; checks accepted.

Women's and children's clothing. Good labels and quality. Moderate prices.

THE RAINBOW RECYCLERY

911 66th Ave. N.
Brooklyn Center
561-4472

Tues., Wed., Fri., 10 a.m.-6 p.m.; Thurs., noon-4 p.m. No credit cards; checks accepted; no returns.

Women's and children's. Maternity sizes 3 to 40. Moderate quality, moderate prices.

TWICE IS NICE

4030 Central Ave. N.E.
Minneapolis
789-0429

Mon.-Sat., 10 a.m.-5 p.m. No credit cards; checks accepted; no returns.

Women's and children's clothes. Merchandise is marginal. Prices are reasonable.

TOO GOOD TO BE THREW

4122 W. Broadway
Robbinsdale
537-7684

Mon.-Fri., 10 a.m.-5 p.m.; Sat., 10 a.m.-4 p.m. No credit cards; checks accepted; no returns.

The majority is women's size 2 to 48. Children's size infant to 12. Nice quality. Moderate prices.

THE SHOWCASE

Oak Park Plaza
10759 University Ave. N.E.
Blaine
757-4703

Mon.-Sat., 10 a.m.-5 p.m.; except Thurs., until 7:30 p.m. No credit cards; checks accepted; no returns.

Women's and children's. Good quality. Moderate prices.

NU-LOOK APPAREL

4956 Penn Ave. S.
Minneapolis
925-0806

Mon.-Sat., 10 a.m.-5 p.m.; except Thurs., until 7 p.m. VISA, Master; checks accepted; no returns.

Mainly women's clothes. Nice selection of maternity, size 6 to 16. Some children's. Good quality. Moderate prices. New samples selling at wholesale prices.

BARBARA'S CONSIGNMENT APPAREL

6418 Bass Lake Rd.
Crystal
533-7676

Mon.-Sat., 10 a.m.-5 p.m.; except Thurs., until 7 p.m. VISA, Master, Shoppers; checks accepted; no returns.

Maternity, women's and children's (infants' to size 8). Good quality. Moderate prices. New samples for women and children.

ONCE AGAIN, INC.

887 S. Smith Ave.
St. Paul
451-8191

Tues.-Sat., 10 a.m.-5 p.m. No credit cards; checks accepted; no returns.

Women's sizes 3 to 15 and extra large 46 and 48. Boys', infant to size 20. Girls', infant to size 14. Some nice labels and quality. Moderate with some items expensive.

TIME AND AGAIN

McKnight/36 Plaza
2124 11th Ave. E.
N. St. Paul
770-0303

Mon.-Fri., 10 a.m.-7 p.m.; Sat., 10 a.m.-5 p.m. No credit cards; checks accepted; returns accepted.

Women's sizes 3 to 40. Girls', infant to size 16. Boys', infant to size 18. Average to good quality. Prices very reasonable to expensive. Children's furniture.

PATTY-KAY'S CLOTHING CONSIGNMENT

478 W. Main
Anoka
427-6837

Mon.-Fri., 9 a.m.-5:30 p.m.; except Thurs., until 8 p.m.; Sat., 10 a.m.-4 p.m. No credit cards; checks accepted; no returns.

Women's size 3 to 22. Children's size 1 to 10. Some maternity. Current fashions. Prices moderate.

THE TRADIN' POST

832 White Bear Ave.
St. Paul
738-9390

Tues.-Fri., 10 a.m.-5:30 p.m.; Sat., 10 a.m.-4:30 p.m. No credit cards; checks accepted; no returns.

Women's size 3 to 40. Children's, infant to 14. Some maternity. Good labels. Prices moderate.

For Men and Women

THE WARDROBE

Market Place Shopping Center
Rice St. & Little Canada Rd.
Little Canada
636-2884

Mon.-Fri., 10 a.m.-9 p.m.; Sat., 10 a.m.-5:30 p.m.; Sun., noon-5 p.m. No credit cards; checks accepted; no returns except on menswear.

Majority is women's clothes, size 3 to 20. Nice selection of menswear. One rack of maternity wear. Good quality. Popular labels. Moderate prices.

THE PINK CLOSET

4024 E. 46th St.
Minneapolis
724-2468

Tues.-Sat., 10 a.m.-5:30 p.m. No credit cards; checks accepted; no returns.

Good selection of both women's and men's clothes. Designer names. Good quality. Furs, accessories. New samples. Reasonable to expensive prices. Some children's clothes.

THE SWITCHING POST

2015 Aldrich Ave. S.
Minneapolis
870-1485

Open September to June, Wed.-Sat., 10 a.m.-3:45 p.m. No credit cards; checks accepted; no returns.

Women's and men's clothing. Designer names. Good quality. Prices reasonable to moderate. Children's clothes occasionally. Lots of furniture, china and household items.

KLOTHES KLOSETT

649 Snelling Ave. S.
St. Paul
698-3484

Mon.-Sat., 10 a.m.-5 p.m. No credit cards; checks accepted; no returns.

Women's and men's clothes and accessories. Small selection of maternity. Occasionally designer items. Good quality and name brands. Moderate to expensive.

THE ELITE REPEAT

1336 Randolph Ave.
St. Paul
699-2315

Mon.-Sat., 10 a.m.-5 p.m. VISA, Master, Shoppers; checks accepted; returns for merchandise exchange.

Women's size 3 to 16. Good selection of men's. Some maternity. Designers and brand names. Good quality. Moderate to expensive. Samples.

ENCORE SHOPPE

242 S. Hamline
St. Paul
699-7522

Mon.-Sat., 10 a.m.-5:30 p.m. No credit cards; checks accepted; no returns.

Women's and men's clothes, some children's. Crowded store. Some good name brands. Moderate prices.

THE OTHER SIDE

2174 3rd St.
White Bear Lake
429-9742

Mon.-Fri., 10 a.m.-6 p.m.; Sat., 10 a.m.-4 p.m. VISA, Master, Shoppers; checks accepted; no returns.

Majority is women's clothing. Some men's. Always have formals and wedding dresses. Good quality. Moderate prices. New samples.

THE CLOTHES EXCHANGE

Lamplighter Shopping Sq.
2712 Douglas Dr.
Crystal
542-9502

Mon.-Sat., 10 a.m.-5 p.m.; except Thurs., until 8 p.m. VISA, Master, Shoppers; checks accepted; no returns.

Women's and some men's clothing. Good quality. Moderate to expensive. Some designer names. Furs and new samples.

For Everybody

THE RECLOTHERY

18336 Minnetonka Blvd.
Deephaven
473-0833

Tues.-Fri., 10 a.m.-5 p.m.; Sat., 10 a.m.-4 p.m. No credit cards; checks accepted; no returns.

Designer women's and men's clothing; some children's. Very good quality. Prices moderate to expensive.

TRINITY CLOTHES HANGER

Trinity Episcopal Church
322 2nd St.
Excelsior
474-8441

Open Sept. to mid-June, Thurs., 10 a.m.-4:30 p.m. and 7-9 p.m.; Fri.-Sat., 10 a.m.-4 p.m. No credit cards; checks accepted; no returns.

Men's, women's and children's. Some fine designer clothes go through here. Reasonable to expensive. This spot is a good find. Consignor gets 2/3 of profits.

ROBBIE'S

5458 Nicollet Ave. S.
Minneapolis
825-5221

Mon.-Sat., 10:30 a.m.-5:30 p.m. No credit cards; checks accepted; no returns.

Women's size 4 to 20. Men's various sizes. Children's, infants' to 6. Popular name brands. Very reasonable.

ANYTHING AT ALL

707 E. Lake St.
Minneapolis
822-5152

Mon.-Fri., 10 a.m.-5 p.m.; except Mon. & Thurs., until 7:30 p.m.; Sat.; 10 a.m.-6 p.m. VISA, Master, Shoppers; checks accepted; no returns.

A thrift shop atmosphere. Small selection of men's, women's and children's clothes. Merchandise is marginal but reasonable.

ONE MORE TYME

1839 E. 38th St.
Minneapolis
724-3222

Mon.-Sat., 10 a.m.-5 p.m. No credit cards; checks accepted; no returns.

Majority is women's. Some men's and children's. Good quality. Prices moderate.

THE GRAND EXCHANGE

1661 Grand Ave.
St. Paul
699-4239

Mon.-Sat., 10 a.m.-5 p.m. No credit cards; checks accepted; no returns.

Majority is women's clothes. Some college-age men's. Children's, infants' to size 16. Good quality. New samples. Moderate prices.

THE AFFORDABLE SHOP

2385 Margaret
St. Paul
777-3616

Tues.-Sat., 10 a.m.-5 p.m. No credit cards; checks accepted; no returns.

Women's size 2 to 50. Men's various sizes. Children's, infants' to 6. Popular name brands. Moderate prices.

For Sports Lovers

PLAY IT AGAIN SPORTS

3505 Hennepin Ave. S.
Minneapolis
824-1231

Tues.-Sat., 11:30 a.m.-6 p.m. No credit cards; checks accepted; no returns.

Save 25% to 75% on used sporting equipment. If you bring yours in to sell, you'll get 60% to 70% of the profit. New activewear samples at discount prices.

Turn Your Clothes into Cash

- Contact a store early in the season (March for spring and summer clothes and July for fall and winter). Make an appointment to bring in your items.
- Stores only want good condition, current style garb. Often they won't take anything that's more than two years old, unless it's a priceless classic. You'll have to wash and press everything before the appointment. But don't do any expensive drycleaning until you know for sure the store will take the outfit.
- In most cases, don't expect to recover half the price you paid for the item. Let the store owner set the price. If you have a really expensive item and are not satisfied with what you'll get from a resale shop, your best bet is to put an ad in the paper and try to sell it yourself.
- The stores mark items down after a certain period; often you must sign a contract with terms that say you agree to settle for less profit if the garment doesn't sell in the beginning of a season. If you don't want to do this, let the store owner know right away. At the end of a season it's your responsibility to pick up the clothes that didn't sell. Otherwise the store will donate them to a charity. You may want to take your own tax credit for the donation.
- A lot of stores don't mail checks out to consignors, but expect you to pick up your own. Inquire about this and mark your calendar with dates to check back with the shop.
- Many stores disclaim responsibility if there's a fire or theft in the shop. If this matters to you, ask about it.

THRIFT STORE SHOPPING

Thrift store shopping is rather like golf. Every time you shop, you're trying to beat your last money-saving score. But it's also the most effective way I know to dress rich on a tight budget. Admittedly, it takes practice and patience. It's easy to find a good wardrobe buy at a neat, well-organized store. The challenge comes when you find it hidden among tightly packed racks or tucked beneath piles of clothing heaped in bins. The more you know, the easier it is to shop.

This section will supply you with inside shopping information and give you the hidden rules of the thrift store game. A lot of shopping amenities are missing at the thrift stores. Some have dressing rooms, some don't. For those of you who have never charted this bargain territory, I've extended the policy section to include parking facilities. Read the store policies carefully, because some stores won't accept checks.

Thrift Store Shopping Strategies

- Look for the best quality and conditioned items on a rack. You can pay $3.00 for junk or $3.00 for a jewel, so use manufacturer's labels and fiber content labels as a guide to quality. Look for designer names and select the natural fabrics (wool, cotton, silk or blends).

- Bring the family's *measurements* (not sizes) and a measuring tape. Often clothes are not marked for size. This will save you shopping time. If you're buying for yourself, try on everything. You can't just go by the size inside the garment. Jeans and cotton blouses shrink. This will save you hassle later, since the majority of stores have a "no return" policy.

- Don't waste your energy going through every garment on the rack. Shop it by color. Stop only when you see the colors you're looking for. If the fabric feels good, and the color is right, then pull the item out and glance quickly for an identifying manufacturer's tag. If you've had your colors analyzed, it helps to bring along your chart.

- Women should never overlook the men's department. Often good blouses and jackets get stuck in with men's shirts and coats.

- Figure in alterations when a garment is an expensive fabric. This is especially true for men's suits. If you buy one for $15 and just the lapels need slimming, your alteration cost will be approximately $25 to $35. Replacement value of the suit is at least $100. So you're still money ahead.

- Before buying anything, check the condition carefully. Avoid anything that is spotted, unless it's marked so low it's worth taking the chance. Wools will probably come clean, but permanent press material won't.

SALVATION ARMY

900 N. Fourth St. (Main Store)
Minneapolis
PHONE: 332-6961

2822 Washington Ave. N.
Minneapolis
PHONE: 529-4077

2615 E. Franklin Ave.
Minneapolis
PHONE: 338-4710

2815 Nicollet Ave. S.
Minneapolis
PHONE: 871-4414

3756 Nicollet Ave. S.
Minneapolis
PHONE: 822-1200

1928 Central Ave. N.E.
Minneapolis
PHONE: 788-6656

1521 Como Ave. S.E.
Minneapolis
PHONE: 331-7833

1326 Coon Rapids Blvd.
Coon Rapids
PHONE: 757-6740

927 Payne Ave.
St. Paul
PHONE: 776-3585

909 Selby Ave.
St. Paul
PHONE: 227-9931

572 University Ave. (UniDale Mall)
St. Paul
PHONE: 224-7061

HOURS: Mon.-Sat., 9 a.m.-5 p.m.; except Coon Rapids, Mon.-Fri., 10 a.m.-9 p.m. and Sat., 9 a.m.-5 p.m., and UniDale Mall, Mon.-Fri., 9 a.m.-9 p.m. and Sat., 9 a.m.-5 p.m.

POLICIES: Checks accepted; no returns; dressing rooms available; parking lots or off street available at all stores; senior and student discount.

There have been seasons when I have completely outfitted myself, shopping *only* at these thrift stores. When people ask, "where did you buy that?" they never suspect a Salvation Army store. Sometimes I say it's from "Salvo's" just to give it a continental flair; others call it "Sally's."

Most of the time, I can't wait to brag about the place and the price. Other thrift stores in town can top some of the Salvation Army's prices, but the volume of clothing donated to this organization is enormous. In this hit or miss shopping game, that's important in adding to your hunting success rate.

The best quality women's clothes are found in sizes 6 to 14, in classic style separates. Women's blazers range from $3 to

$10, skirts from $2 to $8, sweaters from $3 to $4. Men's suits go from $8 to $25, shirts from $1 to $5, children's ski jackets from $3 to $6, jeans from $1.50 to $4.00. Here's a shopping route I use—it may help you beat the hit or miss odds. Begin at the Main (900 North Fourth Street) Minneapolis store where the stock for everything is largest; then travel one mile away to the Washington Avenue Salvation Army store. Finally, head for a "Salvo" store close to home. It won't take much more effort than you'd put into working the "Dales" from end to end.

Salvation Army also gets new donations from retail sources. The bulk of these go to the Main Store location. The largest new donation supply occurs from mid-July to September for summer items and mid-January through February for winter clothes. Often these are ripped or slightly damaged, so inspect carefully. Some of the new items are overpriced, but there are always exceptions. I found one dress selling for $6.00 (retail was $65) that had only the top button missing.

Here's a list of best times to shop at the various Salvation Army Stores. (Take them with a grain of salt—putting out the clothes can be delayed if a store manager gets busy. If it's crucial, call ahead and ask.)

THE MAIN STORE - Clothes put out daily.
WASHINGTON AVE. STORE - Clothes put out daily, but Friday is the best day.
CENTRAL AVE. STORE - Best days to shop are Thursday and Friday.
2815 NICOLLET AVE. STORE - Clothes put out on Wednesday.
3756 NICOLLET AVE. STORE - Clothes put out on Monday or Tuesday.
FRANKLIN AVE. STORE - Best day to shop is Wednesday.
COMO AVE. STORE - Best day to shop is Tuesday afternoon.
COON RAPIDS STORE - Clothes put out on Wednesday and Thursday.
PAYNE AVE. STORE - Clothes put out Thursday through Monday. Best shopping days—Fridays and Saturdays.
UNIDALE MALL - Majority of clothes put out early Saturday afternoon.
SELBY AVE. STORE - Best days to shop are Friday afternoon and Saturday.

GOODWILL STORES

2543 Como Ave.
St. Paul
PHONE: 646-2591
HOURS: Mon.-Fri., 9:30 a.m.-9 p.m.; Sat., 9 a.m.-5:30 p.m.; Sun., 12:30-5:30 p.m.

946 Payne Ave.
St. Paul
PHONE: 646-2591
HOURS: Mon. & Fri., 9 a.m.-9 p.m.; Tues.-Thurs., 9 a.m.-6 p.m.; Sat., 9 a.m.-5 p.m.; Sun., noon-5 p.m.

913 Excelsior Ave.
Hopkins
PHONE: 935-9773
HOURS: Mon.-Fri., 10 a.m.-8 p.m.; Sat., 9 a.m.-5:30 p.m.; Sun., noon-5 p.m.

4020 Bloomington Ave.
Minneapolis
PHONE: 823-4855
HOURS: Mon.-Fri., 9 a.m.-9 p.m.; Sat., 9 a.m.-5:30 p.m.; Sun., 12:30-5:30 p.m.

3000 White Bear Ave.
(across from Maplewood Mall)
Maplewood
PHONE: 770-2401
HOURS: Mon.-Fri., 9 a.m.-9 p.m.; Sat., 9:30 a.m.-5 p.m.; Sun., noon-5 p.m.

POLICIES: Credit cards—Master and VISA; checks accepted; no returns; dressing rooms available; all stores have parking lots; senior discount.

It's no longer just the college crowd shopping second-hand. Goodwill has fashionably outfitted many a middle-class shopper. In fact, when you first walk into one of their stores, you forget you're inside a thrift shop. They are remodeled to resemble discount chains. They're bright, clothes are well displayed, and they're even accepting credit cards. However, the stock is still unpredictable and requires a practiced bargain eye, keeping the taste of shopping adventure alive.

The majority of goods are second-hand; some are new donations from regular stores; but a new tactic is to fill out the merchandise with off-price wares from clothing distributors. Prices are an incentive for return visits. Women's skirts are $3.29, blouses $1.99 to $2.99, men's suits $8.99, children's snowsuits $3.69, and winter coats $5.99 and up. My favorite buy here was a white leather (Miquel Hernandez), very expensive-looking pair of low heels with embroidery on the toes. They were new, never worn. Actually, I didn't find them...another shopper did. I saw them in her cart and I knew there was no way they were going to fit her. Knowing my own hoarding habit of picking up great items and putting them in my cart even when I'm not going to buy them, I decided to ask her about them. She handed over these gorgeous shoes and I ran to the checkout to pay the $1.99 Goodwill price.

A big sale to watch for is the annual 'Drummer Day' sale, the day after Thanksgiving.

THE CLOTHESLINE MINNEAPOLIS JUNIOR LEAGUE THRIFT STORE

3038 Hennepin Ave. S.
Minneapolis
PHONE: 822-3212
HOURS: Mon., 9:30 a.m.-7 p.m.; Tues.-Sat., 9:30 a.m.-5 p.m.
POLICIES: Checks accepted; will hold items for 30 days; returns: store exchange; meter parking.

This store is so well arranged that you almost forget you're in a thrift store. It's a good place for the beginning second-hand shopper to build a first-rate wardrobe. They put out their best clothes in the beginning of each season, so go early. For spring, shop between mid-February and May; for winter, start the first week of August until November. They have men's, women's and children's clothes. But the best selection is in women's clothes, size 6, 8 and 10. New items are put out daily (they always have a mix of drapes and bedspreads, a sprinking of housewares, and a few pieces of furniture).

Look for good buys on the women's dressy clothes and basics: blazers range from $5 to $25, and wool skirts from $7.50 to $15. Men's suits go for $5 to $35. Occasionally they get store donations of new clothes. Last summer they had a donation of sportswear, which sold off the racks as quickly as it was put on. It's no wonder there are some regulars who shop this place every day, just lying in wait for the good stuff to come up!

When you first go into the store, check out the racks directly to the side of the cashier counter. This is where items are hung first before store volunteers put them in the proper place.

Watch for two sales: a popular "gently used" toy sale each year the first week in December, and a Christmas boutique the day after Thanksgiving, with all new gift items.

NEXT TO NEW
ST. PAUL JUNIOR LEAGUE THRIFT STORE

24 W. 7th Place
Downtown St. Paul
PHONE: 222-2061
HOURS: Mon.-Fri., 9:30 a.m.-5:30 p.m.; Sat., 10 a.m.-2 p.m. (Back Room open Wed. & Fri., 10 a.m.-2 p.m.)
POLICIES: Checks accepted; no returns; dressing room available; meter parking.

Next to New has supplied many shoppers with designer labels. The prices lean toward the consignment shop level. Men's suits range from $10 to $50, women's blazers from $10 to $25, wool skirts from $5 to $17.50. The children's clothes are often good quality, but they go fast.

The best time to shop here is when the Back Room is open. This will give you a larger selection to pick through. It's fun to shop those days—everyone crowds in to snatch up bargains off the hangers as soon as they are priced.

They also have a consignment rack that sometimes has top fashion items. These are marked higher than anywhere else in the store. But if you're putting together a working wardrobe and you're short on time, check this out.

Council Thrift Shop

3210 Bloomington Ave. S.
Minneapolis
PHONE: 729-6131
HOURS: Mon., 10 a.m.-8 p.m.; Tues.-Sat., 10 a.m.-5 p.m.; during the summer they close Mon. evenings at 6:30 p.m.
POLICIES: Checks accepted; returns: exchange only; lay-by: 30 days; dressing room available; off-street parking; delivery referral.

Anyone putting together a working wardrobe has to stop here. This store is operated by the National Council of Jewish Women and the designer names that come through are frequently real finds. Every time I shop, there are Jones of New York, Calvin Kleins and Evan Picones hanging on the racks, not always in my size, but the excitement of seeing them keeps me hunting.

The best selection is women's sizes 6 to 14; skirts range from $3 to $15, blazers are $8 to $15. You'll see lots of sweaters, shoes and slacks, too. The men's clothes are some of the most fashionable you'll find at a thrift store, and suits range from $15 to $35. Children's clothes are very spotty. If you do find something, it'll be marked low. But the bargains I've passed up here because I couldn't make a quick decision give me nightmares.

Often, the Council Thrift Shop gets new store donations. One that I recall was from a well-known shoe store in town that went out of business. Current style all-leather women's shoes priced $8 to $15.

This store is not stocked by seasons. When it's winter, you'll still find summer items, which is great if you're looking for cruisewear. Clothes are put in the store daily.

Lots O' Savings Shoppe

942 Payne Ave.
St. Paul
PHONE: 774-5809
HOURS: Tues.-Sat., 10 a.m.-4 p.m.
POLICIES: Checks accepted; no returns; dressing rooms available; off-street parking.

This store is positioned well for serious thrift shoppers—it's located right between a Salvation Army and a Goodwill store, giving you three bargain stops within a couple of blocks! Items are restocked daily, and the store has a reputation for considering prices as bargainable, even though the prices are already cheap. Men's suits range from $3.50 to $10, slacks from $1.00 to $4.00. Women's skirts are $.75 to $2.50 and dresses are $1.00 to $8.00.

Watch for special bag sales in March and August, when you can stuff whatever you can get into a bag and buy it for $3.00.

MINNEAPOLIS YMCA THRIFT SHOP

1130 Nicollet Mall
Downtown Minneapolis
PHONE: 332-0501, ext. 161
HOURS: Mon.-Fri., 10 a.m.-5 p.m.; except Tues., until 8 p.m.
POLICIES: Checks accepted; no returns; dressing room available; meter parking.

The Y's thrift store can hold some bargains, especially for the downtown Minneapolis working crowd. The more frequent your visits, the better the chances for a good find. The store is small and easy to shop; most prices are moderate. Some great name brand labels pass through here for both men and women. Look for a small selection of children's clothes and household wares.

STEEPLE PEOPLE THRIFT STORE

715 W. Franklin Ave.
Minneapolis
PHONE: 871-8305
HOURS: Thurs., 10 a.m.-8 p.m.; Fri., 10 a.m.-5:30 p.m.; Sat., 10 a.m.-5 p.m.
POLICIES: Checks accepted; no returns; dressing room available; off-street parking.

At times a price tag here will reflect a higher value than you would expect in a thrift store. Men's suits range from $3.00 to $25, shirts $.50 to $3.00, women's suits $2.00 to $7.00, kids' jeans $.25 to $2.00. Lots of household bric-a-brac. Don't let the small size of this store mislead you. It takes some time to shop. Often there are treasures hidden here if you're persistent in your pursuit. The shoe section, in particular, holds a few.

Shop this store early on Thursdays. That's when the stock is replenished for the week. Check out the jewelry case, because some good pieces glide through here.

REACHOUT THRIFT STORE

417 E. Lake St.
Minneapolis
PHONE: 827-5606
HOURS: Mon.-Sat., 9 a.m.-9 p.m.
POLICIES: Checks accepted; no returns; no dressing rooms; off-street parking.

At times the clothes seem overpriced here, but then you stumble on something great and it keeps you coming back. Men's suits will range from $5.00 to $20.00, women's skirts from $2.00 to $4.00. There's a fairly good selection of children's clothes. The store is maintained with just enough disorder to pique the hunter's interest.

DISABLED AMERICAN VETERANS' THRIFT STORE

1808 Emerson Ave. N.
Minneapolis
PHONE: 522-0047
HOURS: Mon.-Sat., 9 a.m.-9 p.m.
POLICIES: Cash or money orders; no returns; no dressing rooms; parking lot available.

We are talking about some serious digging here. This place is large and it's packed with all types of clothes, household items, furniture, appliances. One of those "you name it, we've had it at one time or another" stores. Prices are very cheap on items that should be cheap. But when you get into some of the better things, you can end up paying a lot of money, especially for the effort involved. Men's suits range from $4.00 to $60, men's slacks from $.10 to $20, women's skirts from $.10 to $20. What will keep you coming back is the chance that good things do slip by the pricers—those can be a steal.

New stock is put out on Tuesdays and Saturdays at about 11:30 a.m. That's the time to shop here.

WORN-A-BIT

436 N. Smith
St. Paul
PHONE: 291-9639
HOURS: Mon.-Fri., 9 a.m.-4:45 p.m.; Sat., 9 a.m.-3 p.m.
POLICIES: No checks; cash only; no dressing rooms; off-street parking.

When you pull up to this thrift store it looks questionable on the outside, and at first glance, the inside seems to hold little promise. But there are finds here for the bargain hunter short on money and long on time (and energy!). This store has rows and rows of clothing bins. In the front, by the door, there's a rack of long dresses. Occasionally you'll find a wedding dress or some spectacular slinky thing. Coats are hung along the wall and sometimes hold a prize. I found a beige leather women's Fifties style coat, mint condition, for $3.00, the last time I was here. Nothing is marked. Just gather your goods, take them to the counter and the staff will tell you the prices. If you love books, save some time to browse through the shelves.

ST. VINCENT DE PAUL

461 W. 7th St.
St. Paul
PHONE: 227-1332
HOURS: Mon.-Fri., 9:30 a.m.-2:30 p.m.; Sat., 10 a.m.-2:30 p.m.
POLICIES: Checks accepted; no returns; dressing room available; off-street parking.

St. Vincent's store can be intriguing. Sometimes there's absolutely nothing in the place that will interest you, yet other times, it's great. Dresses sell for $2.00 and $3.00, men's suits are $3.50 to $5.00, and shoes are $.50 to $1.00. I have found some of the best shoe deals here. Nothing is marked, so you have to bring it to the counter and ask. (You can do some bargaining here and depending on the volunteer that day, you can have some fun.) In the back of this building there's a room with odds and ends of furniture. Housewares are very spotty. Once I did find a French gourmet 3-tier pie cooling rack for $2.00 (I think that's what it is!) I don't bake pies, so it doubles as my letter file.

THE ECONOMY CENTERS

1001 E. Franklin Ave. S.
Minneapolis
PHONE: 871-1551
HOURS: Tues.-Sat., 10 a.m.-3:45 p.m.

2064 W. Broadway N.
Minneapolis
PHONE: 521-5159
HOURS: Tues.-Sat., 9 a.m.-3 p.m.

POLICIES: Checks accepted; no returns; dressing room available; off-street parking.

Bring along small change when you shop here. Most of the clothes sell for $1.00 or less, and most you won't want, even for that price. But as always, in this unpredictable shopping arena—you never know. There just might be something hidden. There are some household items and old (and odd) appliances, too.

A lot of male shoppers have claimed some good buys here.

AMERICAN COUNCIL OF THE BLIND THRIFT STORE

4713 36th Ave. N.
Crystal
PHONE: 522-7738

633 Minnehaha Ave.
West St. Paul
PHONE: 488-5553

HOURS: Mon.-Sat., 9 a.m.-9 p.m.
POLICIES: Cash only; no returns; no dressing rooms; off-street parking.

These stores are large and packed with racks of clothes for the whole family. The staff isn't too fussy about what they put in this store. The prices, however, are so cheap that maybe it's worth all the careful inspecting you'll need to do. Men's suits range from $1.09 to $3.99, women's skirts $.59 to $1.99, and coats from $1.09 to $5.99. So, if you do find a treasure here it could beat garage sale prices. Some household items and furniture available.

The searching here requires the perseverance of a professional picker.

MORNING MARKET
ST. PAUL ACADEMY UPPER SCHOOL

1712 Randolph Ave.
St. Paul
PHONE: 698-2451
HOURS: Store only open from day after Labor Day to April 30th each year; Mon.-Fri., 8:30 a.m.-1 p.m.; closed during school holiday vacations.
POLICIES: Checks accepted; no returns; dressing room available; parking lot on Davern and Randolph.

If you can swerve off your normal shopping path, visit this little shop. Most of the donations come from St. Paul Academy families and alumni. Some big bargains fly out this door. Would you believe an Oscar De La Renta evening dress was here (briefly) for $4.00? Some of the best buys here are the children's clothes. There's always a ton of jeans, selling for $2.00 a pair. Nice men's suits go for $15.00. Women's blazers are $3.50 to $10.00, and skirts $2.50 to $7.00.

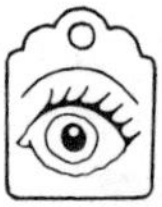

The last weekend in April, before they close up shop, they sell out everything in the store at unbelievable prices. Look also for a small selection of toys and housewares.

VALUE VILLAGE

6412 Penn Ave. S.
Minneapolis
PHONE: 866-3633
HOURS: Mon.-Fri., 10 a.m.-6 p.m.; except Thurs., until 9 p.m.; Sat., 10 a.m.-5 p.m.; Sun., 1 p.m.-5 p.m.
POLICIES: Checks accepted; no returns; dressing rooms available; off-street parking; delivery on furniture extra.

Even avid rummage sale shoppers will agree the prices are decent at Value Village. You'll find lots of children's clothes, most of it selling for $.25. Women's skirts and blouses start at $.50 and men's suits range from $3.00 to $15. Of course there's some digging to discover just the right bargain.

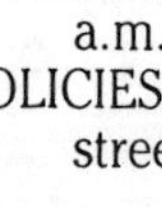

A real bonus at this thrift store is their Call File. If you're looking for something, they will fill out an index card and when it comes into the store, give you a call. One hunter

saved herself shopping time and money and bought her electric roaster oven for $8.00 with the help of this service.

Housewares are restocked on Tuesdays and there are some good buys on these. Furniture is also available. Miscellaneous items are set out every day.

TATTERS

2922 Lyndale Ave. S.
Minneapolis
PHONE: 823-5285
HOURS: Mon.-Fri. 10 a.m.-8 p.m.; Sat. 10 a.m.-6 p.m.; Sun. noon-6 p.m.
POLICIES: Credit cards—VISA and Master; checks accepted; hold for 24 hours, or 10 days with a deposit.

The recycled threads at Tatters have taken the rumble seat to their New Wave neighbors. The new-item takeover in the store is all first quality, with the emphasis on flashy. Stylized male or female shoppers will have no trouble gleaning garb ideas from the store displays, because this place is forward in fun fashions. There's still a supply of military goods in the New Wave madness and a nice selection of Fifties and Sixties clothes.

Some merchandise is a little pricey for the tattered pocketbook, but if you sign their mailing list you'll get 20% off coupons. Stock is put out daily but they do gear up for the Saturday shopper.

THE CORNER STORE

900 W. Lake St.
Minneapolis
PHONE: 823-1270
HOURS: Mon.-Fri., 11 a.m.-6 p.m.; Sat., 10 a.m.-6 p.m.
POLICIES: Credit cards—VISA and Master; checks accepted; lay-by: 30 days; returns: exchange only.

This store has a real corner on the vintage clothing market from the 1870s to the 1960s. I personally could die for the man's silk tie with the painted nude lady inside. It's a real collectible and *not* for sale. Men and women shed their business suits and shop for funky classics here. Men's suits range from $20 to $50, women's suits from $15 to $50, skirts from $5 to $15. All the clothes are handled with care by the owner, except those in the back, where you'll find a little room full of unpressed bargains priced at $3 to $5. There's a fun selection of kitschy Fifties furniture and home accessories, too.

REPEAT PERFORMANCE

707 W. 34th St.
Minneapolis
PHONE: 824-3035
HOURS: Mon.-Fri., 1 p.m.-6 p.m.; Sat., 11 a.m.-5:30 p.m.
POLICIES: Checks accepted; lay-by: negotiable; returns: exchange only.

You can create a distinct dressing style from the racks at Repeat Performance. This well-organized shop has mint condition vintage clothes for men and women. Some of the prices may knock your bobby socks off. But maybe not, if you love Forties and Fifties clothes. Men's suits are $30 to $50, women's suits are $15 to $40, shoes (a great selection) are $7.00. The costume jewelry ranges from rhinestone to art deco and the display is large. This place is a real gem for anyone collecting the old baubles.

You can exchange your vintage clothes for store merchandise.

URBAN CHIC AT THE POOR MAN'S STORE

2451 Nicollet Ave.
Minneapolis
PHONE: 870-8751
HOURS: Mon.-Sat., 1-6 p.m.; except Thurs., until 8 p.m.
POLICIES: Checks accepted; lay-by: 30 days; returns: exchange only.

This new addition to the Poor Man's Store is a boon for the bizarre New Wave dresser as well as the vintage shopper. We are talking about some high ticket items here, with women's Forties suits ranging from $32 to $125 and men's from $30 to $89. Rumor has it the staff may do some bargaining. Local designer fashions are available and the jewelry is a princely sight. The Poor Man's Store has some reasonably priced furniture, too. You'll see everything here.

Thursdays and Fridays are the best furniture hunting days.

JETT

604 W. 26th St.
Minneapolis
PHONE: 872-4322
HOURS: Wed.-Sat., noon-6 p.m.
POLICIES: Checks accepted; lay-by: 30 days; no returns.

You'll walk down a few steps into an apartment building to get to this little shop. The most recent clothes are from the Fifties and they go as far back in time as possible. When there is a real oldy, you'll pay a little more for it. The merchandise leans toward wearable rather than costume items. These are moderately priced: men's suits are $25 to $45, women's dresses, $4 to $12. But the real specialty is the costume jewelry. You'll find classic black jet, wacky Sixties styles, chunky bracelets and one-of-a-kind specials, mostly priced at $1 to $5. There's a jewelry sale every month.

The best day to shop is Wednesday.

LA MODE

5 W. 15th St.
Minneapolis
PHONE: 870-1751
HOURS: Tues.-Sat., noon-6 p.m.
POLICIES: Credit cards—VISA, Master and American Express; checks accepted; will hold items for 1 week; returns: exchange only.

La Mode is an interesting little shop with beautiful condition Fifties and Sixties clothes for men and women. This is the type of spot I envision New York designers preying on to inspire their next season's collection. Men's suits range from $24 to $45, slacks from $8 to $20, and women's suits from $16 to $40.

They have a huge storage room in the back, so if you can't find what you're looking for, let the salesperson know.

LOIS'S ATTIC

2710 Lyndale Ave. S.
Minneapolis
PHONE: 872-1070
HOURS: Tues.-Sat., 1 p.m.-7:30 p.m.
POLICIES: Checks accepted; returns: exchange only.

Lois's Attic can best be described as eclectic. It's cluttered with early period and vintage clothes (men's and women's), collectables, and furniture. Not only do you have to look under things, but be sure to look up, too—there's more hanging from the ceiling. It's a store that definitely requires some shopping time.

I go to chat with Lois, who is filled with stories about every item in the shop. One day I bought Gary Cooper's wife's hunting jacket for $4.00. Just that tidbit alone was worth more to me than the coat. When they are in stock, her Twenties dresses and teddies are worth viewing. Prices hit everyone's budget, from unbelievably cheap to more expensive.

ELSIE'S SUPER SAVERS

3105 Nicollet Ave.
Minneapolis
PHONE: 825-5627
HOURS: Mon.-Sat., 10 a.m.-5 p.m.
POLICIES: Checks accepted; lay-by: 30 days; no returns.

Merchandise is catch-as-catch-can at this store. But one item you can always depend on is vintage hats. Chances are Elsie will be wearing one when you stop by The best selection of clothing is size 16 and up, with smaller sizes at various times. The last time I was there, Elsie had a window stacked with pointed-toe shoes, and the time before that, it was "I Love Lucy" style dresses. Prices range from dirt cheap to expensive. Some of the merchandise is on consignment. But Elsie loves to bargain, so don't be shy.

GRAND ADDICTIONS

1460 Grand Ave.
St. Paul
PHONE: 690-3165
HOURS: Mon.-Sat., 11 a.m.-5 p.m.
POLICIES: Checks accepted; lay-by: two weeks; no returns.

The neon scene in the window at the front of this store suggests some futuristic finds inside, but vintage clothing will flash you back to the early 1900s. The largest selection is men's and women's Fifties attire. Beaded cashmere sweaters sell for $12.00; women's wool gab skirts for $5.00. Prices are very reasonable. There's an assortment of men's clothes in the basement, usually complete with tuxedos.

GRAND NOUVEAU

236 Snelling Ave. S.
St. Paul
PHONE: None
HOURS: Winter Hours: Tues.-Sun., noon-6 p.m.; Summer Hours: Tues.-Thurs., noon-8 p.m.; Fri. & Sat., noon-6 p.m.
POLICIES: Checks accepted; lay-by: negotiable; returns: exchange only.

High school and college students love this store. It's inexpensive, crammed full of Fifties and Sixties clothes, and crowded with rainbow-haired shoppers. During Halloween the store is mobbed. Jayne, the owner, has a real knack for putting together the absurd. Clothes are not always in perfect condition and you'll find a larger variety of select vintage items elsewhere. But this shop is on the saving edge in the New Wave clothes market.

RAGSTOCK

Warehouse Store
10th St. & Washington Ave.
Minneapolis
PHONE: 333-6576
HOURS: Mon.-Thurs., 9 a.m.-9 p.m.; Fri. & Sat., 9 a.m.-6 p.m.; Sun., noon-5 p.m. (except during summers)

2547 W. Hwy. 10
Moundsview
PHONE: 786-8954
HOURS: Mon.-Fri., 10 a.m.-9 p.m.; Sat., 9 a.m.-6 p.m.; Sun., noon-5 p.m.

Dinkytown
315 14th Ave. S.E.
Minneapolis
PHONE: 331-6064
HOURS: Mon.-Fri., 8:30 a.m.-6 p.m.; except Thurs., until 8 p.m.; Sat., 9 a.m.-5 p.m.

8913 Penn Ave. S.
Bloomington
PHONE: 881-6411
HOURS: Mon.-Fri., 9:30 a.m.-8 p.m.; Sat., 9:30 a.m.-5 p.m.; Sun., noon-5 p.m.

Newest Location
1433 W. Lake St.
Minneapolis
PHONE: 823-6690
HOURS: Mon.-Sat. 10 a.m.-9 p.m.; Sun. noon-5 p.m.

POLICIES: Credit cards—VISA and Master; checks accepted; no lay-by; no returns on used merchandise; returns for new merchandise: exchange only.

At Ragstock, the recycled racks are picked with rigor. You can assemble a forward fashion, or grab backward for the vintage times. The mix of military items makes for great fatigue chic. Whatever you choose, the campy clothes will set you apart from the civilized.

This company obtains new imports from all over the world. In the second-hand industry, it's the kingpin of rag merchants.

So your selections will often be "one of a kind." A lot of people think of Ragstock when they are invited to a Fifties bash or Halloween party. But teens and college students hunt down unisex wardrobes there, finding reasonably priced irregulars in jeans and sweat clothes to provide the basics, with foreign military surplus (Belgium, England, Italy, France) to add a more expensive flair.

If you're short on imagination, shop the well-displayed stock at the neighborhood Ragstock branch stores. The main warehouse store holds the largest selection and the best prices for those willing to plunge into the bins to uproot a bargain.

ZIMMERMAN DRY GOODS

1702 Grand Ave.
St. Paul
PHONE: 699-4273
HOURS: Mon., 9 a.m.-8 p.m.; Tues.-Sat., 9 a.m.-5:30 p.m.
POLICIES: No credit cards; checks accepted; lay-by: negotiable; refunds: exchange only.

This store specializes in authentic used foreign military wear. The day I shopped, Italian fatigues were selling for $10.99—very fashionable, with elastic on the cuffs and zippers on the sides. The shipment had just gone on the shelves and the atmosphere was charged, with both men and women grabbing to get their sizes. Shop here frequently and eventually you'll view garb from every country that has a standing army. Prices are very reasonable. The store also carries khakis, T-shirts, backpacks, and soft luggage at 35% to 50% discounts.

There's always a good assortment of military pants, but some foreign wars are fought with more flair than others. You've got to grab them when you see them. They may never travel through Zimmerman's again.

HARRIS WAREHOUSE & CANVAS SALES

501 30th Ave. S.E.
Minneapolis
PHONE: 331-1321
HOURS: Mon.-Sat., 8:30 a.m.-5:30 p.m.; except Mon. & Thurs., until 8:30 p.m.
POLICIES: Checks accepted; lay-by: flexible; no returns on used merchandise; returns on new merchandise: cash or credit.

Harris Warehouse is another one of those shopping experiences. The place is filled with old military gear, closeouts on Levis and Nikes, and canvas boat covers. The merchandise sure doesn't seem compatible, but there certainly is a blend of bargains. The best deals are on the closeouts and sample clothes, marked 30% to 50% off. The military surplus is marked at the going rate, which can be expensive if you're looking for something that's really hot, like Navy flight jackets.

Watch for the big sales in July, August or February for bigger markdowns.

PART II

FOR THE HOME

CHAPTER 6

NEW HOME FURNISHINGS

Whether you're remodeling, replacing an appliance or just adding to the linen closet, the variety of bargain shopping arenas you'll find in the Twin Cities will improve your bottom line substantially. Furniture shoppers can curl up with catalogs and fabric swatches and order exactly what they want, or they can visit liquidators and wholesalers' showrooms. Or how about hitting the second-hand thrift stores and taking your chances? For the ever-faithful bargain hunter who loves to shop around, this chapter will add to your money-saving repertory.

Furniture, Carpet, and Appliances

CURLEY'S FURNITURE LIBRARY

2010 S. Lexington Ave.
Mendota Heights
PHONE: 452-1010
HOURS: Mon.-Fri., 10 a.m.-9 p.m.
POLICIES: Checks accepted; lay-by: negotiable; no returns; delivery extra.

Even if you're not in the market for anything, stop by Curley's just for the fun of it. Here's a few of Curley's quips to my probing questions. "If you need your furniture today it will take three months; if there's no hurry, we can get it for you yesterday." Or "So you want something that wears well? I have never had anybody say they wanted something that would fall apart quickly." On the matter of delivery, "Yes, if you don't mind a green truck with butterflies on it. Otherwise we can come after dark."

But I'll tell you what they take very seriously here: quality. They sell furniture, beds and carpeting at 50% to 60% below regular retailers. You can order from over 1,000 different manufacturers. You can't get Ethan Allen furniture, but Curley will match you up with similar quality and styles. Some people shop around first and come to Curley's with the exact brand, style and model number. Others just go in with an idea in mind and sit and flip through catalogs, fabric swatches, and wood samples until they spot what they want.

Curley never misrepresents what he sells. His staff knows the quality of the furniture from each company they order from very well. They'll let you know when a manufacturer is good or not. There is no showroom to speak of, but while you're browsing through pictures and samples, you may get sodas, coffee—even lunch if you've missed it.

CONTRACT SALES

PHONE: 475-1147 (get address when you set up appointment)
POLICIES: Checks only; lay-by: negotiable; no returns on custom orders; delivery extra; orders take 4 to 6 weeks.

You can call Contract Sales and make an appointment. Then you custom order from their furniture catalogs and select the items you want, in the fabric you choose. Here are just some of the lines you can order from: Thomasville, Hekman, Casa Stradiveri, Isenberg wood tables, outdoor furniture, wicker, brass and several lamp lines. They canot order Ethan Allen or Drexel.

Your furniture will arrive in 4 to 6 weeks at their warehouse. Delivery to your home is extra but very reasonable (a large sofa is $15). Or you can do the lifting yourself.

If you already know what you want and have a specific name brand, just call Contract Sales and they will give you a comparison price quote.

JACK L. RUBENSTEIN/WHOLESALE

PHONE: 922-4781 or 929-7581; ask for Joel or Fred
HOURS: Mon.-Fri., 8:15 a.m.-5:45 p.m.; Sat., 8:15 a.m.-noon
POLICIES: Checks accepted; no lay-by; no returns; full factory warranties apply.

Believe me, knowing about Rubenstein's is a lead no serious bargain hunter can do without. You will get hefty discounts on furs, jewelry, carpeting, furniture, *cars*, vacuum cleaners, and sewing machines, by ordering through Jack. All you have to do is call with a description of what you're looking for, and he will get you into "not open to the public" wholesale showrooms where you can select what you want.

I suppose you're wondering what the catch is. There isn't any. Jack Rubenstein has been doing this for 39 years. All he does is get you the wholesale price, then add a nominal profit for himself. But you're still saving a lot below retail (less so in the competitive electronic, appliance and TV category). Jack's crazy wholesale buying phone business also gives you a great way to check out prices you've found. He'll let you know if he can beat the price you found, or else tell you if you already have a good one. It's a great service for those of us who feel guilty later if we didn't get something for the best price.

GOTTLIEB CARPET AND FURNITURE CO.

2750 Johnson St. N.E.
Minneapolis
PHONE: 781-1313

8940 Lyndale Ave. S.
Bloomington
PHONE: 884-7799

HOURS: Mon., 9 a.m.-8 p.m.; Tues.-Wed., Fri., 9 a.m.-5:30 p.m.; during winter only, Thurs., 9 a.m.-8 p.m.
POLICIES: Checks accepted; lay-by: negotiable; returns: negotiable; delivery extra.

You'll save 40% on brand name furniture and carpeting ordered through Gottlieb. You will select from manufacturers' catalogs but the staff will work with you to make the job easy. None of the goods are seconds or damaged. Count on a large supply of carpet samples to choose from.

MURAN BROS.

6413 Lyndale Ave. S.
Richfield
PHONE: 866-3753
HOURS: Mon.-Fri., 10 a.m.-6 p.m.; Sat., 9 a.m.-5 p.m.
POLICIES: Credit cards—Master and VISA; checks accepted; lay-by: 90 days; returns: exchange only; special orders take 2 to 12 weeks; delivery extra.

Muran's has a showroom with a fairly good selection of sofas and other furniture. Al Muran also orders from 75 manufacturers such as Kroehler, Davis, Land O' Nod, Ashley and more. Discounts vary from item to item, but they will beat any price you come up with. Some used furniture is available, too.

LONDON SALES

10726 France Ave. S.
Bloomington
PHONE: 884-3900
HOURS: Mon.-Fri., 9 a.m.-8 p.m.; Sat., 9 a.m.-6 p.m.
POLICIES: Credit cards—Master and VISA; checks accepted; lay-by: 90 days; returns: cash or credit; delivery extra.

The furniture inventory changes frequently at Jeff London's showroom, where the merchandise is closeouts, damaged goods and samples. Some name brands are available—Broyhill, Burlington, Thomasville—all at 25% to 50% below regular retail prices. You'll find lamps, pictures and home accessories, too.

KROWN SALES

7478 Washington Ave. S.
Eden Prairie
PHONE: 944-6288
HOURS: Mon.-Fri., 10 a.m.-9 p.m.; Sat., 10 a.m.-5 p.m.; Sun., noon-6 p.m.
POLICIES: Credit cards—VISA and Master; checks accepted; financing available; 30-day money-back guarantee; delivery referral.

Krown Sales liquidates furniture. Some of the owners of this store are manufacturers' furniture representatives. When furniture is discontinued, overstocked or samples are left, Krown gets an early pick of the furniture leftovers.

Shopping in this store requires a real sense of direction—the interconnecting showrooms make it easy to get lost! But the furniture goes on and on in the maze of 65 rooms and hallways. Prices are discounted 20% to 35%, and sometimes more, depending on how "right" they can buy the liquidated items. Sofas average $199 and loveseats $149.

This store is for the shopper who has definite decorating ideas. Interior design help isn't built into the low prices.

BROADWAY DISCOUNT STORE

1000 W. Broadway
Minneapolis
PHONE: 529-9577
HOURS: Mon.-Fri., 9 a.m.-8 p.m.; Sat., 9 a.m.-6 p.m.

POLICIES: Credit cards—VISA, Master and Shoppers; checks accepted; lay-by: 5% down and 5% payments for 1 year; refunds: exchange.

Manager Bill Franklin will help out your decorating budget with 40% to 50% savings on moderate quality furnishings. He also carries the extras: TV's, stereos and appliances. You can special order from manufacturers' catalogs, but you won't get the same deep in-stock discounts. The store goods are all closeouts, overstocks, or discontinued patterns, and they change monthly.

Shop in the beginning of the month when the prices are reduced even more for quicker turnover.

THE UNPAINTED PLACE

1601 Hennepin Ave.
Minneapolis
PHONE: 339-1500
HOURS: Mon.-Fri., 9 a.m.-6 p.m.; except Mon. & Thurs., until 8 p.m.; Sat., 9 a.m.-4 p.m.

2005 E. Lake St.
Minneapolis
PHONE: 721-3346
HOURS: Mon.-Fri., 9:30 a.m.-8:30 p.m.; Sat., 9:30 a.m.-5 p.m.; Sun., noon-5 p.m.

POLICIES: Credit cards—Master, VISA and Shoppers; checks accepted; lay-by: negotiable; returns: 30 days; delivery extra.

The Unpainted Place has a reputation for manufacturing high quality unfinished furniture. Discounts range from 15% to 40%. And, as owner David Fellman points out, there's the satisfaction of refinishing your own pieces. How do you measure the value of that?

Dressers range from $50 to $200, a cedar-lined oak storage chest is $135, and a twin-size, three-drawer birch platform bed is $165. If you're remodeling the kitchen, you may want to check out the unfinished oak and birch cabinets. You can fill an 8-foot space for $300 to $400.

When you stop by the store, pick up a catalog and sign their mailing list for news about special sales.

TREASURE ISLAND

4200 W. Lake St.
Minneapolis
PHONE: 927-7913
HOURS: Mon.-Fri., 9 a.m.-6 p.m.; Sat., 9 a.m.-5:30 p.m.; Sun., noon-5 p.m.
POLICIES: Credit cards—VISA, Master and Shoppers; checks accepted; lay-by: 9 months; returns: credit or exchange; delivery extra.

Treasure Island is a mecca for parents searching for kids' furnishings—from cribs to canopy beds. This store has always downplayed the fact that they sell infants' and childrens' furniture at discount prices. The reason is that they distribute furniture to other regular retailers. You'll find the good name brands: Childcraft, Simmons, Bassett, Lullabye, Henry Link, Dixie, and more. Sometimes this store's prices will be competitive with Penney's, La Belle's or Target. When you have a specific item in mind, just pick up the phone and make a quick comparison. Where Treasure Island really wins is in selection. They are well stocked with all the treasures of a kid's room.

DAYTON'S OUTLET STORE

701 Industrial Blvd.
Minneapolis
PHONE: 623-7111
HOURS: Mon.-Fri., 9 a.m.-9 p.m.; Sat., 9 a.m.-6 p.m.; Sun., noon-6 p.m.
POLICIES: Credit cards—Daytons; checks accepted; no lay-by; returns accepted unless item is sold as is; delivery extra.

Dayton's outlet gets the returned merchandise, dented goods and discontinued styles that come from the retail stores. If you're looking for a TV, stereo, or VCR equipment, you should call just to comparison shop. There's some furniture up front; sofas and recliners seem to be the regular items. If you're interested in carpeting and rugs, you can wander back into the warehouse.

But the good deals are better when Dayton's runs their "Warehouse Sales," every two to three months. To find out when, call the number above. If a date has been set, they will let you know (usually the sales run on weekends for two days). You must get there on the first day to get the heavily discounted merchandise. Go at 8 a.m. and join the crowd lining up early. Housewares, lamps, china, wallpaper, and odds and ends are also a good buy.

When the doors open, if you're a furniture buyer, head right for the "must go" area down the middle aisle of the warehouse near the refreshments. That's where the best deals will be.

SEARS RETAIL OUTLET STORE

2700 Winter St. N.E.
Minneapolis
PHONE: 379-5600
HOURS: Mon.-Fri., 10 a.m.-6 p.m.; except Mon. & Fri., until 9 p.m.; Sat., 9 a.m.-5 p.m.
POLICIES: Credit cards—Sears; checks accepted; all warranties apply; returns: cash or credit, satisfaction guaranteed.

This outlet store is Sears' clearinghouse for discontinued, few of a kind, slightly damaged, and overstocked furniture, bedding and appliances. The persevering bargain hunter is going to find some good deals here. Some of the items are repaired by Sears, and carry a full warranty. Most of the stock is reduced 20% to 50% from Sears' original price. Do-it-yourselfers can dig around for the home improvements merchandise.

Shipments arrive daily, so shop often.

LABELLE'S CATALOG SHOWROOMS

St. Paul Showroon
1925 Suburban Ave.
St. Paul
PHONE: 739-4900

Roseville Showroom
1750 W. Hwy. 36
Roseville
PHONE: 636-9300

Richfield Showroom
7701 Nicollet Ave.
Richfield
PHONE: 861-7111

Burnsville Showroom
1350 W. Co. Rd. 42
Burnsville
PHONE: 435-2400

Brooklyn Center Showroom
5925 Earle Brown Dr.
Brooklyn Center
PHONE: 566-7755

St. Anthony Showroom
2500 38th Ave. N.E.
St. Anthony
PHONE: 781-8090

Minnetonka Showroom
13513 Ridgedale Dr.
Minnetonka

Direct Ordering Tele-LaBelle Phone: 933-4848

HOURS: Mon.-Fri., 10 a.m.-9 p.m.; Sat., 10 a.m.-6 p.m.; Sun., noon-5 p.m.
POLICIES: Credit cards—Master and VISA; checks accepted; lay-by: only in certain departments; returns: cash or credit.

La Belle's is a great place to do some comparison pricing on toys, furniture, small appliances, electronics, cameras, and jewelry. Stop at any showroom and flip through the catalogs, and while you're there, sign up to get a one of your own. If you're short on time, call the direct phone ordering number to save a trip and find out if the showroom near you has what you need in stock. (If it doesn't, the clerk can direct you to the store that does.) You will find discounts here, but they will not be comparable to some of the other sources in this book.

Around all major holidays—Christmas, Easter, Mother's and Father's Day—watch the Sunday Minneapolis and St. Paul newspapers for special promotions.

BIRNBERG'S CATALOG SHOWROOMS

1933 University Ave.
St. Paul
PHONE: 645-1313
HOURS: Mon., 9 a.m.-8:30 p.m.; Tues.-Fri., 9 a.m.-5:30 p.m.; Sat. 9 a.m.-4 p.m. (except mid-June to Sept. 1, closes Sat. at 1 p.m.)
POLICIES: Credit cards—Master and VISA; checks accepted; lay-by: negotiable; returns: cash or credit on everything but items with a serial number (they can be returned for repairs only). Shipment available by UPS.

Birnberg's has been quietly selling good name brands to the public at a 30% to 60% savings for 20 years. They are known for their giftware and they even offer Bridal Registry. During the holidays, this store really draws the Yuletide shoppers. There's a wide selection of jewelry—diamonds, 14-Karat gold jewelry, Seiko watches. In housewares you'll find silver, china, dishes, giftware, small appliances, electronics, and televisions (brands like Lennox, General Electric, Panasonic, and Toastmaster). Sporting goods and even baby furniture and accessories round out the list.

A large catalog is published annually, featuring merchandise that will be available for the whole year. When Birnberg's makes an inventory changeover, overstocks are ticketed with a red tag and sold at drastic reductions. Just go to the showroom, pick up a free catalog, and browse through the store displays.

They have nine special sales a year. Sign the mailing list and you'll receive advance notice.

BETTER BEDS

PHONE: 861-3360
HOURS: By appointment only, 8 a.m.-10 p.m., Mon.-Sat.
POLICIES: Checks accepted; lay-by available; no returns; no deliveries.

Better Beds manufactures futons for the retail market. They also sell to the public—and anytime you can go directly to the source, you're going to save money. But price isn't the only good feature here. Quality is excellent, and the variety of custom orders they can handle is unlimited. How about a futon for an infant's crib, or one made to fit the back of your van? And for those of you who really want plush comfort, you can get your futon stuffed with wool.

Better Beds specializes in three styles of all-cotton futons: the 6-inch traditional style, the 8-inch American style, and the two-inch foam core style. Prices range from $55 for a single up to $155 for a 2-inch foam king size. There are also several styles of wood-frame sofa beds to fit the futons.

GABBERTS ODDS & ENDS ROOM

3501 W. 69th St.
Edina
PHONE: 927-1500
HOURS: Mon.-Fri., 10 a.m.-9 p.m.; Sat., 10 a.m.-6 p.m.; Sun., noon-5 p.m.

POLICIES: Credit cards—Master and VISA; checks accepted; no lay-by; no returns.

Gabberts is known for quality furniture as a regular retailer, but they do have an "odds and ends" room that may pay off for the persistent furniture shopper. Pieces move in and out of this room without any predictability. Look for good deals on slightly damaged floor models, discontinued items, or perhaps off-color furniture finds.

THE CEDAR BOX CO.

Corner of Hiawatha & 22nd Ave.
Minneapolis
PHONE: 332-4287
HOURS: Mon.-Thurs., 7:30 a.m.-4 p.m.; Fri., 7 a.m.-3:30 p.m.
POLICIES: Checks accepted; no lay-by; no returns.

Students and first apartment dwellers will love this spot. Owner Jeff Gershone makes and sells containers and boxes for displays—some of them are pretty oddball sizes. But most of them work for record collections and books, and make shelving or great end tables. The prices range from $2 to $8.

Call first because you never know if they will be stocked or not. When they are, you can dig to your heart's content and come out with a cheap decorating coup.

KOVAL'S

4317 Excelsior Blvd.
St. Louis Park
PHONE: 920-6144
HOURS: Tues.-Thurs., 9 a.m.-7:30 p.m.; Mon. & Fri., 9 a.m.-5:30 p.m.; Sat., 9 a.m.-4:30 p.m.
POLICIES: Checks accepted; financing available; lay-by negotiable; returns: cash or credit, satisfaction guaranteed; full warranties apply; delivery extra.

In major appliances, if you want all the new colors, current styling and good brand names (General Electric, Whirlpool, Litton, Jenn Air, RCA), Ben Koval's is the place to shop. But he does encourage you to shop around before you come, so you can appreciate his discounts. No fancy fixtures here, but all the appliances are first quality.

REIS TARGO

3650 Central N.E.
Minneapolis
PHONE: 781-3331

9056 Lyndale Ave. S.
Minneapolis
PHONE: 888-5407

3808 Chicago Ave.
Minneapolis
PHONE: 823-5213

HOURS: Mon.-Thurs., 9 a.m.-8:30 p.m.; Fri.-Sat., 9 a.m.-5 p.m.
POLICIES: Credit cards—VISA and Master; checks accepted; financing available; returns: on stock items only; *no* returns on special orders.

Reis Targo has good name brands in appliances, TVs and stereos, always marked 20% below suggested retail prices. But if you see it for less within 90 days from the time you made your purchase (be sure to save your receipt), you can claim a refund for the price difference. Look for Litton microwaves, Zenith TVs, Whirlpool appliances, and Tappan ranges, just to name a few. Special orders are also available at a savings.

SWEEN LUNDEEN

322 S. Fourth St.
Minneapolis
PHONE: 332-1333
HOURS: Mon.-Fri., 9 a.m.-5:15 p.m.; Sat., 8 a.m.-noon
POLICIES: Credit cards—Master and VISA; checks accepted; no lay-by; returns: in original packages, cash or credit.

The downtown Minneapolis crowd is most familiar with Sween Lundeen's wares. To first-time shoppers this store may look like a pawn shop from the outside. There's quite a variety of merchandise sitting in the window, from watches to cutlery. You'll save 20% to 30% on name brand microwaves, stereos, tape recorders and televisions (Sanyo, Quasar, Panasonic, for instance). If you select an off-brand, you can save up to 50%. Watches are always marked down 35% to 40% and gold chains sell at half-price.

GIMBLE'S HOME ENTERTAINMENT CENTER

468 N. Lexington Ave.
St. Paul
PHONE: 644-1312
HOURS: Tues-Fri., 10 a.m.-6 p.m.; except Thurs., until 8 p.m.; Sat., 10 a.m.-5 p.m.
POLICIES: Credit cards—Master, VISA and Shoppers; checks accepted; lay-by: flexible; all warranties apply; returns: within 7 days.

Henry Gimble stocks all types of home electronics, priced 12% to 25% below retail prices. Look for TVs, stereos, and more in Panasonic, Sony, Marantz, and Zenith brand names.

Ask about trading in your old piece of equipment...you might reduce the price even more.

Linen, China, Silver, and Cookware

HOME-KO BED & BATH OUTLETS

Golden Valley Shopping Center
Hwy 55 & Winnetka Ave.
Golden Valley
PHONE: 544-5914

Village North Shopping Center
7587 Brooklyn Blvd.
Brooklyn Center
PHONE: 566-2681

Valley West Shopping Center
Old Shakopee Rd. & France Ave. S.
Bloomington
PHONE: 888-2448

Har Mar Mall
2100 N. Snelling Ave.
Roseville
PHONE: 633-4496

HOURS: Mon.-Fri., 10 a.m.-9 p.m.; Sat., 10 a.m.-5:30 p.m.; Sun., noon-5 p.m.
POLICIES: Credit cards—VISA, Master and Shoppers; checks accepted; will hold items for 7 days; returns accepted.

Home-Ko has been hawking off-price bed and bath bundles for eight years. The savings here are 20% to 60% below regular retail prices. Home-Ko doesn't compete with Target or K-Mart or discount chain store prices; it goes up against major department stores. Some shoppers, not realizing this, walk into a store and comment that the prices are too high, but it may be that their expectations are off the mark.

There's no muslin sold here. The merchandise is all name brand (Martex, Fieldcrest, Springmaid, Martex, J. P. Stevens, Utica, Dakotah), both perfect and #1 irregular manufacturers' overstocks and closeouts. The lowest prices, of course, will be on the irregulars, whose flaws won't impair wearability.

Home-Ko has added Super Premium quality matching decorator bedroom items that compete with any of the fancy-fixtured stores. They have dust ruffles, pillow shams, comforters...you name it. The discount works like this. If the set is $400 at those 'other' stores, Home-Ko's price is about $300. Shipments arrive weekly. I can't pinpoint a best shopping day, but the stores do gear up for the Friday and Saturday shopper.

Two sales to watch for: the July Anniversary sale and the pre-Christmas sale in October. That's when all the holiday towels, tablecloths and linens will be in stock.

LINEN CENTER

Eden Prairie Outlet Centre
12475 Plaza Dr.
Eden Prairie
PHONE: 941-8942

Ridge Square Shopping Center
13029 Ridgedale Dr.
Minnetonka
PHONE: 542-9574

Southview Shopping Center
1869 S. Robert St.
West St. Paul
PHONE: 451-3665

Target Center
7054 York Ave. S.
Edina
PHONE: 920-5706

HOURS: Mon.-Fri., 9:30 a.m.-9 p.m.; Sat., 9:30 a.m.-6 p.m.; Sun., 11 a.m.-5 p.m.
POLICIES: Credit cards—Master and VISA; checks accepted; no lay-by; returns: cash or credit.

No clearance sales are held at the Linen Center stores—just White Sale prices, offered every day. The savings range from 20% to 60% below retail prices. The stores are well-stocked with brand name (Wamsutta, Laura Ashley, Burlington, Cannon) coordinated sheets, shower curtains, towels, blankets, bedspreads, and curtains for the well-decorated bed or bath. You'll find some irregulars and #1 seconds. All discontinued patterns will be flagged with a red tag. Mini-blinds are marked 65% below regular retail prices.

Before you start your shopping, check out the bargain table. Each store has one; it holds a mix of bed and bath markdowns. If it is first quality you're after, look on the wall shelves.

LINEN OUTLET ANGEL INDUSTRIES

421 S. Main St.
Stillwater
PHONE: 430-1286
HOURS: Mon.-Sat., 10 a.m.-5 p.m.; Sun., 1-5 p.m. (hours subject to change)

488 S. Robert
West St. Paul
PHONE: 224-7591
HOURS: Mon.-Fri., 7 a.m.-5 p.m.

POLICIES: Checks; lay-by: negotiable, returns: exchange only.

The Linen Outlet is owned by Angel Industries. They manufacture a Cadillac line of placemats, napkins, table linens, toaster covers, pot holders and other kitchen coordinates, distributing to posh stores all over the country. They use lots of ginghams and calicos for the city dweller with a country decor home. The outlet stores carry their discontinued styles with a mix of creatively crafted remnant items. You'll save at least 40%. Placemats are $2.50 apiece and napkins $1.50. The true factory outlet store is right at the manufacturing plant on Robert Street. The Stillwater outlet is what they call the "frosting on the cake," selling craft items and displaying a larger variety of linens. But for the bargain hunter who thrives on a factory atmosphere, the Robert Street store (where you have to search for the outlet inside the plant) is heaven. At both Linen Outlets, they love their customers and are very helpful.

OFF THE TOP

7058 York Ave. S.
Edina
PHONE: 922-5531
HOURS: Mon.-Fri., 10 a.m.-9:30 p.m.; Sat., 9:30 a.m.-7 p.m.; Sun., noon-5 p.m.

POLICIES: Credit cards—Master, VISA and American Express; checks accepted; no lay-by; refunds: cash within 30 days.

Off the Top has such a slick, high-class look, you would never suspect everything in here is overstocks, closeouts, cancelled orders, or discontinued patterns. Owner Dave Mitchell isn't trying to hide the fact, either—there's no bull in this china shop. He proudly displays good name brand china, dinnerware, stemware, glassware and flatware, all priced at 20% to 70% below regular retail prices. You'll see Mikasa, Sango, Nikko, Colony, Noritake and more. Take your chances on finding what you want when you want it. But if you're buying dinnerware, you can special order some of the extras, like bowls and cups.

Ask about the free monogramming service on glassware bought here. Sign the mailing list for unadvertised specials.

CHELSEA FAYRE

PHONE: 698-3070
HOURS: Thurs., 10 a.m.-5 p.m. (Call Mon.-Fri., 10 a.m.-5 p.m., for special appointments.)
POLICIES: Checks accepted; no lay-by; returns: exchange only in 30 days; 33% to 50% deposit at time of ordering; free gift wrap; delivery 2-4 weeks.

Chelsea Fayre is a home business that offers a special ordering service for china, crystal, stoneware, stainless, lucite and silver. All top of the line name brands are available, exactly as you would find in a regular department store. No discontinued patterns here. Let me name a few. In china there's Royal Doulton, Minton, Fitz & Floyd, Hornsea, Hutschenreuther, Metlox, Royal Worcester, Spode, Wedgwood. In stoneware, there's Denby, Franciscan. In crystal stemware, Ceska, Gorham, Galway, Ittala, Josair, Pepi Hermann, Svend Jensen. In flatware, Community, International, Oneida, Supreme, Gorham, Towle, Wallace.

The minimum discount is 20% below retail prices. However, let me explain how you can really save on this service. Throughout the year manufacturers offer special 40% off promotions to the regular department stores to pass on to their customers. During those times, you will get the 40% off *plus* an additional 15% to 20% when you order through Chelsea Fayre. You don't even have to watch for these special sale times. Burniece, the owner, will do it for you. She gets advance notices of all manufacturers' promotions, and when your style or pattern is going to be discounted, she will give you a call.

Chelsea Fayre offers a personalized Bridal Registry service for china, crystal, and flatware, so bargain-hunting brides can get the same price breaks for their guests. Giftware is also available. The drawback here is you can't use credit cards, or make returns except for store exchanges, and you will have to put down a deposit with your order and wait for a few weeks to get the goods. But if you want the high quality wares at a lower ticket price, this is the place to call.

COLLECTOR'S CABINET

PHONE: 698-9609 (call for an appointment)
POLICIES: Checks accepted; no lay-by; returns: exchange only.

Make an appointment and meet with Liz in her home. You can page through catalogs and select your Waterford Crystal or buy from her stock at 25% to 35% below regular retail prices. She also sells Lalique and Baccarat crystal at 30% to 50% off on selected items. If you collect Hummels, call to see what she has in stock at 20% below retail prices.

CARRINGTON'S

909 W. 50th St.
Minneapolis.
PHONE: 825-2437
HOURS: Mon.-Sat., 10 a.m.-6 p.m.; except Thurs., until 8 p.m.
POLICIES: Silverplate only (also new and antique clocks); credit cards—Master and Visa; checks accepted; lay-by: 90 days; no returns on silverplate.

See description under The Silver Hunter, below.

ADELE STERLING

PHONE: 690-3670 (by appointment only)
POLICIES: Sterling flatware only; checks accepted; free delivery service; satisfaction guaranteed; orders take 2 to 4 weeks.

See description under The Silver Hunter, below.

THE SILVER HUNTER

PHONE: 927-5468 (by appointment only)
POLICIES: Sterling and silverplate flatware; checks accepted; lay-by: 6 months; returns: within 10 days; free pick up and delivery services; flatware repair service available.

Have you inherited Grandma's flatware and now want to complete the set—but find that the pattern is discontinued? Or maybe you've lost a treasured sterling piece. Well, don't waste your precious searching time. I've located sterling and silverplate pattern finders. Given some time, these services can locate some of the most elusive flatware patterns. Replacements from inactive or antique styles will be second-hand but polished to look like new. Active pattern orders can also be filled.

You'll save a lot of money by using these services. On sterling, the cost is based on the current spot metal prices and the weight (a small markup is tacked on, depending on the pattern). If sterling prices are down, it's a good time to buy. Currently at The Silver Hunter, a second-hand, four-piece place setting of Wallace Rosepoint is $85.00. At a catalog discount store the price is $139; at a major department store sale the price is $266. At Carrington's, where they specialize in silverplate patterns, a spoon replacement is about $5.00, knives and forks, $7.00.

The services will identify your pattern too...for free.

NORDIC WARE OUTLET NORTHLAND PRODUCTS

5120 Cedar Lake Rd.
Cedar Lake R. & Hwy. 100
Minneapolis
PHONE: 920-2888
HOURS: Open only on the *first full weekend* each month; Fri., noon-9 p.m.; Sat., 9 a.m.-5 p.m.; Sun., 10 a.m.-5 p.m.
POLICIES: Credit cards—VISA, Master, American Express and Shoppers; checks accepted; no lay-by; returns: cash or credit.

This factory outlet sells Northland Aluminum Products that are seconds or discontinued at 50% and more below the regular retail price. You'll find barbeque grills, Nordic Ware aluminum cookware, microwave accessories, small electric woks, and a complete line of terra cotta clay baking dishes.

Call and get on their mailing list.

PLASTICS, INC.

214 Ryan Ave.
St. Paul
PHONE: 227-7371
HOURS: Mon.-Fri., 9 a.m.-4:30 p.m.; Sat., 10 a.m.-1 p.m.
POLICIES: Checks accepted; no lay-by; no returns.

Cooks and crafters will profit from a trip here. Plastics, Inc. sells first quality (at regular retail prices) and seconds in bacon racks, cake pans, muffin tins, baking sheets, etc.—for use in both microwave and conventional oven cooking. Plenty of plastic tumblers, bowls, mugs and picnic ware. Except for the first quality items, the discount here ranges from 50% to 75% below retail. Crafters can nickel and dime their way into some project materials, too. Plastic trays can be converted to vanity decor. Old plastic cups—I'll let you use your own imagination.

Twice a year, Plastics, Inc. has special sales that go deep on the discounts. These are scheduled each year in spring and fall, held on the same weekends we go through the daylight saving time change. You know, spring forward, fall back.

Paint, Wall Coverings, Tile and Lighting

POST WALLCOVERING

Ridge Square North
13023 Ridgedale Dr.
Minnetonka
PHONE: 544-7575, or toll free phone ordering number 1-800-521-0650
HOURS FOR STORE: Mon.-Fri., 9 a.m.-9 p.m.; Sat., 10 a.m.-6 p.m.; Sun., noon-5 p.m.

POLICIES: Checks accepted; no deposits necessary; freight and delivery service free; ordering 7 to 10 days; no returns except on defective coverings or wrong pattern sent.

If you've ever ordered wallcoverings by phone from Post's toll free number, you know that they can get you any residential pattern you're looking for. The savings is 27% below the suggested retail price and 10% off on wallpaper book fabrics. Now they have a local wallcovering showroom where you will get the same deal, plus design help and wallpaper books to make your selection easier.

BUDGET PAINT AND WALLPAPER

4009 Minnehaha Ave.
Minneapolis
PHONE: 724-7676
HOURS: Mon.-Fri., 9 a.m.-5:30 p.m.; except Mon. & Thurs., until 9 p.m.; Sat., 9 a.m.-5 p.m.
POLICIES: Credit cards—Master, VISA and American Express; checks accepted; returns: cash or credit.

This is a small store, but they have a large selection of wallpaper, paint and all the sundries. You'll save 40% to 80% on any in-stock wallpaper, and for catalog orders you'll save 20% to 30%. Be sure to check out the discontinued patterns in the basement, where you'll find wallpaper for $1.99 a roll. Budget has been a favorite of bargain hunters for many years, long before the discount wallpaper shops hit town. You'll find this store cheaper than most.

WALLPAPER CITY

1510 Nicollet Ave.
Minneapolis
PHONE: 871-2414
HOURS: Mon.-Sat., 10 a.m.-6 p.m.
POLICIES: Credit cards—Master and VISA; checks accepted; returns: cash for in-stock merchandise, special order returns have a 20% restocking charge.

This store carries a full line of wallpaper, paint, mini-blinds, even carpet samples. Wallpaper book orders will average 20% savings. In-stock selections can range 40% to 80% below retail prices. Bargain tables for hours of rummaging!

WALLPAPER TODAY

5717 Excelsior Blvd.
St. Louis Park
PHONE: 929-7126

1732 Lexington Ave. N.
Roseville
PHONE: 488-1707

HOURS: Mon.-Fri., 9:30 a.m.-9 p.m.; Sat., 9:30 a.m.-5 p.m.; Sun., noon-5 p.m.
POLICIES: Credit cards—VISA and Master; checks accepted; returns: first quality wallpaper only.

It's easy to shop here, thanks to large-size displays of the wallpaper. You'll save 20% to 50% on any wallcovering in stock, which includes both first quality and seconds. If you order from the catalogs, you'll get a 10% to 30% discount. If you're just covering a small area, check through the odds and ends bin. These stores carry wallpaper and adhesives only; prices can start as low as $1.99 a roll and go as high as $100 a roll.

Instruction tapes are available for in-store listening—then you have to rely on your memory until you get home.

WALL TO WALLPAPER

2149 Ford Parkway
St. Paul
PHONE: 699-5617
HOURS: Mon.-Fri., 9 a.m.-6 p.m.; except Mon. & Thurs., until 9 p.m.; Sat., 9 a.m.-5 p.m.
POLICIES: Credit cards—VISA and Master; checks accepted; returns: cash on in-stock wallpaper only.

If you select a wallpaper from the in-stock supply, you'll save 25% to 70%. Catalog wallpaper orders are sold at regular retail prices. Paint is high quality and sells for 20% below retail prices. Lots of helpful services and pamphlets are available. Look for mini-blinds selling at 25% off.

DIAMOND VOGEL PAINT CENTERS

2020 N. Second St.
Minneapolis
PHONE: 521-4707

6315 Cedar Ave.
Minneapolis
PHONE: 869-7581

HOURS: Mon.-Fri., 7:30 a.m.-5 p.m.; Sat., 8 a.m.-noon.

POLICIES: Credit cards—Master and VISA; checks accepted; returns: cash on in-stock merchandise only.

Diamond Vogel sells high quality interior/exterior paint at 10% to 15% below regular retail prices. If you do some shopping around be sure to compare to equally high grade brand names to see the value of the savings. Custom coloring is free. Lots of paint supplies and free information pamphlets for the do-it-yourselfer.

La Petite Allied Aluminum Manufacturing Co.

7341 Commerce Lane
Fridley
PHONE: 571-7341
HOURS: Mon.-Fri., 10 a.m.-8 p.m.; Sat., 10 a.m.-5 p.m.
POLICIES: Credit cards—Master, VISA and Shoppers; checks accepted; lay-by: 30 days; no returns; delivery charge $2.50; measuring charge $3.00 per window—minimum $30 service.

Allied Aluminum specializes in storm windows, doors and similar items, but for their La Petite outlet they custom order 1-inch mini-blinds for windows. You'll save 40% to 70% here on custom blinds. If you have standard size windows, forget it...there are better deals in town. But if your picture window is a brute, this is the place to get a good deal.

You can select from 50 colors and they will mix or stripe the colors at an additional charge. Delivery takes a week to 10 days.

Call for a free color brochure with window measuring instructions. Or if you break into a sweat just pulling out the yardstick, call and they will talk you through each step.

Muska Lighting Center

700 Grand Ave.
St. Paul
PHONE: 227-8881
HOURS: Mon.-Fri., 9 a.m.-5:30 p.m.; except Mon. & Thurs., until 9 p.m.; Sat., 9 a.m.-5 p.m.

POLICIES: Credit cards—VISA, Master, American Express and Shoppers; checks accepted; will hold with a deposit; returns: cash, credit or exchange on in-stock merchandise in 14 days; manufacturers' warranties for one year.

Bill Muska features ceiling and wall light fixtures, all sold at 40% below regular retail prices. Track lights, table and floor lamps and landscape lighting are not included in this 40% discount. The service here is great and the brands are top quality.

LIGHT FACTORY, INC.

2665 Fourth Ave.
Anoka
PHONE: 421-6810
HOURS: Mon.-Fri., 9 a.m.-5 p.m.; except Thurs., until 8 p.m.; Sat., 9 a.m.-3 p.m.
POLICIES: Credit cards—VISA, Masters and Shoppers; checks accepted; lay-by: 90 days; returns: cash or credit.

Here's a big variety of ceiling fixtures, outdoor lights, fans, and some table lamps, all at 40% below retail prices. Many are closeouts or overstocks, but the brand names are good...Eagle Southwest, Spring Serama, Nova, Quoizol.

Watch for a big sale at 50% to 70% off in March and April each year.

FREEMAN'S LIGHTING CONCEPTS CLOSEOUT ROOM

1255 W. Larpenteur
Roseville
PHONE: 644-4790
HOURS: Mon.-Fri., 10 a.m.-9 p.m.; Sat., 10 a.m.-6 p.m.; Sun., noon-5 p.m.
POLICIES: Credit cards—VISA, Master, Shoppers and American Express; checks accepted; no lay-by; no returns.

You can lighten up your remodeling budget at a 40% savings. Track lighting, lamps, fixtures and ceiling fans are banished from most of Freeman's store locations when there's a scratch, dent, or discontinued style. Most of the fixtures work; some may have been repaired. But if that's the case, the prices will go even lower. The stock varies, so frequent trips are a must.

Twice a year, at Freeman's Warehouse at 7435 Washington Ave. S. in Edina (941-6410), they have a huge lighting sale. Everything is sold at 75% or more off retail prices. Call for sale dates in March and September.

TILE FACTORY OUTLETS

1007 Excelsior Ave. E.
Hopkins
PHONE: 938-8088

8017 Nicollet Ave. S.
Bloomington
PHONE: 881-3340

5736 Lakeland Ave. N.
Crystal
PHONE: 535-1772

HOURS: Mon.-Fri., 11 a.m.-8 p.m.; Sat., 10 a.m.-5 p.m.; Sun., noon-4 p.m.
POLICIES: Credit cards—VISA and Master; checks accepted; return: full refund on unused tile; deposit on tile installation equipment.

Even the do-it-yourselfer who's all thumbs will love this ceramic specialty store. All the mystery is taken out of laying your own tile. The salespeople freely give cutting and grouting demonstrations and the instruction booklets are not the type you get stuck with on Christmas Eve—they are easily deciphered. Expect savings of 44% to 77% below high quality retail grade tile prices. You'll find glazed and unglazed tile, mosaics, Italian marble, all in good name brands: American Olean, Cisa, Huntington Florida, Sideral. This company manufactures some of its own quarry tile, but also orders from large quality manufacturers' tested and rated tile stock.

It's important to select the right strength tile for each spot in your home if you want it to last a long time. If you're planning a large job, give yourself some ordering time during March to September. These are the busiest months.

No need to invest in any one-time-use tile tools. Just put down a deposit and get free use of the store's equipment.

Remodeling and Renovation Items

MERILLAT INDUSTRIES INC.

21755 Cedar Ave. S.
Lakeville
PHONE: 469-5444; be sure to call first
HOURS: Sat. only, 8 a.m.-noon
POLICIES: Checks or cash.

If you're remodeling the kitchen, check this spot out before you buy cabinets. Merillat Industries is the second largest kitchen cabinet maker in the country, and this location is where they assemble the goods. On Saturdays only, they sell their discontinued and second items to the public. You can save 40% to 60% and sometimes more, making it worth the trip! The cabinets are structurally sound but some may be damaged.

RENOVATION CONCEPTS

213 Washington Ave. N.
Minneapolis
PHONE: 333-5766
HOURS: Tues.-Fri., 8:30 a.m.-5 p.m.; Sat., 10 a.m.-2 p.m.
POLICIES: Credit cards—VISA and Master; checks accepted; no lay-by; returns: subject to 20% restocking charge.

Renovation Concepts specializes in unique building materials for new and old homes. The majority sell for 10% to 30% below regular retail prices. That is, if you could even find some of these supplies at regular retail stores. You'll find 60 different tin ceiling patterns ranging from $2.50 to $3.25 per square foot. There are oak door casings and wainscoating, even Victorian gabled porch railings. You can order from over 45 different manufacturer's catalogs. They do have a few in-stock items.

If you're working with a contractor, steer him to this place to order at wholesale prices.

Liquidation Shopping Strategies

- Inquire about the return or exchange policies. Save your receipts.

- Ask about what type of goods you're buying (factory closeouts, seconds, etc.). Find out if the warranty still applies.

- Look for name brands and avoid the cheaper imports, especially on tools and pots and pans.

- Most liquidators offer a 50% to 70% savings, but you'll still need to compare prices between each liquidator and discount stores.

- If you're a serious shopper, go frequently, since stock changes often.

- Know the key terms of liquidation shopping. *First quality merchandise* is in perfect condition, though not necessarily sold in season. *Irregular and second quality items* have minor flaws that shouldn't affect wear. Clothing must be marked if it's a second. Check carefully—seconds have more damage than irregulars, though they're sometimes repaired. *Blems or blemished goods* are merchandise with cosmetic flaws (scratches, dents, etc.) that still work perfectly. *Closeouts and discontinued or cancelled goods* can be first or second quality or irregular items that are usually no longer being produced.

C.O.M.B. CO.

6850 Wayzata Blvd.
Golden Valley
PHONE: 541-9700

3070 W. Hwy. 13
Burnsville
PHONE: 890-8296

3161 Hadley Ave. N.
Oakdale
PHONE: 770-2672

Hi-Lake Shopping Center
2216 E. Lake St.
Minneapolis
PHONE: 724-0077

250 N.E. Osborne Rd.
Fridley
PHONE: 572-3711

12580 Plaza Dr.
Eden Prairie
PHONE: 944-6400

HOURS: Mon.-Fri., 9 a.m.-9 p.m.; Sat., 10 a.m.-6 p.m.; Sun., 10 a.m.-5 p.m.

POLICIES: Credit cards—VISA and Master; checks accepted; no lay-by; returns: within 14 days; delivery extra; warranties don't always apply, so ask the salesperson.

It's that element of surprise that makes bargain hunters play the game of liquidation shopping. On one trip you'll find a great deal—the next time nothing. You have to make buying decisions on the spot. So the pressure is on you to know regular retail prices and spot quality.

One avid C.O.M.B. shopper bought a reconditioned Mitsubishi Video recorder for $400, but he knew this brand was selling for $1200 new at regular retail. That was three years ago, and it is still working.

You'll see the craziest things here—and what's crazier, there's actually a buyer for most of it. They have even sold World War II French mine detectors! Popular items that are always available are tools, housewares, kitchen gadgets, electronics and, once in a while, clothes.

Set aside some time to shop C.O.M.B. It can take one to two hours to really comb the store. But the excitement when you find something will thrill you as much as the savings, which are usually about 50%.

If you're a glutton for shopping punishment, you'll find the largest array of merchandise is located in the Wayzata Boulevard and Fridley stores.

AX MAN SURPLUS

1639 University Ave.
St. Paul
PHONE: 646-8653
HOURS: Mon.-Fri., 9 a.m.-6 p.m.; Sat., 9 a.m.-5 p.m.
POLICIES: Checks accepted; lay-by: negotiable; returns: cash unless sold as is.

Jess Liberman's store has always attracted a wide range of customers, from the handyman in overalls to the pinstriped do-it-yourselfer to the needlepointer looking for picture frames for her handiwork. There's an ever-changing inventory, but you can always count on some electronics and housewares that didn't fly the first time out in the retail market. Some of the weird items can only be appreciated by a select few. Anyone for used airline seat belts or 1976 Bicentennial placemats? Well, whatever you come up with, you'll find the prices right.

CRAZY LOUIE'S

839 University Ave.
St. Paul
PHONE: 291-8035
HOURS: Mon.-Fri., 9 a.m.-9 p.m.; Sat., 9 a.m.-5 p.m.; Sun., 11 a.m.-5 p.m.
POLICIES: Credit cards—VISA, Masters and Shoppers; checks accepted; lay-by: 30 days; 90-day guarantee for returns; warranties apply.

This place is worth the trip just to see the free museum of old cars and model trains. Usually there are some useful housewares, beauty products, and electronic gear. You *can* go crazy at Louie's: all you need is some time to do it in. Kids love this place.

THE SURPLUS STORE

1254 W. Seventh St.
St. Paul
PHONE: 227-7136
HOURS: Mon.-Fri., 9:30 a.m.-5:30 p.m.; Sat., 9 a.m.-5 p.m.

See description under Blaine Discount Center, below.

BLAINE DISCOUNT CENTER

10611 University Ave.
Blaine
PHONE: 757-4333
HOURS: Mon.-Fri., 9:30 a.m.-8 p.m.; Sat., 9 a.m.-6 p.m.; Sun., noon-5 p.m.

POLICIES: Credit cards—Master and VISA; checks accepted; no lay-by; returns: cash or credit.

These stores are owned by Roger Hovet. Each store is filled with an unpredictable supply of liquidated merchandise from food to toys to automobile engine hoses. Typical of this type of shopping, I stopped at The Surplus Store one day just to browse and couldn't resist the French imported chocolate honey-filled cookies, two packages for $1.00. I didn't need any cookies. I wasn't even *hungry*, but I was really excited to find gourmet shop quality treats selling so cheap. The bargain hunter will know Target and K-Mart prices on the children's items before shopping here. There are some kitchen gadgets, but not enough to plan on unless you just want to take your chances.

LIQUIDATION CENTER

1113 Excelsior Ave. E.
Hopkins
PHONE: 933-6717
HOURS: Mon.-Fri., 9 a.m.-6 p.m.; Sat., 9 a.m.-5 p.m.; Sun., noon-5 p.m.
POLICIES: Credit cards—VISA and Master; checks accepted; returns: credit or exchange in 10 days; full warranties apply.

The Liquidation Center does not carry any refurbished or damaged goods. Most of their stock is from closeouts, bankruptcies and samples. For those who want hardware mixed with housewares, the stock can prove satisfying. Bob and Lee Liberman, the father-son owners, also sell clothes, food, gift items, stereos and greeting cards.

THE BARGAIN OUTLET

6575 Cahill Ave. E.
Inver Grove Heights
PHONE: 457-8933
HOURS: Mon.-Tues., Sat., 9:30 a.m.-5:30 p.m.; Wed.-Fri., 9:30 a.m.-9 p.m.; Sun.. 1-5 p.m.
POLICIES: Checks accepted; returns: exchange only; 60-day warranties apply.

The Bargain Outlet is similar to a dime store. Dan and Cathy Schroeder specialize in T-shirts (a 50/50 cotton blend, for $1.99; transfers for another $1.50), and always have a variety of general merchandise. They try to keep the imported goods at a minimum. Discounts range from 20% to 70%.

CHAPTER 7

SECOND-HAND HOME FURNISHINGS AND HOUSEHOLD GOODS

Redecorating your home with second-hand furnishings is the best way to buy quality goods and still cushion your budget. Consignment furniture and thrift stores offer a good selection of the older wooden pieces that have already stood the test of time. There's no guesswork—you can see for yourself how well they have performed over the years. Each store has its own special atmosphere. Patience is the key word for this buying route. You'll probably have to make a few runs before you uncover your decorating treasure. But the reward is in the character of the goods you get and in all the money you've saved. And, of course, in the bragging that goes with finding a good deal.

ESTATE SALES

Buying furniture at estate sales is hit or miss shopping that can take a whole day. But it's an adventurous way to buy home furnishings for less, especially when you're decorating your first home or apartment. You can find bedroom sets, occasional tables, sofas, chairs, diningroom sets, china, lots of kitchen items, and usually plenty of linens. But if it's a big sale, the sale conductor will probably hand out numbers and only let in a few people at a time. Standing in line is part of the modus operandi.

Here's a list of some of the Estate Sale Conductors in the Twin Cities. If you can't keep track through the newspapers, give these people a call and they can tell you if they have a sale coming up soon.

DOROTHY ROBB	473-3095
THOMAS MURPHY	521-8510
BADGE HENDERIKSON, INC.	377-2123
ELIZABETH DAVIES	823-4243
CARROLL SHEPHERD	473-1554
DONALD DONAHUE	291-7254
JANICE ANDREWS	228-9713
JUDY KING	429-4068
MARY MARSDEN	224-2237
MAGGIE'S CORNER	298-0913
THE SWITCHING POST	870-1485

Estate Sale Strategies

- Watch the Wednesday and Thursday papers, since sales are held toward the end of the week or on weekends. In the *St. Paul Pioneer Press* look in the classified ads under Household Goods. In the *Minneapolis Tribune* look in the classifieds under Estate Sales.
- If you see a major item you like and it is only the first day of a two-day sale, don't panic. Often people don't buy the big furniture items the first day. Usually they have to go home and get other family members' input. Do the same, but do it quickly if you really love it. On the second day the prices will start coming down, so the wait may be worth it.
- Unless absolutely necessary, most professionals try to avoid giving an estate sale during the Christmas holidays. But if you do happen on one, it is a good time to shop. You're not competing with so many buyers, and prices will be lower.
- Estate sales conducted in upper crust neighborhoods will charge more for identical items, so know the true value of goods you buy.
- A well conducted estate sale will have the condition of an item marked on the tag. If there's a chip or crack it may say "as is." But buyer beware: inspection is still up to you.
- Before you buy, consider how you're going to cart your find home. Ask if the people conducting the sale have access to delivery. If they do, it is usually at an extra charge.
- Inquire if the person conducting the sale has a "call file." If so, you list what you're looking for. Then in the future if a sale comes up with the item you want, you will be notified about the sale date.

Consignment Stores

H & B GALLERIES

2729 Hennepin Ave.
Minneapolis
PHONE: 874-6436
HOURS: Tues.-Sat., 10 a.m.-4:30 p.m.
POLICIES: Checks accepted; lay-by: 30 to 60 days; no returns, but can take out an item on paid approval; referrals for delivery.

Everything in this store is on consignment. They have a large selection of quality used furniture and accessories with a few antiques mixed in the stock. As one bargain hunter described this shop, "It's elegant but affordable. The best deals are on sofas. A friend of mind found two down sofas here that people are constantly raving about." Sofa prices range from $125 to $450, dressers $75 to $200, coffee tables $75 to $300, and there are tons of lamps. Furniture moves quickly. You may have to scout for a couple of weeks to find just the right item.

If you're selling your furniture, this is a good spot. You'll get 70% of the profits.

THE SWITCHING POST

2015 Aldrich Ave. S.
Minneapolis
PHONE: 870-1485
HOURS: Wed.-Sat., 10 a.m.-3:45 p.m; from last week in June until first week in September, open Saturdays only.
POLICIES: Checks accepted; lay-by: 60 days; no returns; no delivery.

This consignment house is run by the Minneapolis League of Catholic Women. They get some good used furniture. Prices for sofas range from $150 to $400, occasional tables from $50 to $150. They sell china and sterling. There's a linen room located on the third floor that holds some good buys in draperies and bedspreads. Down in the basement are all the odds and ends. Unmatched wood chairs sell for $15, and dish collectors make frequent sweeps through the lower level.

ANYTHING AT ALL

707 E. Lake St.
Minneapolis
PHONE: 822-5152
HOURS: Mon.-Fri., 10 a.m.-5 p.m.; except Mon. & Thurs., until 7:30 p.m.; Sat., 10 a.m.-6 p.m.
POLICIES: Credit cards—VISA, Master and Shoppers; checks accepted; money-back guarantee on mechanical or electrical items, no returns on other merchandise; delivery extra.

Anything at All is a consignment shop that looks like a thrift store. It has a lot of furniture, from very cheap to very fine. Sofas range from $40 to $175, dressers from $15 to $100, wood dining room sets from $80 to $200. Many bargain hunters have had great luck here. It's cluttered and takes some patience to rummage. Some of the household gadgets seem overpriced.

AARDVARK TREASURES

1332 Randolph Ave.
St. Paul
PHONE: 698-6995
HOURS: Tues.-Sat., 10 a.m.-5 p.m.
POLICIES: Checks accepted; lay-by: 30 to 90 days; returns: within 1 week.

When you're looking for just the right accent piece to add a unique look to your room, Aardvark Treasures is worth a stop; it specializes in small collectable home accessories. Small piecrust tables range from $40 to $240, table lamps from $12 to $55. With five owners, there's lots of variety in this shop.

They do take consignments. Your trash may be someone else's treasure. Stroll through this store and see what's become a hot collectable.

GALLERY ANEW

6822 Hemlock Lane
Maple Grove
PHONE: 424-6903
HOURS: Mon.-Thurs., 11 a.m.-6:30 p.m.; Fri.-Sat., 10 a.m.-5 p.m.
POLICIES: Checks accepted; lay-by: flexible; returns: within 10 days.

Gallery Anew is a consignment store selling new, used and antique pictures. You'll find contemporary to traditional styles in prices that range from $1 to $300. If you're changing the living room around again, this may be just the place to sell the pictures that don't fit your decorating style anymore. You'll get up to 50% of the selling price. Or maybe you're a painter. Here's a place to peddle your wares without having to sit in the hot sun.

Don't overlook the box of used picture frames and mats. Ready-made frames and custom framing are also available.

Charitable Thrift Stores

SALVATION ARMY THRIFT STORES

Main Store, 900 N. Fourth St.
Minneapolis
PHONE: 332-6961

1928 Central Ave. N.E.
Minneapolis
PHONE: 788-6656

1521 Como Ave. S.E.
Minneapolis
PHONE: 331-7833

1326 N.W. Coon Rapids Blvd.
Coon Rapids
PHONE: 757-6740

2615 Franklin Ave. E.
Minneapolis
PHONE: 338-4710

2815 Nicollet Ave.
Minneapolis
PHONE: 871-4414

3756 Nicollet Ave.
Minneapolis
PHONE: 822-1200

2822 Washington Ave. N.
Minneapolis
PHONE: 529-4077

909 Selby Ave.
St. Paul
PHONE: 227-9931

927 Payne Ave.
St. Paul
PHONE: 776-3585

Uni-Dale Mall
572 University Ave.
St. Paul
PHONE: 224-7061

HOURS: Mon.-Sat., 9 a.m.-5 p.m.; except Coon Rapids, Mon.-Fri., 10 a.m.-9 p.m.; Sat., 9 a.m.-5 p.m., and Uni-Dale Mall, Mon.-Fri., 9 a.m.-9 p.m.; Sat., 9 a.m.-5 p.m.
POLICIES: Checks accepted; no lay-by; 30-day replacement or repair on major appliances; no returns on other merchandise; no delivery.

Salvation Army Thrift stores get a good mix of furniture and appliances donated all the time. Major appliances are repaired and carry a 30-day warranty. A large portion of the furniture is reupholstered and refinished by the Army's repair departments. At the Main Store you'll find the largest selection of antiques, collectables, used furniture, appliances, reconditioned mattresses and books. Also at the Main Store is the infamous basement full of junk and "as is" merchandise, plus trunks, filing cabinets, and shelves. You never know what you'll find. Some neighborhood stores to check also for a good selection of furniture are on Payne Avenue in St. Paul, Washington Avenue in Minneapolis, 3756 Nicollet Avenue in Minneapolis, and the Coon Rapids store.

One Salvation Army regular had this to share. "They have an interesting stock of used furniture, sometimes a bit high priced, but you can find a good piece here." Salvation Army also gets donations from new retail furniture stores and sometimes you'll hit it on a day when they have just put out a shipment. Sofas range from $50 to $300, dressers start at $45, lamps at $5. You'll also find linens, curtains, TVs—and even used cars (at the Main Store only). The good inexpensive furniture goes fast. And of course there's no guarantee you'll find what you want on your first pass through. Plan your trips around these furniture shipment days.

THE MAIN STORE - Delivery arrives daily.

WASHINGTON AVE. STORE - Delivery arrives on Wednesday morning.

CENTRAL AVE. STORE - Delivery arrives on Wednesday.

2815 NICOLLET AVE. STORE - Delivery arrives Monday afternoon.

3756 NICOLLET AVE. STORE - Delivery arrives on Monday.

FRANKLIN AVE. STORE - Delivery arrives on Monday morning.

COMO AVE. STORE - Delivery arrives on Tuesday.

COON RAPIDS STORE - Delivery arrives on Tuesday.

PAYNE AVE. STORE - Delivery arrives on Thursday.

UNI-DALE MALL - Delivery arrives Friday around 3 p.m.

SELBY AVE. STORE - Delivery arrives on Friday morning around 9:30 a.m.

Best deals will always be on the "as is" furniture. If a large item has been around for a while, try bargaining with the store manager.

GOODWILL STORES

4020 Bloomington Ave.
Minneapolis
PHONE: 823-4855
HOURS: Mon.-Fri., 9 a.m.-9 p.m.; Sat., 9 a.m.-5:30 p.m.; Sun., 12:30-5:30 p.m.

Main Store, 2543 Como Ave.
St. Paul
PHONE: 646-2591
HOURS: Mon.-Fri., 9:30 a.m.-9 p.m.; Sat., 9 a.m.-5:30 p.m.; Sun., 12:30-5:30 p.m.

913 Excelsior Ave. W.
Hopkins
PHONE: 935-9773
HOURS: Mon.-Fri., 10 a.m.-8 p.m.; Sat., 9 a.m.-5:30 p.m.; Sun., noon-5 p.m.

946 Payne Ave.
St. Paul
PHONE: 776-3185
HOURS: Mon. & Fri., 9 a.m.-9 p.m.; Tues.-Thurs., 9 a.m.-6 p.m.; Sat., 9 a.m.-5:30 p.m.; Sun., noon-5 p.m.

3000 White Bear Ave.
Maplewood
PHONE: 770-2401
HOURS: Mon.-Fri., 9 a.m.-9 p.m.; Sat., 9:30 a.m.-5 p.m.; Sun., noon-5 p.m.

POLICIES: Credit cards—Master and VISA; Checks accepted; lay-by: for furniture priced $50 or more, put 33% down and they will hold one for one week; no returns; no delivery.

In the Main Goodwill Store on Como Avenue you'll find some good wood furniture that Goodwill has reupholstered. It's usually put out in the morning during the week and the prices start at $75. In the back of this store you'll also find a small array of "as is" items. They don't carry appliances, but you can find color TVs ranging from $10 to $120. There are curtains and linens—Goodwill is even buying some manufacturers' closeouts and overstocks on towels and household items. Many times you'll run across items donated from new stores.

If you're in the market for a used car, go to the Main Store and look over the list of availabilities. You may have to shop frequently, but you never know what treasure you'll turn over.

SALVAGE ARMY VETS OF WORLD WAR II

9 East 16th St.
Minneapolis
PHONE: 874-7728
HOURS: Mon.-Thurs., 9 a.m.-5 p.m.; Fri.-Sat., 9 a.m.-6 p.m.
POLICIES: Checks accepted; lay-by: negotiable; no returns; delivery extra.

You're going to find a large supply of used furniture here. But prepare yourself for the hunt: this place is big, so shop when your energy is high. Sofas range from $50 to $150, hideabeds $95 to $175, dressers from $18 to $125, and dining room sets $115 to $245. Don't expect to find antiques; they only show up occasionally.

STEEPLE PEOPLE THRIFT STORE

715 W. Franklin Ave.
Minneapolis
PHONE: 871-8305
HOURS: Thurs., 10 a.m.-8 p.m.; Fri., 10 a.m.-5:30 p.m.; Sat., 10 a.m.-5 p.m.
POLICIES: Checks accepted; 10% down will hold for 2 weeks; returns: exchange only; delivery extra.

This little thrift store holds precious memories for me, because I managed it a few years back for Hennepin Methodist Church. Since it's only open three days a week, if you're going to seriously shop this place, you have to get there the minute it opens on Thursdays. That's when all the goodies have been stocked for the week. You'll be competing with every scrounger who knows how good Steeple People can be.

I remember the time (you never forget the bargains that got away) I sold a poster to a dealer for fifty cents. He later informed me it was a collectable and worth at least $250. And the worst part was, when I unrolled it as I was ringing it up, I saw it was titled "The Bargain Hunter." Since that day, I have never passed a poster without checking it out.

Occasionally a good sofa, dresser, end table or bedroom set will wedge its way into the store. Because the place is small, the staff really can't keep large furniture around for very long, so you can try bargaining on those pieces with the manager. Everything in the store is donated and volunteers from the church spend a lot of time weeding out the items in bad condition.

REACHOUT THRIFT STORE

417 E. Lake St.
Minneapolis
PHONE: 827-5606
HOURS: Mon.-Sat., 9 a.m.-9 p.m.
POLICIES: Checks accepted; no lay-by; no returns; delivery extra.

Reachout has good used furniture, all of it sold "as is," but some of it in excellent condition. Their best items are the wood pieces, though some are overpriced. People doing their own reupholstering will find good deals. Sofas range from $10 to $150. When an old ornate wood dresser comes in, it can range from $69 to $170. In the back warehouse area, you'll find all sorts of household miscellany. Merchandise is put out every day.

SALVAGE STORES

A salvage safari can produce some rare finds for the do-it-yourselfer, especially one renovating an old home, and will inspire those with a decorating flair. Scroungers have fun, and exercise fanatics work up a sweat that beats any aerobic routine.

If you're a novice in the scrap hunt, here are a couple tips to keep you on target. Be sure to bring along any measurements you need, a flashlight (because there are some dark corners), and a measuring tape. Dress for the hunt: don't wear open toe shoes; wear hard soles for protection. If you can, avoid shopping on Saturdays; you'll get more assistance during the week.

BAUER BROS. SALVAGE

174 Arlington Ave.
St. Paul
PHONE: 489-9044
HOURS: Mon.-Fri., 7:30 a.m.-5 p.m.; Sat., 7:30 a.m.-noon
POLICIES: Checks accepted; lay-by: negotiable; returns: cash or exchange; delivery extra.

Remember that wonderful copper lady who presided over the Copper Squirrel on Hennepin Avenue in downtown Minneapolis for so many years? She now graces this salvage yard. If you're nostalgic at all, you'll enjoy picking through these and other remains of some familiar sites in the Twin Cities.

The first time you shop at Bauer's, give yourself some time. Stop at the office first and tell the staff what you're looking for. Someone will steer you in the general direction of your quarry. Don't expect a lot of service—the hunt is yours. If you're looking for solid wood doors, they are here, somewhere, for $20 to $45. Wooden hand railings are priced from $.50 to $1.00 per foot. Room radiators are priced $5 to $7 per section.You'll always find window screens, maybe not the right size, but worth looking for at $5.00 apiece. If you're looking for built-in buffets or leaded glass windows, ask to be taken to the garage behind the office.

Don't be afraid to bargain. You may not get anywhere, but it's almost expected that you'll try.

ALL-STATE SALVAGE

1354 Jackson St.
St. Paul
PHONE: 488-6675
HOURS: Tues.-Fri., 9 a.m.-5 p.m.; Sat., 9 a.m.-3 p.m.
POLICIES: Credit cards—VISA; Checks accepted; lay-by: 30 days on large items; no returns after 1 week.

There are always surprises when you shop here. You just don't know what you'll find. But one thing is for sure—you *will* find a lot. Do-it-yourselfers, building contractors, plumbers, and carpenters make regular runs through All-State. Wood doors average $15 to $45, French doors $45 to $100, and toilets $27.50. At this yard, the owner, Vern Denzin, buys up estates and also damaged or lost merchandise from truck lines, so you can run into some good furniture deals. Wood dressers range from $15 to $150, and dining room sets from $150 to $500. Remember, it takes shopping stamina to sift through this salvage!

S & B SALVAGE

607 Washington Ave. N.
Minneapolis
PHONE: 881-5767 (call before you shop—they may be conducting a sale)
HOURS: Mon.-Fri., 9 a.m.-5 p.m.
POLICIES: Credit cards—Master and VISA; checks accepted; lay-by: negotiable; returns: for store credit.

S & B Salvage is an old-style liquidator, going to store sites and selling right down to the walls (they liquidated the leftovers at the old Donaldson's store in downtown Minneapolis). Remnants from these on-site sales are brought to the home base, which is the huge sixth floor of an old warehouse on Washington Avenue. There you can find the furniture remains of a closed Holiday Inn or lighting fixtures and shelving from a long-defunct business. You just never know what you'll uncover. If you've got the time, stop here. Whatever you find will be at a good price.

FRANK PLUMBING SALES

1101 Washington Ave. S.
Minneapolis
PHONE: 338-7609
HOURS: Mon.-Fri., 8:30 a.m.-5:30 p.m.; Sat., 8:30 a.m.-4 p.m.
POLICIES: Checks accepted; no lay-by; returns; refunds minus a 15% restocking charge; delivery extra.

If you're remodeling a bathroom, you need to know about Frank's. This place is a storehouse of hard-to-find plumbing fixtures, with a large supply of sinks and tubs. One of their specialties is the old pedestal sinks and claw-footed tubs, all reconditioned with new porcelain finishes. At first, prices seem hefty, but the old fixtures are difficult to find and the new reproductions, if you can find any in the style you want, are more costly than Frank's. You'll be happy you found this spot.

Frank's also buys up manufacturers' closeouts, overstocks, and seconds on new tubs and sinks. On these you'll save 15% to 60% below the regular retail price. Some of the items have only a cosmetic flaw in the finish.

When you're trying to replace a broken plumbing part, be sure to bring the piece along with you. Chances are they can match any thingamajig you're looking for. And have they got toilet tank covers? Every size imaginable, in prices ranging from $10 to $14.

CORT FURNITURE RENTAL CLEARANCE CENTER

8925 Lyndale Ave. S.
Bloomington
PHONE: 884-5622
HOURS: Mon.-Thurs., 9 a.m.-8 p.m.; Fri., 9 a.m.-5:30 p.m.; Sat., 10 a.m.-4 p.m.

1901 W. Hwy. 36
Roseville
PHONE: 631-2811
HOURS: Mon.-Thurs., 10 a.m.-7 p.m.; Fri., 10 a.m.-5:30 p.m.; Sat., 10 a.m.-4 p.m.

POLICIES: Credit cards—VISA and Master; checks accepted; hold furniture for 10 days; returns: cash, minus a 10% restocking charge; delivery extra.

Thanks to mobile business executives, the rental furniture business is booming, and every year the quality of rental furniture keeps getting better. This means the buyer looking for a good deal can cash in by shopping the clearance centers, where all the used rental furniture awaits a permanent home. You'll find contemporary, traditional, and country styling in sofas, chairs, tables, dining room sets, bedroom sets, and accessories. The prices are at least 50% below a regular retailer.

Do a background check on the furniture you're interested in. Some items were merely sitting in model homes; others may not have been popular rental choices; and some will be slightly damaged. Good name brands are available, like Chrome Craft in contemporary styling, Peters Remington in the wood occasional tables and Stratford in the upholstered furniture and recliners. A sofa selling for $150 to $300 at Cort will compare to a $500 to $600 sofa at retail price, while at the high end, a sofa at Cort selling for $900 compares to a $4,000 retail sofa. The Lyndale Avenue store has the largest selection.

Watch for these special times to shop. There's a big sale in October, with a lot of the Parade of Homes Models' furniture. Another good sale is in April. Throughout the year, the best time to shop is around the 5th day of each month, when the rental furniture has been returned.

RECYCLED MUSIC SYSTEMS

3531 11th Ave. S.
Minneapolis
PHONE: 721-3295
HOURS: Mon.-Fri., must make an appointment
POLICIES: Checks accepted, lay-by: negotiable; returns: cash within 7 days; 30-day full guarantee on merchandise.

There aren't too many audiophiles in town who haven't heard about Recycled Music Systems. Al Peterman has been selling used audio gear out of his basement for 14 years. He buys trade-ins from the audio stores in town—turntables, receivers, speakers, cassette decks, amplifier tuners—goes over them with a repairman's eye, and fixes anything necessary. A few times a year he travels the country, buying up stereo and audio gear from pawn shops outside military bases. He also finds used video equipment and new computer accessories (printers, monitors, modems).

You can save 25% to 65% off list prices on the stereo equipment. There are no car stereos or Walkmans here. If you would like to know what he has in stock, just give Al a call. Al's is the place to get a good deal on sound equipment.

If you're looking for something in particular and Al doesn't have it, he will list you on his computerized database and phone you when he gets it.

CHAPTER 8

FABRIC, CRAFT, AND UPHOLSTERY SUPPLIES

Now that we have two large fabric retailers in town, Minnesota Fabrics and Northwest Fabrics, home sewers are having a field day with the two stores offering competitive deals to claim their dressmaking dollars. The smart sewer gets on these stores' mailing lists and gets notified about all the specials. One edge that Northwest Fabrics has is the bargain area in the back of their stores.

A few sources of savings are listed in other sections of this book. For first quality woolens, see the Shoppers Factory Outlet (p. 30) and the Wool-n-Shop (p. 7). For coat fabrics, visit the Sharpe Factory Store (p. 26). And for wool batting materials for quilts, check out the Twin Cities Carding Mill (p. 174). When it comes to fabric sales, the favorite for sewing bargain hunters is the Minnetonka Mills Fabric Sale, held in April and September each year. No remnants here! Call them at 935-2663 to get on their mailing list. (Incidentally, "odd lots," "mill-ends," "bolt-ends," and "remnants" are all words that describe fabric leftovers. They save you a wad if you buy carefully.)

Unless otherwise noted, you can assume that returns aren't accepted in yard goods, patterns, and other supplies.

Sewing and Craft Supplies

THE AMERICAN SEWING GUILD

P.O. Box 35513
Minneapolis, MN 55435
PHONE: (612) 941-8885
HOURS: Mon.-Fri., 9 a.m.-4:30 p.m.

This guild offers many benefits to the home sewer. If you don't belong yet, seriously consider joining. Often they get fabric discounts for members, but they also have neighborhood sewing support groups where you are updated on the latest sewing trends. Here's some information from their recent newsletter.

The major pattern manufacturers offer a special toll-free help hotline. If you're having any problems with their pattern, you can call these customer service numbers and they will help you through it.

VOGUE/BUTTERICK®	1-800-221-2670
SIMPLICITY®	1-800-223-1664
BURDA PATTERNS®	1-800-241-6887
McCALLS®	1-800-255-2764

(At McCalls they will be offering a discount pattern service. Give them a call.)

REMNANT STORE

1010 Excelsior Ave. W.
Hopkins
PHONE: 938-6238
HOURS: Mon.-Tues., Fri., 9 a.m.-7:30 p.m.; Wed.-Thurs., Sat., 9 a.m.-5:30 p.m.; Sun., noon-5 p.m.
POLICIES: No credit cards; checks accepted.

This place is a storehouse of Munsingwear fabric. In fact, Jack McCarthy, the owner, is a former employee of that company. What you'll find here is what Munsingwear specializes in—knit material. There's a lot of T-shirt knits, some lingerie fabrics and notions. The savings are 35% to 40% below regular retail, but there's no skimping on service. The fabric is first quality, second quality, and includes remnants. The better quality is sold by the yard; the rest is in bins and is sold by weight. They have a good selection of knit collars, cuffs, and ribbon. Knit blend fabric is $1.25 a yard.

Get on their mailing list for special sales.

KIEFFER LINGERIE SUPPLIES

1625 Hennepin Ave.
Minneapolis
PHONE: 332-3395
HOURS: Mon.-Fri., 9 a.m.-4:30 p.m.; Sat., 9 a.m.-1 p.m.
POLICIES: No credit cards; checks accepted.

If you're sewing lingerie, here's where to shop. This place is by no means fancy, but it has some real bargains. You'll find swimwear fabric, lots of lace and trims, and bolts of wide lingerie fabric (some first quality and many mill seconds). The prices are lower than wholesale. Fabric goes from $3.00 to $5.50 a yard, with the best prices on their sale tables and on the fabric sold by the pound (this can be as little as fifty cents a pound). Kieffer also carries "Sew Lovely" and "Kwik Sew" patterns ranging from $1.50 to $3.75.

You'll need some time to shop here...it is pretty much self-service.

BROTEX COMPANY

800 N. Hampden
St. Paul
PHONE: 645-5721
HOURS: Mon.-Fri., 9 a.m.-5 p.m.; Sat., 9 a.m.-3 p.m.
POLICIES: Credit cards—Shoppers; checks accepted.

Home sewers, crafters, and quilters dedicated to digging (and I mean digging) out a bargain eventually find their way to Brotex. The savings is 20% to 50% off fabric bolts, mill-ends, cone yarn, some first quality fabric and discontinued sewing patterns. They also have "barrel goods," fabric sold by the pound. Be sure to check everything carefully before you buy, since none of the flaws are marked. Also check out the flyer in the store to see what's on special that day. There's no selection of wool here or 100% natural fabrics; most are blends. Poly/cotton is priced $1.79 to $3.98 a yard.

BEMIDJI WOOLEN MILLS, INC. FACTORY AND MILL STORE

P.O. Box 277
Bemidji, MN 56601 (Send for a free catalog.)
Location:
Third & Irvine Ave.
Bemidji
(Four blocks from Paul Bunyan and Babe,
225 miles north of the Twin Cities.)
PHONE: (218) 751-5166
MILL STORE HOURS: Mon.-Sat., 8 a.m.-5:30 p.m.; closed on major holidays.
POLICIES: Credit cards—VISA and Master.

Maybe it's stretching things to include Bemidji in this book, but if you can't make the trip, call or write Bemidji Woolen Mills and get their free catalog. Bemidji Woolen Mills has wonderful bargains on both clothing and fabrics. A 60-inch wide wool blend (85% wool/15% nylon) sells for $10.95 a yard. You can also order 100% Pendelton wool starting at $15.95 a yard. Knitters can take their pick of homespun yarn at $1.95 for a 4-ounce skein of 100% wool, 4-ply knitting worsted, in natural or natural grey.

You'll get a bigger selection, of course, if you visit the store, where they always have mill ends, remnants, and yarn sold by the bag. The savings at this factory outlet store is about 50% below retail, sometimes more. In clothing you'll find down jackets, men's heavyweight coats, hunting jackets, blankets, sweaters, wool socks, and much more.

FARIBO WOOLENS FACTORY STORE

1500 Second Ave. N.W.
Faribault, MN 55021
(45 minutes south of Burnsville on Hwy. 35W)
PHONE: (507) 334-6444
HOURS: Mon.-Sat., 9 a.m.-5:30 p.m.; Sun., 1-5 p.m.
POLICIES: Credit cards—VISA, Master and American Express; checks accepted; returns: cash or credit, irregular blankets for merchandise exchange; all sales final.

If you are adept at making your own coats or suits, a fabric treasure awaits you at Faribo Woolens Factory Store. You can buy 100% wool, 90-inch wide, blanket ends (available in various lengths). The cost is hard to gauge since it is sold by the pound, but it is very reasonable. The drawback is that you're taking your chances on color and pattern selection each time you stop by. It really depends on what Faribo is manufacturing at the time. It could be a black-and-red plaid or a navy...you just never know. Another incentive to hit the road might be the blankets and afghans that are sold for 40% to 50% below major department store prices. These are irregulars, but often the flaw is slight. The blankets can be mail ordered...just write Faribo Woolens for a free catalog. However, the blanket ends *cannot* be ordered by mail.

S. R. HARRIS INDUSTRIES

5100 County Rd. 18
New Hope
PHONE: 535-3050
HOURS: Mon.-Thurs., 8 a.m.-9 p.m.; Fri., 8 a.m.-10 p.m.; Sat., 8:30 a.m.-6 p.m.; Sun., 11 a.m.-5 p.m.
POLICIES: Credit cards—VISA and Master; checks accepted; returns: cash or credit.

At S. R. Harris you are going to find a lot of fabric and thread and a warehouse atmosphere. Some shoppers arrive when Harris opens (8:30 a.m.) and are still around at noon. It takes time to shop. You cut and measure your own fabric, which is largely mill overruns and closeouts, but you will find first quality, too. One of the bargains is the Evan Picone wool, selling for $6.99 a yard. One home sewer, who is somewhat critical of their fabric selection, did concede, "when S. R. Harris has the Evan Picone fabric, it is a good deal. But you have to know good fabric before you shop here." Check everything carefully before you buy in order to avoid any irregularities showing up later when you get home. Many shoppers love the bargains on thread...30 core Levi topstitch thread sells for 99 cents a spool. Designer corduroy is $4.99 a yard, and denim is $2.99 a yard. The savings here is over 50%.

Twice a year, Sid Harris has his famous "Midnite Madness Sale." On the first day of this sale, if you don't get there early, you don't get in the door—it is that popular! The sales are usually scheduled for the end of May and the 1st of Septem-

ber. There's no mailing list, so savvy sewers start calling here in April and August just to keep tabs on the sale date. During the year, watch for weekly specials advertised in the *Minneapolis Tribune* Thursday or Sunday paper.

KNIT KITS, INC.

216 Third Ave. N.
Minneapolis, MN 55401
Note: this is a mailing address only—no walk-in shopping.
PHONE: 332-0361
HOURS TO CALL: Mon.-Fri., 9 a.m.-5 p.m.
POLICIES: Credit cards—VISA and Master; checks accepted.

Actually, Knit Kits no longer sells kits, and they don't have any walk-in customer service. You order by mail. Call or write for their catalog; there's a $1.00 charge with $15.00 as the minimum order. The catalog lists Carter's infant wear fabric, stretch terry for pajamas; knit fabrics for sweatshirts, T-shirts and underwear; and cotton calicos. Most of the fabric is not found in regular stores and is used only by major manufacturers. You'll save 30% to 50%.

Delivery normally takes five days, but during the busy season, mid-September to mid-November, it can take up to two weeks.

ANGEL INDUSTRIES

488 S. Robert
West St. Paul
PHONE: 224-7591
HOURS: Mon.-Fri., 7 a.m.-5 p.m.
POLICIES: Checks accepted; no returns.

This linen manufacturing firm buys directly from the best fabric mills in the country. There are bolts and bolts of calico and gingham in 50/50 cotton/poly blends. One shopper bought fabric for her daughter's bedroom, finding all the prints she needed from dust ruffle to curtains. All the goods are first quality. Veteran quilters and crafters know and love this place.

The first time you stop, go to the receptionist and you will get a personal tour. They are real angels here—they treat you well.

YARN BARN

Midland Shopping Center
Winnetka & Medicine Lake Rd.
New Hope
PHONE: 541-0070
HOURS: Mon.-Fri., 10 a.m.-5 p.m.; Sat., 10 a.m.-4 p.m.
POLICIES: Credit cards—Master and VISA; checks accepted; returns: credit only.

You'll save 30% to 50% below regular retail prices at the Yarn Barn. They specialize in service and savings. Their yarn is first quality mill ends and closeouts in good brand names...Bernat, Ulltex, Pingouin, Brunswick. The 100% wool is sold in bags at 60 cents an ounce; of course this means that you will spend some time rolling it into skeins. Acrylic is sold on the skein. Colors will vary, but whatever you choose, there is usually enough for what you're making. Patterns, notions, and cone yarn are also available.

LEE'S APRON CO.

Wyman Bldg.
400 First Ave. N.
Minneapolis
PHONE: 332-2035
HOURS: Mon.-Fri., 10-11:30 a.m.; 1-2 p.m.
POLICIES: Cash only.

If you quilt or do appliqué work, you must know about this spot. You can buy pre-cut cotton scraps for 15 cents a pound. It is best to call them first and find out how much they have in stock that day. Or if you're in downtown Minneapolis and want to take a chance, stop in during the hours listed.

CALICO CORNERS

7101 France Ave.
Edina
PHONE: 925-5600

Fairdale Shopping Center
2325 Fairview Ave.
Roseville
PHONE: 636-5112

HOURS: Mon. & Thurs., 10 a.m.-9 p.m.; Tues.-Wed., Fri., 10 a.m.-6 p.m.; Sat., 10 a.m.-5 p.m.; Sun., 1 p.m.-5 p.m.

POLICIES: Credit cards—Master and VISA; checks accepted

There's no child-proof Herculon here. Calico Corners specializes in printed cottons or cottons with rayon and other blends for drapes or upholstering. Printed cottons range from $3.95 to $11.95 a yard. A couple of years ago a friend of mine was redecorating with a country flair and found fabric here for $5.00 less a yard than at other stores. She snatched it up and covered 18 floor pillows for $79.00.

The fabric is first quality, second quality, bolt ends, and remnants, but the staff will carefully inspect the fabric with you for flaws and offer lots of service to help you with any decorating problems you may be working around. You'll find notions, drapery hardware, and upholstering supplies, not necessarily any off-priced, but the fabric itself is where you can get the bargain.

Two special sales to watch for come during the beginning of March and the beginning of August.

Upholstery Supplies

MINNESOTA FOAM PRODUCTS CO.

6523 Bass Lake Rd.
Crystal
PHONE: 535-5855
HOURS: Mon.-Fri., 8:30 a.m.-5 p.m.; odd-dated Sat., 8:30 a.m.-4 p.m.
POLICIES: Checks accepted; flexible lay-by.

Minnesota Foam Products is a foam cushion distributor, so you'll find a great selection of foam rubber cushions, have any size cut to fit your needs, and buy some upholstery to cover it in one stop. The foam wares run the gamut on quality and prices, though all the upholstery fabric is first quality. The brand names are tops: Waverly, Schumacher, LaFrance, Kirsch, and lots of vinyls. There's an unbelievable array to choose from. If you order from the floor stock, you can save up to 50% over retail prices. If you custom order, your savings go to about 25%, depending on the amount of material you need. Fabric ranges from $5 to $45 a yard, and vinyls from $9 to $28 a yard.

Check this spot first for quality and selection. Special sale times are in February and September.

DO-IT-YOURSELF UPHOLSTERY SUPPLY

1558 W. Larpenteur Ave.
St. Paul
PHONE: 645-7211
HOURS: Mon.-Fri., 9:30 a.m.-5:30 p.m., except Thurs., until 7:30 p.m.; Sat., 9:30 a.m.-4 p.m.
POLICIES: Checks accepted.

You can save 40% to 60% off regular retail prices here on upholstery fabric. It's mill-ends, closeouts and some first quality. Fabric ranges from $5 to $25 a yard. They also have all the supplies you need to cover the job.

A-1 FOAM-N-FABRICS

7608 Lyndale Ave. S.
Richfield
PHONE: 861-5255
HOURS: Mon.-Fri., 9 a.m.-6 p.m., except Thurs. until 7:30 p.m.; Sat., 10 a.m.-3 p.m.
POLICIES: Checks accepted.

If you're still on a fabric run, check out A-1, where the remnants are $2.50 a yard. Their first quality fabrics go to $15.00. You'll find upholstery supplies and foam rubber cushions here, too.

A tip from upholsterers is to always put your money into a good cushion, one that's tightly sealed with dacron wrapping. That will keep your foam from deteriorating and getting flaky, and your upholstery cover will wrinkle less.

KAISER MANUFACTURING

9445 Brookview Rd.
Woodbury
PHONE: 739-7411
HOURS: Mon.-Fri., 9 a.m.-5 p.m., except Wed., until 9 p.m.; Sat., 9 a.m.-12 p.m.
POLICIES: Checks accepted.

Kaiser is really diversified. You won't believe some of the things you'll spot here. They have upholstery fabric for furniture and boats for $5 to $35 a yard, canvas for boat covers; awning material for your home; rope for barges, decoration, tug of war and macrame; and indoor/outdoor carpeting for boats or homes. There's no shortage of selection in anything, but if you don't find the upholstery fabric you want, you can go through the books and have it ordered. Prices are very good. For some, it may be quite a drive, but if you need anything mentioned, it's worth the trip.

CHAPTER 9

REPAIR SERVICES

If you have a broken treasure in the attic that has sentimental or even antique value, you'll be money ahead by having it fixed. This is also true whenever you figure that to replace an item, whether it's clothing or furniture, it would cost you at least 50% more than your repair cost. And if you're an avid second-hand shopper, you know that a find that needs fixing may well be your best bargain. To save searching time looking for reputable and sometimes unusual repair services, take a look through this chapter.

Furniture, Housewares, and Lighting

CILEK WOOD FURNITURE REPAIR

1501 Randolph Ave.
St. Paul
PHONE: 699-4022
HOURS: Mon.-Fri., 8 a.m.-6 p.m.; Sat., 8 a.m.-2 p.m.
POLICIES: Checks accepted.

Gene Cilek has been fixing wooden chairs for 25 years. He guarantees that once he repairs a piece, it's fixed for life. His prices only range from $10 to $45, no matter what the job. Gene's specialty is regluing, with the average price to have a chair reglued $25. He can also transform a completely broken chair with pieces missing into brand new for $45. Or he will hand-carve a missing chair spindle for $15. So before you toss a chair because it looks like it's an impossible repair job, bring it to Gene Cilek—he'll love the challenge.

MOHN'S LAMPTRICIAN

925 W. Lake St.
Minneapolis
PHONE: 923-4243
HOURS: Mon., noon-8 p.m.; Tues.-Fri., 9 a.m.-5:30 p.m.
POLICIES: No credit cards; checks accepted.

At Mohn's, lamp repair and replacement parts are the specialty. That wasn't always the case for owner Tom Davies. Before he took early retirement, he was a Senior Research Scientist at Honeywell. He welcomes any challenge you can give him. Lamp transformations include (just to get your imagination going) blow torches, trumpets, parking meters...the list goes on.

The cost to rewire and replace a socket on a table lamp is under $10 for the *whole* job. To rewire a chandelier with glass arms costs $6.50 an arm. A metal arm chandelier costs less (if you're a garage sale shopper this information will help you bargain on a broken light fixture). If you want to fix it yourself, Tom can give you some pointers. Chances are the parts you'll need are in his shop. Glass chandelier prisms cost $.56 to $5.00.

If you're looking for a St. Paul counterpart to Mohn's, check out Brinkman Service Co., 286 S. Snelling Ave., 698-8577. They are more expensive, but maybe the distance works better for you.

MICHAEL'S LAMPS

3101 W. 50th St.
Edina
PHONE: 926-9147
HOURS: Mon.-Fri., 9:30 a.m.-5:30 p.m.; Sat., 9 a.m.-5 p.m.
POLICIES: Credit cards—VISA and Master

Michael's specializes in everything to do with lamps, but especially *shades*. If the number of lamp shades available still doesn't turn up that difficult-to-find shade, they can special order it for you. A 14-inch lined silk blend drum shade costs $48.75. A similar shade, unlined, is $37. If you want a shade recovered, Michael's will send it out, but generally that's a costly job and you're better off to buy it new.

BRITE IDEAS

134 S. Tenth St.
Minneapolis
PHONE: 332-0683
HOURS: Mon., noon-5 p.m.; Tues.-Fri., 9:30 a.m.-5 p.m.; Sat., 9:30 a.m.-10 p.m.
POLICIES: Credit cards—Master and VISA; checks accepted.

If you are looking for a shade to match your decorating fabrics, Brite Ideas is a good first stop. Bring your own fabric and they will laminate a lamp shade to your size specifications. Or you can choose from their decorator fabrics. Whether you go with a personal touch or a custom shade, the cost is the same. Or you can spend less and select from a wide range of ready-made fabric shades.

Metal, Glass, and Wicker

JOYNER'S SILVER SHOP

7716 Lakeland Ave. N.
Brooklyn Park
Mailing Address: P.O. Box 262, Osseo, MN 55369
PHONE: 425-2104
HOURS: Mon.-Fri., 8 a.m.-4:30 p.m.
POLICIES: No credit cards; checks accepted.

Joyner's has been in the business of restoring silver, brass, copper, nickel, chrome and other precious metal platings for over 40 years. They do excellent quality work. They will repair, polish or plate your silverware and help you keep your set intact, fix broken brass lamp bases, or get pewter repaired.

The minimum charge for any order is $30. Each repair piece requires its own special work, so they prefer that you bring your item in for a free estimate. You will save money by going directly to Joyner's rather than a department store for your silver repairs, because chances are, the store would have sent it out to Joyner's anyway.

Plan ahead for repairs here, because from October to December, Joyner's is swamped getting silver repaired for the Thanksgiving and Christmas holidays.

WILLIAM MARVEY COMPANY

1540 St. Clair Ave.
St. Paul
PHONE: 698-0762
HOURS: Mon.-Fri., 8 a.m.-5:15 p.m.; Sat., 8:30 a.m.-4 p.m.

Bill Marvy is probably best known for his barber-supply business and the fact that he is the sole maker of barber poles in North America. What isn't as well known is his excellent work in polishing brass and copper. Nor is it well known that he was once called on to do emergency graffiti removal service in a State Department's brass elevator. Marvy's forte, however, is not graffiti, but brass beds. You can have an old standard double-size brass headboard polished for $260. When he is finished it looks...*marvelous* (a comparable quality new brass bed costs about $950). Copper wash boilers cost $39 without a cover and $43 with a cover to shine up.

Pick up and delivery service is available in the Twin Cities and some suburbs for $20 to $40.

If you're missing casters for any bed, take a tip from Marvy's. They send everyone over to Skarnes Inc., 2907 Franklin Ave., Minneapolis, 339-9141. You'll save about 30% on some of the casters they have in stock, but you can also special order hard-to-find items.

KAEMPFER GLASS AND CRYSTAL REPAIR

1599 Selby Ave.
St. Paul
PHONE: 644-0763
HOURS: Wed.-Sat., 9-11:30 a.m. and 1-6 p.m.
POLICIES: No credit cards; checks accepted; workmanship guaranteed; call to make an appointment.

David Kaempfer has spent 11 years developing techniques to fix broken china, crystal and ceramic. He will remove chips from the rims of glasses for $2.50 to $7.00. He can also restore decorative china pieces (not regular dinner plates) at a very reasonable price. Just bring in your fragile treasures and he will give you an estimate. Most of the better department stores bring their problem pieces to him.

FORD MCNUTT GLASS CO.

144 Glenwood
Minneapolis
PHONE: 338-6963
HOURS: Mon.-Fri., 8 a.m.-4:30 p.m.
POLICIES: No credit cards; checks accepted.

Bring mirrors that need resilvering to Ford McNutt. The cost is $8.00 per square foot and the minimum charge is $16.00. They will also make mirrors for the same price. This company has been around for 95 years.

I must tell you, though, if you have an antique mirror and the silver back is fading, you may want to keep it as is. Some experts say the value will go down if you tamper and have it resilvered.

LIZ HEISLER AMERICAN CLASSICS

4944 Xerxes Ave. S.
Minneapolis
PHONE: 926-2509, or 487-1349
HOURS: Mon.-Sat., 10:30 a.m.-5 p.m.; Sun., noon-4 p.m.
POLICIES: Checks accepted; she will give you a *definite* price quote; workmanship guaranteed.

Liz Heisler has a section in American Classic Antiques where she sells her wickerware, specializing in the older pieces. She's also known in the Twin Cities for her excellent wicker, cane and rush repair work (she does all fiber seats). In fact, the New York editor for *House Beautiful* even tracked her down (she has been featured in that magazine twice).

If you have a cane-seated chair that is the set-in type, the average repair costs $25. If the chair has drilled seat holes, count the holes and multiply the number of holes times 65 cents. The figure you come up with is the cost of that repair. Wicker repair is done strictly on a bid basis, after Liz has examined it.

Most antique dealers in town go to Liz for their repairs, and she makes it a point not to charge regular consumers any more than dealers (believe me, the dealers are known for looking for a good price). If you can't reach her at one number, try the other. She can also arrange to meet St. Paul customers at her Selby Avenue warehouse in St. Paul. But if you meet her at

American Classics, it will give you a chance to shop a fun antique corner that houses several good stores.

REED WEAVER
MISSY HEFFELFINGER CHEYNEY

PHONE: 926-4638
HOURS: Mon.-Fri., 9 a.m.-5 p.m. Call for an appointment.
POLICIES: No credit cards; checks accepted; workmanship guaranteed.

Missy Heffelfinger Cheyney repairs and restores old wicker. She will only quote prices once she has seen the damage, but once she starts the work the wait for the repair is much shorter than her name. She has been offering this service in her home for about six years. So give her a call when you need your wicker promptly. She also custom designs wicker furniture and accessories.

Clocks and Watches

DONALD EMPSON
CLOCKMAKER/WATCHMAKER

889 Grand Ave.
St. Paul
PHONE: 227-5216
HOURS: Tues.-Sat., 10 a.m.-5 p.m.
POLICIES: Checks accepted.

Donald Empson has been tampering with time in the basement of this antique shop (use the side door) for 15 years. He specializes in antique pocket watches. The average repair price for those is $75. He also fixes antique clocks and watches. He doesn't do Big Bens or cuckoo clocks. Stop and see him for a free estimate.

DARYL CARLSON, CLOCKSMITH

1516 E. Lake, 2nd Floor
Minneapolis
PHONE: 721-8888
HOURS: Mon.-Sat., 10 a.m.-5 p.m. (closed Tuesdays)

Daryl Carlson specializes in Grandfather clock repair. The average service charge is $45. He doesn't do watch repair, but he does fix music boxes and mechanical metronomes.

Electrical and Small Appliances

THE ELECTRONIC CO-OP

3464 Minnehaha Ave. S.
Minneapolis
PHONE: 724-3629
HOURS: Mon.-Fri., 10 a.m.-6 p.m.; Sat., 10 a.m.-4 p.m.
POLICIES: Credit cards—VISA and Master; checks accepted; returns: repaired items for sale have a 30-day minimum warranty.

This shop specializes in repairing stereo gear (audio gear, to the enthusiasts) and televisions. The Co-op will take on turntables, tape decks, speaker systems, tuners, amplifiers...you name it. One of the great things about this place is that they also specialize in classic tube equipment and they routinely take 20% off audio and TV tubes when they do a repair. They offer a 90-day warranty on their work. Bring your gear in for a free estimate. They will quote you a fair flat fee. If the job doesn't take as long as figured, you'll get charged *less* than the quote. If the repair requires more extensive work, you will be called before the job is tackled.

An interesting sideline here is that the Co-op will take your castoffs on consignment to resell. Which also means that if you're looking for used reconditioned gear (stereo and TVs), you may find it here at a good price. I've heard they're bargainable on these items.

VINTAGE RADIO SERVICE

310 N. First St.
2nd Floor
Downtown Minneapolis
PHONE: 339-6270
HOURS: Sat., noon-4 p.m.; weekdays by appointment

Steve Raymer has only been officially in this business for seven years, but he's been repairing radios since he was 14. He says he does "anything with tubes, except TVs." This includes antique car radios, juke box amplifiers, and he specializes in radios from the Twenties to the Sixties. Steve will give you a free estimate before he does any work, and you can decide whether it's worth it or not. (Incidentally, all the old radios are repairable. The problem with them is that when they stop working, they usually need to be rebuilt and most repair people don't want the job. Not Steve—he's dedicated to it.) The price to rebuild a floor model vintage radio is $125. Plastic car radios, rebuilt, cost $50 to $100. All of Steve's work is guaranteed for a year.

If you're driving by, look for the neon RCA Victor sign in the warehouse window on the second floor. If the light's on, Steve is there.

BRAND SERVICE CENTER

2225 University Ave.
St. Paul
PHONE: 645-9371
HOURS: Mon.-Fri., 8:30 a.m.-5 p.m.; Sat., 9 a.m.-1 p.m.
POLICIES: No credit cards; checks accepted; returns: cash or store credit on mechanical parts but no returns on electrical parts.

This shop does amazing work repairing small (and sometimes large) appliances. If you have ever tried to fix one of your own small appliances, you know how frustrating it can be. Here's just a few of the items they'll tackle: blenders, can openers, coffee makers, curling irons, fans, food processors, garden tools, irons, oven broilers, toasters, woks, shavers, mixers, lawn mowers, vacuums. Their prices are very reasonable. They offer a 90-day warranty on their repair work, and they can get parts for over 75 major brands. So if you're still determined to do your own fixing after you get an estimate, you can buy your parts here.

Once you get an estimate, if the cost to buy a new appliance is only a little more than the repair, opt for the new.

DEY APPLIANCE

525 Snelling Ave. N.
St. Paul
PHONE: 647-0171
HOURS: Mon.-Fri., 8 a.m.-5:30 p.m.; except Thurs., until 9 p.m.; Sat., 8 a.m.-noon
POLICIES: Credit cards—Master, VISA and Shoppers; checks accepted.

Adolph Dey sells only parts for all major appliances, washers, dryers, dishwashers, etc., so his store is a great place for the do-it-yourselfer. Bring in your model and serial numbers or a sample of the part. He has a huge inventory of parts, and they can special order odd ones for you. The prices are standard, but the advantage here is that 90% of what you might need is in stock.

Clothes

NOKOMIS SHOE SHOP

4950 34th Ave.
Minneapolis
PHONE: 724-1406
HOURS: Mon.-Fri., 8 a.m.-6 p.m.; except Thurs., until 9 p.m.; Sat., 9 a.m.-5 p.m.; Sun., noon-4 p.m.
POLICIES: Credit cards—VISA and Master; checks accepted.

Nokomis carries Red Wing shoes and boots. In the repair service area, they can handle anything in leather and they do it reasonably. To replace zippers in leather or suede coats costs $10. Of course, they also fix boots and shoes. But the real bonus here is the unusual repairs that they take on: $7.50 to repair rips in tarps or boat covers, $5 to $7 for replacing antique trunk handles. This is also the spot where many photographers get their leather camera cases repaired. They really take pride in their work here.

DON'S LEATHER CLEANING

4308 E. Lake St.
Minneapolis
PHONE: 721-4881
HOURS: Mon.-Fri., 7:30 a.m.-5 p.m.; Sat., 8 a.m.-noon (Sat. hours effective only Oct.-March)
POLICIES: Checks accepted; free pick-up and delivery.

Better leather garments are investment items that last for a long time. But when you must have them cleaned, you start questioning the price of that investment. Well, at Don's it will cost you a reasonable $20-$25 for an average leather or suede coat cleaning. They are really experts in this field and all the cleaning is done right on the premises. Nothing is sent out. For years many cleaners in the Twin Cities sent all their leathers to Don's. Now some of those cleaners have their own special equipment to do the job. But at Don's they have been doing this for 13 years. They also have a complete leather repair service.

HARVEY LEWIS FURS

Lumber Exchange Bldg., Room 830
10 S. Fifth St.
Downtown Minneapolis
PHONE: 333-2629 (you can call Mon.-Fri., 9 a.m.-9 p.m., for information)
HOURS: Mon.-Fri., 9 a.m.-4 p.m.; Sat., 9 a.m.-12:30 p.m.
POLICIES: No credit cards; checks accepted; lay-by: 1/3 down and monthly payments; fur storage and cleaning available.

You name the repair—Harvey Lewis Furs can do it. Lewis Gale has been doing furs in the Lumber Exchange Building for 28 years. Before that he worked for many reputable furriers in town. To reline a full-length fur ranges in cost from $85 to $110;

to restyle a fur collar averages $48 to $58. The price for fixing average rips is $7.50 to $16.00.

Cleaning and storage are also available. To clean a full-length mink, the cost is $20.00. A full-length Persian lamb, muskrat or rabbit is $18.75. This shop averages about 30% less for its repair service compared to other furriers in town. Mr. Gale is wonderful to work with, and so helpful. He will give you estimates over the phone and take time to answer any questions. He really is a fur craftsman. A few years ago he made Carl Eller a wolf coat. *That* must have been a big job to tackle!

BELL TWIN CITY FUR CO.

PHONE: 927-5454 (by appointment only)
HOURS TO CALL: Mon.-Fri., 9 a.m.-8 p.m.; Sun., noon-4 p.m.
POLICIES: No credit cards; checks accepted; returns: cash or credit, within 1 week.

Pat Shirley Bell's father, a furrier, learned his trade in Poland, and passed his expertise on to Pat. She's been in business for forty years, quietly operating out of her home. Now her daughter is part of this fur-selling and repairing operation. Make an appointment and bring in your furs for a free estimate on repairs. They remodel, restyle and repair furs that date back from the 1800's to now (if a fur is unfixable it is easy to detect because it won't even hold a new stitch).

Repairs start at $35, including minor rips. Relining a coat can range from $65 to $100. Restyling a new collar is $100 to $125. So, before you throw out Grandma's fur because it is too big, consider this—you can have a coat cut down from a size 20 to a size 8.

They also buy furs outright. In fact, they travel the East Coast for many furs, new and used, and then sell them by appointment.

WIZARD WEAVERS

Suite 509, Syndicate Bldg.
84 S. Sixth St.
Minneapolis
PHONE: 338-6413
HOURS: Mon.-Fri., 9:30 a.m.-5:15 p.m.

POLICIES: No credit cards; checks accepted.

Have you ever dropped a cigarette on your best suit? Well, Wizard Weavers can salvage holes in clothing. Filling in most holes costs at least $12; the average cigarette burn will cost you $20 to $25. Not bad, if you can save a $150 to $200 suit. The Wizards use a special repair process of reweaving and semi-weaving. In most cases the repair won't even show, but you'll find out ahead of time if the job will leave any tell-tale signs. You can also get a free estimate. All work is satisfaction guaranteed; the wait averages about two weeks. The Wizards also repair linens and tablecloths.

FRENCHWORKS VINTAGE CLOTHING MAKEOVERS AND REPAIRS

PHONE: 927-9762 (All work done by appointment.)
HOURS TO CALL: Mon.-Sat., 9 a.m.-8 p.m.
POLICIES: Checks accepted.

Most people shy away from doing alterations on vintage clothes. Cynthia French Koehler welcomes the job, probably because she loves the period styles. Restoration and rebeading is her specialty. In fact, for a $5.00 finder's charge she will scout out the old beads to replace your missing ones. She also does custom work, and will copy your favorite threadworn piece. Her charges: to narrow shoulders $10 to $18; to take in or let out coat side seams, $8.00; to shorten sleeves, $6 to $8. On slacks, to have the waist, seat and crotch shortened is $15.00. Alterations take five days to two weeks.

When you're buying vintage, keep these tips in mind: a suit can usually be brought down two sizes at most. If it is too small in the shoulders, forget it. But if it fits in the shoulders and is just too big in the waist or hips, no problem.

DARLING CLEANERS

4805 Nicollet Ave. S.
Minneapolis
PHONE: 827-5461
HOURS: Mon.-Fri., 7:30 a.m.-5 p.m.; Sat., 9 a.m.-noon.

POLICIES: Credit cards—Master and VISA; checks accepted; free pickup and delivery service.

We are fortunate to have a cleaners like Darling in the Twin Cities. They are specialists in the cleaning and restoration of delicate, old and unusual items. They still press table linens by hand, using turn-of-the-century curtain stretchers. There are only three companies left like this in the nation! They have table linens sent to them from all over the country.

The owner, Al Soeffker, invented the only lamp shade cleaning machine anywhere. To get a standard 12-by-14 inch silk-lined shade cleaned, the cost is $8.50, a real savings when you consider the replacement cost.

Darling has cleaned things you wouldn't believe...car convertible tops, private jets—just to name the bizarre. But the list of things you should know about includes tapestries, fabric luggage, down comforters, fabric book covers, fabric gun cases, golf bags, needlepoint handbags, bed pillows, vintage clothing, antique quilts, and fabric headboards—it just goes on and on.

Darling is great about giving you information and prices over the phone.

Upholstery

GOODWILL STORES UPHOLSTERING SERVICE

2534 Como Ave.
St. Paul
(Go to the north end of building, to the office entrance.)
PHONE: 646-2591
HOURS: Mon.-Fri. 9:30 a.m.-9 p.m.; Sat., 9 a.m.-5:30 p.m.; Sun., 12:30-5:30 p.m.
POLICIES: Credit cards—VISA and Master; checks accepted; workmanship warranteed for 90 days.

Goodwill has an upholstering service available to the public. The cost is at *least* 35% below other upholstery shops. All you have to do is call the main store and ask to speak to someone in the upholstering department. Set up an appointment and then bring in your furniture measurements. Once you get there, you can choose from 60 different fabric swatches, or you may want to use your own fabric.

Goodwill gives a written estimate on your job, describing exactly what they will do and how much it will cost. All work is guaranteed. This upholstery department has a trained supervisor in charge, but you should know that your item will be worked on by people who are learning the trade. The wait is two weeks. They will upholster anything—no job is too big or too small. Pick up and delivery are *not* available.

Sporting Goods

FREEWHEEL BIKE CO-OP

1812 S. Sixth St.
Minneapolis
PHONE: 339-2219
HOURS: Mon.-Fri., 11 a.m.-8 p.m.; Sat., 10 a.m.-6 p.m.; Sun., noon-4 p.m.
POLICIES: Credit cards—VISA, Master and Shoppers.

Freewheel is a worker-owned co-op that has been around for ten years. The people here are knowledgeable, dedicated and extremely helpful. They do all types of bike repair at Freewheel, ranging from trikes to fussy racers' bikes. A one-speed bike checkup costs $12. You can have tune-ups, overhauls, painting, and rebuilding all done at reasonable prices. Or you can do your own repairs here: use their tools and get a little assistance by scheduling time in their repair clinic, to really save money.

THE GOLF CLUB HOSPITAL

4308 Bryant Ave. S.
Minneapolis
PHONE: 825-5389
HOURS: Mon.-Fri., 9 a.m.-5 p.m.; Sat., 9 a.m.-noon
POLICIES: Checks accepted.

Put some swing into your next golf game and save your money for the caddy! The Golf Club Hospital repairs clubs and 50%

of their business is sent by the Pro shops. But if you bring your clubs here you'll save 10% to 25% on the repairs. Club re-gripping averages $3.00; re-heading woods with top of the line heads is $27 to $35; and re-shafting woods and irons is $14.50 to $15.50 a club. Most repairs only take a few days. Refinishing ($15.00 a club) can take two to three weeks. The Hospital is an authorized repair center for Wilson and AMF Ben Hogan brands, and they offer 30 different golf club repairs.

Miscellaneous Services

TWIN CITIES CARDING MILL

209 Washington Ave. N.
Minneapolis, MN 55401
PHONE: 332-6528
HOURS: Mon.-Fri., 11 a.m.-5 p.m.; Sat., noon-5 p.m.
POLICIES: Credit cards—Master and VISA.

About a year ago, Twin Cities Carding Mill bought the Badger Carding Mill in Chippewa Falls, Wisconsin, and moved it to Minneapolis (somehow this news was unheralded in the local press). Unless you read farm journals or are active in the Weaver's Guild, you're probably not familiar with their services. This place is great if you have an heirloom quilt that's lost its loft. They will wash, recard and refill your quilt for $2.00 a pound of wool batting. They can also add new wool to increase the loft. If you're a quilter, weaver or knitter, you can buy new wool batt here for $6.00 a pound.

Those who raise sheep will also welcome this service. Bring in any amount of fleece after shearing and have the raw grease wool washed for $1.25 a pound. This service is also available by mail.

E. & W. OPTICAL BINOCULAR REPAIR

2420 E. Hennepin Ave.
Minneapolis
PHONE: 331-1187
HOURS: Mon.-Fri., 9 a.m.-5:30 p.m.; open additional hours throughout the year

POLICIES: Credit cards—Master and VISA.

Astronomy buffs will love Harold Watson's shop. E. & W. does optical and mechanical repairs on binoculars and telescopes. They also have binocular replacement eyecups and new cases available. The average binocular repair costs $22.50 and takes two weeks. Many of the new binoculars are made out of plastic. So if you have an older metal pair and you're really attached to it, let E. & W. evaluate the quality and advise you on whether it's worth the repair.

If you're an estate sale shopper, often you'll run across binoculars for sale. The best old brands to look for are Bausch & Lomb, Zeiss, and Leitz. Post-World War II binoculars are generally worth $100. You can identify these by looking for a blue reflection in the lens. Or ask the person conducting the estate sale for the age of the binoculars. If they don't know, their ignorance leaves you wide open for bargaining.

THOMAS HARDY PIANO TUNING AND REPAIR

PHONE: 227-1784 (This is his answering service, but he's prompt in returning calls.)
POLICIES: Checks accepted.

Thomas Hardy has been flexing his fingers in this business full-time for several years. He has a B.A. in music and taught music for 15 years in Cottage Grove. He travels to tune anywhere in the Twin Cities and suburbs. He will come out and give you a free estimate on repairs. His tuning takes two to two-and-a-half hours and his standard charge is $35.

MINNEAPOLIS TECHNICAL INSTITUTE

1415 Hennepin Ave.
Minneapolis
PHONE: 370-9400
HOURS: Mon.-Fri., 9 a.m.-4 p.m.
POLICIES: No services mid-June to mid-July; checks accepted; no pickup or delivery service. you must make an appointment.

MTI offers all types of repair services to help their students gain experience. Fees are minimal, but sometimes the hassle or wait isn't worth the savings. It is best to call MTI and ask them to send you a free catalog of their services. This will give you a listing of all the instructors' names and phone numbers where you can get more information about the availability of the service and repair time. Some of the services available are alterations, small appliance repair, shoe repair, radio and TV repair, upholstering, and auto and truck repairs.

PART III

SPECIAL PLACES AND TIMES TO SHOP

Chapter 10

OUTLET MALLS AND ONE-STOP OUTLET STORES

One-stop off-price shopping malls are increasingly common in the Twin Cities, as new malls are being constructed and old malls are being renovated. This marketing approach has dismayed some diehard bargain hunters, who love the old-time confusion and clutter of traditional sources.

At these new outlet centers and malls, the facilities are bright and easy to shop in, and customers who value their time and pleasant surroundings as much as their budget can bargain hunt in comfort. In this chapter, you'll get an overview of some of the existing Twin Cities' malls.

Policies at these stores vary, though most accept checks and credit cards and many allow credit or refunds on returns. Call the numbers listed if you're in doubt about a particular store's policies.

EDEN PRAIRIE OUTLET CENTRE

I-494 and Hwy. 5 West
(near Menards)
Eden Prairie

HOURS: Mon.-Fri., 9:30 a.m.-9 p.m.; Sat., 9:30 a.m.-6 p.m.; Sun., 11 a.m.-5 p.m.

This off-price mall opened in the Twin Cities with a real bang, drawing bargain hunters from all over. Many were disappointed by the quality of the goods, the prices, and even with some of the stores in the mall.

Interestingly, the owners and developers of the Centre are eager to discuss those problems. In fact, they have made a few changes already. Some of the original stores are gone. New stores are coming into the mall and are adding a stronger selection of fashions while still meeting the mall's stipulation that they must carry name brands at prices that can't be beat anywhere else in town. A few of the existing stores always did have good quality and prices, so it will be worthwhile to keep an eye out for future changes and see if the Centre offers more of the promised bargains in the future.

AMBROSIA CHOCOLATE & COCOA

PHONE: 944-5228

If you're going to try candy making, this store has all the supplies, chocolate, molds, and books to show you how to do it, at a savings. You can treat your sweet tooth while you're here, too.

ANDERCRAFT WOODS, INC.

PHONE: 944-5237

In this family business, the Andersons treat their customers well. It is a specialized store for handcrafted bird feeders, nativity scenes, and great prices on high quality oak furniture reproductions. If you feed the birds, you can get a 10-lb. bag of thistle seed for $9.72 here.

BANNISTER'S

PHONE: 944-5332

An excellent off-price shoe store where you'll save up to 50% below retail prices. I found women's Evan Picone and Liz Claiborne shoes, plus Freeman's shoes for men. But there are 40 other major brands that are just as popular. Right next door they have a good selection of athletic shoes. If you get a chance, look through the purses in the front of the store—you'll find some good designer names.

CAN'DA FASHIONS

PHONE: 944-0988

Women's size 5 to 18 suits, blazers, and sportswear are abundant here. It's hard to compare savings, however, when you can't recognize the labels. None were familiar to me.

D LU FURNITURE INDUSTRIES

PHONE: 944-5244

The D Lu company manufactures all the furniture displayed in this store. It is geared to a very special furniture buyer, one with rustic styling tastes. You can custom order fabric and wood finishes.

DICKENS DISCOUNT BOOKS

PHONE: 944-5240

This bookstore specializes in good prices on *New York Times* bestsellers in hardcover and paperback. Plus you'll find the shelves stocked with various other books, all discounted.

LUCKY LEAVES

PHONE: 944-5410

Here's a kiosk where you design your own accessories with gold chains (you can have these cut to any length), leaves, and shells. Bracelets, rings, and necklaces are all made in a special process combining gold and sterling. The effect of this process is stunning, and it keeps the prices down. The finish is guaranteed not to tarnish.

FAMOUS FOOTWEAR

PHONE: 944-5310

(See p. 55 for a description.)

FASHION LINK

PHONE: 944-5230

Upbeat styles for juniors and women. The brand names on jeans were great, but the prices on some were higher than I expected, even if they were French made. Lots of moderate quality sportswear and dresses, in a somewhat limited selection.

FASHIONS FOR LESS

PHONE: 944-5099

Men's and women's fashions with the style emphasis for teens. Familiar moderately priced brand names in sportswear and casual styles.

FRUGAL FRANK'S

PHONE: 944-5288

Brand name shoes, athletic shoes, and accessories for men, women, and children. Tucked on the shelves in various places are some good shoe buys.

HOUSEWARE OUTLET STORE

PHONE: 944-5455

Good prices on name brand kitchen gadgets. It's fun to browse through the aisles of aluminum cookware and bakeware—sort of an old dime store atmosphere.

KIDSMART

PHONE: 944-5264

(See p. 41 for description.)

THE KNIT PIKKER

PHONE: 944-5172

This unusual store combines children's apparel with some great ragg wool mittens and scarves. Then if you travel to their back wall, you'll find cone yarn in a variety of colors.

KUPPENHEIMER FACTORY STORE

PHONE: 944-5622

(See p. 36 for description.)

LE GRANDE

PHONE: 944-5171

Another fun kiosk—you can test your scenter with all their perfume reproductions. Le Grande has a long list of expensive perfumes that they have duplicated. See how close they come to your favorite scent, at a price that is a lot cheaper.

LINEN CENTER

PHONE: 941-8942

(See p. 119 for description.)

MID-AMERICA SHOE FACTORY OUTLET

PHONE: 944-5263

You'll rummage a bit when you go through this shoe store, but that's okay—it will remind you that you're bargain hunting. It's hit or miss shopping with limited sizes in men's and women's brand name footwear.

MOUNTAIN CAMPER FACTORY OUTLET

PHONE: 944-5268

Campers will find some savings on good quality gear here. They carry a complete line of Camel products, including tents and outerwear.

OUTERWEAR PLUS

PHONE: 944-5616

Outerwear Plus manufactures good quality coats and jackets for men and women using Ultra Suede, leather and wool fabrics. The savings are 40% to 60% off retail prices. They also carry sportswear; the day I shopped there was a supply of Merona irregulars. You can sign a Merona call sheet and they will phone you when the next shipment arrives.

HOUSE OF LARGE SIZES

PHONE: 944-8289

(See p. 22 for description.)

WINONA KNITTING MILLS FACTORY OUTLET

PHONE: 944-5190

(See p. 27 for description.)

QUANNON COMPUTERS

PHONE: 944-5616

Hardware and software for Columbia and other IBM-compatible systems, as well as software for Apple. Printers and monitors are also available, all at a good discount.

SPORTS STUFF

PHONE: 944-5267

Sports and athletic wear for the whole family, but merchandise is limited.

THE TOY CELLAR

PHONE: 941-8200

You'll find brand name toys: some manufacturers' overruns, some current items. (Good stocking stuffers.) Only comparison shoppers will know how good a deal they are getting.

TWO PLUS TWO

PHONE: 944-0350

Costume jewelry. Lots of pierced earrings, many selling at six pairs for $5.00.

TREASURE CHEST

PHONE: 944-5188

14-Karat gold jewelry, selling at a discount.

SAN FRANCISCO GLASS

PHONE: 941-9341

Great prices on crystal and everyday glassware, gift items, and glass animal art pieces. I saw wine glasses (seconds) for $1.99 that were selling for at least 10 times that price at a regular retail store.

THE WALLET WORKS

PHONE: 941-3852

Very good prices on wallets, with a huge selection to choose from. Purses and luggage also available.

WINSTON'S

PHONE: 944-5335

Men's and women's clothing and accessories. When you first walk in, you feel like you're in a department store. The name brands are good; there's just not enough selection in each category. Discounts of 20% to 50% below retail prices.

NEW HOPE FACTORY OUTLET MALL

42nd St. and Winnetka Ave.
New Hope

HOURS: Vary from store to store.

This off-price mall has a no-frills atmosphere. The decor is not even close to the Dales, but you get the impression that rents are reasonable enough for the businesses to pass on the savings to shoppers.

BANK'S

PHONE: 533-4248

(See p. 47 for description.)

HANDS AND FEET

PHONE: 535-0010

Whatever warms the hands and feet—that's what you'll find in this store, most of the time at 50% savings. There is also jewelry and odds and ends, to boot.

THE GIFT OUTLET

PHONE: 535-3623

A wide assortment of household gift items is slashed 50% to 70% below retail price here. The merchandise includes tableware; cutlery; bed, bath, and kitchen linens; and glassware. All the items are factory closeouts.

THE PAPER OUTLET

PHONE: 533-7629

Here's a party-planning store with paper and plastic cups, napkins, tablecloths—whatever you need to set a festive table. Savings are 10% to 30% below the suggested retail price.

ELEGANT INTERIORS

PHONE: 537-0055

Draperies, carpets, and all types of window treatments can be custom ordered through this great off-price service. The savings range from 25% to 70%. There's a huge assortment of top-of-the-line drapery fabrics and an interior designer to help you with the choices. Check out the drapery closeout rack for even bigger savings.

WATER BEDS OF MINNESOTA

PHONE: 533-0309

You can expect low-tide prices—as low as $99—with a wide variety of models to choose from. And if you find a lower price elsewhere, Water Beds of Minnesota will meet it.

DISCOUNT DECORATING

PHONE: 535-2287

A mere 1,000 colors of paint to choose from, starting at $5.99. Expect 20% off on wallpaper orders, or 30% to 70% savings if you order paper that's in stock. Mini-blinds are cut 25% to 35% and inside/outside lighting fixtures are discounted 50% to 75%.

CHILDREN'S FACTORY OUTLET

PHONE: 533-9159

Parents will recognize the children's name brands and appreciate the savings here—20% to 60% below retail prices. The majority of the stock is first quality current styles for boys and girls, infant to size 14.

BOOKS PLUS

PHONE: 536-0238

You'll save at this book exchange, which sells used paperbacks at half the cover price. But you'll save the most by building credit when you recycle your own paperbacks. Gift items are also available.

THE COST CUTTERS

PHONE: 533-2975

This family haircutters shop starts their reasonable cuts at $6. No appointments are needed (but they'll only cut clean hair for the $6 rate).

LOEHMANN'S PLAZA

98th and Normandale
Blvd.
Bloomington

HOURS: Vary from store to store.

This plaza is probably one of the oldest off-price malls in the Twin Cities. The Loehmann's store dominates the center.

LOEHMANN'S

PHONE: 835-2510

(See p. 4 for description.)

LANCER'S OUTLET STORE

PHONE: 831-0114

(See p. 13 for description.)

FAMOUS FOOTWEAR

PHONE: 835-0676

(See p. 55 for description.)

PREMIUM OUTLET STORE

PHONE: 835-6588

Premium liquidates discontinued gift catalog merchandise. You will see just about anything here: small appliances, watches, glassware, luggage, lamps, power tools. The savings can only be evaluated by the Target or LaBelle's comparison shopper. A very unusual feature of this store is that they will redeem Gold Bond stamps for their store merchandise. Remember them?

SOFA AND CHAIRS

PHONE: 831-7027

You can always get 20% off on upholstered furniture, tables and lamps. This is a custom order store, with 30- to 40-day delivery. (Sofa and Chairs has another location in Robbinsdale.)

HAR MAR MALL

2100 N. Snelling Ave.
Roseville

HOURS: Vary from store to store.

Of course the major off-price retailer at Har Mar Mall is Marshall's. But Har Mar is also filled with a good percentage of off-price stores, and they are continuing to sign leases with other discounting businesses.

MARSHALL'S

PHONE: 636-6688

(See p. 49 for description.)

BEATA'S IN FASHION

PHONE: 636-4004

The savings at Beata's is 15% to 60% on women's size 6 to 18 and junior's size 3 to 13 clothing. Fashions are upbeat and the quality is good. (Beata's has another location in the Signal Hills Shopping Center in West St. Paul.)

COATS GALORE

PHONE: 633-6983

You can find women's coats, blazers, and sportswear in sizes 6 to 16 plus winter coats in half sizes here. The brand names range from moderate to higher quality, and the markdown ranges from 20% to 50%.

GLAD RAGS

PHONE: 636-6569

Glad Rags carries both women's and junior's clothing but the majority of styles are geared for juniors. The savings vary, but seem to range from 20% to 50%. (Glad Rags has nine other Twin Cities locations.)

FABULOUS FAKES

PHONE: 633-8660

The fakes really are fabulous at this store. They feature gold-filled chains (ranging from $14 to $72) and cubic zirconia, the diamond look-alike, in men's and women's rings, plus pendants, earrings and bracelets. You can also get 14-Karat gold.

EXTRA SPECIAL

PHONE: 633-8918

(See p. 23 for description.)

FAMOUS FOOTWEAR

PHONE: 636-3398

(See p. 55 for description.)

HIT OR MISS

PHONE: 633-9884

(See p. 8 for description.)

HOME-KO BED AND BATH

PHONE: 633-4496

(See p. 118 for description.)

PLAY IT AGAIN

PHONE: 636-6666

This is a children's consignment store. (See p. 74 for description.)

UNITED STORES

PHONE: 631-0260

(See p. 54 for description.)

THE BOOKSHOP

PHONE: 636-3176

The Bookshop features second-hand paperback books priced at half the cover cost. They will take trade-ins, but it's best to give them a call first. They do have limits on what they will accept.

CHAPTER 11

AUCTIONS AND FLEA MARKETS

If you've really got the bargain hunting bug, and haven't explored the fun (and savings) of auctions and flea markets, you've got a treat in store for you. Auctions challenge your game-playing instincts; flea markets test your self-restraint—they're like giant garage sales.

Until now, it wasn't possible to find out where and when goods changed hands through these channels in one organized listing. But now, armed with the information in this chapter, you can plan on attending these bonanzas and sharing the treasures.

AUCTIONS

Auctions can be entertaining affairs where beginners and experienced bargainers compete head to head. There's always the chance that you'll get what you need (or fancy) at 40% to 50% discounts. There's also the chance that the passion to buy something—anything—can overpower your good sense. If you have never attended an auction before, you may feel safer going the first time as an observer. Whenever you're serious about buying, make sure you attend the early inspection session. Here's a list of Twin Cities auctions that will tempt you with a variety of goods.

It's best to shop auctions with cash or certified checks. If you plan to use a personal check, call ahead for special policies (some places approve checks before the bidding starts, sometimes as long as several days in advance).

MAIN ST. PAUL POST OFFICE

180 E. Kellogg Blvd.
St. Paul
PHONE: 293-3083

In our towns, mail that gets lost or damaged makes its way to the dead parcel office at the downtown St. Paul Post Office. About ten times a year, all the unclaimed items get auctioned off. If you call the number listed above, you can get on the mailing list and be notified about the next sale.

On the Saturday of the sale, you can pick up a catalog listing the merchandise, which is sold by the bin—you have to buy the whole binful to get what you want. In the past, I've run into electronics, books, clothing, china, linens—even furs. Inspection is always held for two hours before the auction starts.

Because of the bin system of bidding, you may want to bring along a few friends to increase the likelihood of making use of all the items in a bin you want to buy—and to share the finds.

U.S. CUSTOMS OFFICE

PHONE: 349-3990

Once a year, usually in the spring, Customs auctions its confiscated goods at their Minneapolis/St. Paul International Airport office. Since this is a low-profile auction with almost no publicity, the only way you can track it is by calling the information number periodically and inquiring when the sale will be held.

STATE OF MINNESOTA CAR AUCTIONS

PHONE: 296-6131

The State holds about four used car and truck auctions a year. Call the information number listed here to get on the sale flyer mailing list. Most of the vehicles have been used by the Department of Transportation and other State offices. There are some good deals on American-made cars, most at least four years old.

MINNEAPOLIS AND ST. PAUL POLICE BIKE AUCTIONS

PHONE: 292-3637 for St. Paul; 348-2932 for Minneapolis

In spring, summer and fall, both cities' police departments hold bike auctions to clear out bikes recovered from thefts and losses. The knowledgeable bike buyer can get a good deal. Keep tabs on the next auction by calling the information number.

ROYAL STAR LIQUIDATORS

7565 S. Concord Blvd.
Inver Grove Heights
PHONE: 455-1931

During the fall and winter months, Royal Star holds auctions on Friday and Saturday nights. Inspection is at 6:00 p.m.; the auctions start at 7:00 p.m. In the summer months, sales are held on Wednesday and Saturday nights. This company has four buyers scouring the country for new, antique and collectable merchandise. You'll see everything from autos to weapons here. The auction house is huge and the bidding moves quickly, so be on your guard against getting swept away in the excitement.

ROSE GALLERIES

1123 W. County Rd. B
Roseville
PHONE: 484-1415

Rose Galleries specialize in fine home furnishings, antiques, and once a month, offer a jewelry auction. Inspection time is on Tuesdays from 5-8 p.m. and Wednesdays from 11 a.m.-6 p.m. The auctions are every Wednesday night at 6:00 p.m.

FLEA MARKETS

Flea markets can be great for entertainment and surprises. You can do some real wheeling and dealing, and there's always the chance you can walk off with a treasure. Real antiques are no longer plentiful, with new furniture, household items and imports taking over the table, but you can pick up real bargains if you know your stuff. The serious flea market shoppers arrive at the summer markets during the pre-dawn hours when dealers are setting up for the day.

To be safe, bring along cash and assume the policy is that all sales are final.

MANN FRANCE AVENUE DRIVE-IN

7800 France Ave. S.
Bloomington
PHONE: 835-7441

HOURS: Sun., 7 a.m.-4 p.m., May to September

Both new and old items.

MIDWAY SHOPPING CENTER

University and Snelling Ave. (back parking lot)
St. Paul

HOURS: Sat., 7 a.m.-4 p.m., May to September

A garage sale atmosphere with older items.

ALDRICH ARENA

1850 White Bear Ave.
St. Paul
PHONE: 457-8416

HOURS: Fri., 7 a.m.-6 p.m.; Sat.-Sun., 7 a.m.-4 p.m.

A garage sale atmosphere with older items.

PINE CITY FLEA MARKET

Pine County Fairgrounds just north of Pine City on Hwy 61.
PHONE: 1-629-6924

HOURS: Wed., 5 a.m.-noon, May to September

This flea market has been around for a long time and is very popular. They have at least

120 vendors. You'll see everything from produce to collectables.

SUPER FLEA MARKET

1865 University Ave.
St. Paul
PHONE: 644-2912

HOURS: Fri., noon-6 p.m.; Sat., 9 a.m.-6 p.m.; Sun., 10 a.m.-5 p.m.

Expect a mix of both old and new items and a large supply of new liquidated furniture, reasonably priced.

OSOWSKI ORCHARD FUN MARKET

Take Hwy. 94 west to Hwy. 75; first Monticello exit.
PHONE: 1-295-2121

HOURS: Fri. 4-9 p.m.; Sat.-Sun., 9 a.m.-5 p.m., year round.

This large indoor/outdoor market has lots of new merchandise with some collectables. Entertainment includes music, food and people watching.

CAMBRIDGE FLEA MARKET

Hwy. 95 in Cambridge, next to Erickson's Grocery Store
PHONE: 1-689-4300

HOURS: Tues., 6 a.m.-noon, year round.

Lots of old items and garage sale type goods.

WRIGHT COUNTY'S SWAPPER'S MEET

Go 3 miles west of Annandale on Hwy. 55. Turn north on Hwy. 136 and travel two miles to the first gravel road on your right. You'll see the flea market sign.
PHONE: 1-274-8071

HOURS: Sat. 8 a.m.-4 p.m.; Sun. 9 a.m.-4 p.m., year round.

Lots of antiques, collectables, and secondhand items.

CHAPTER 12

THE BARGAIN HUNTER'S CALENDAR

Good news for bargain hunters! Department stores and other regular retailers in the Twin Cities are changing their sale tactics. Some are going head to head with the off-price stores with special sales. One great bargain opportunity in the past year was held once a month at Dayton's. Their Old Fashioned Bargain Days were responsible for plenty of "I got a good deal" stories. Dayton's is no longer running those sales, but they do offer similar bargains when they hold their special 12-hour sales.

Another source of bargains that you shouldn't overlook is aired every Monday through Friday at 3 p.m., right in your own living room. KSTP TV's Good Company Show features daily Super Bargains. The show's staff negotiates special 50%-off deals with Twin Cities retailers and restaurant owners, then passes the bargains on to viewers.

To help you track retail sales throughout the year, I have developed a Bargain Hunter's Calendar—a list of traditional sales and markdown periods you can refer to, month by month. If you're in the market for a special item, check the Calendar and keep a sharp eye on the papers for sale notices (or call the numbers I've listed for further information). You'll find Dayton's major sales listed in the Calendar; I contacted the other major retailers in the area so they could be listed, too, but they were reluctant to share their sale information. You should know, though, that Donaldson's opens its warehouse at various times each year for special sales on furniture, housewares, and appliances. The only problem is that you'll have to keep tabs by calling 721-5305.

I haven't included Target or K-Mart in the Calendar, only because they are such obvious places to save money, year-round, for all shoppers. Both stores print weekly sale flyers that are inserted in the Minneapolis and St. Paul Sunday papers. Incidentally, if you buy merchandise at K-Mart or Target and later see it advertised on sale at the same discount chain for less, you have thirty days from your date of purchase to bring your sales receipt to the store and collect the difference.

In other chapters of this book, you'll find special sale times for most of the stores I've listed. But the Bargain Hunter's Calendar will help you keep tabs on special, hard-to-find and under-publicized sales, for both new and second-hand merchandise.

From April 15th to October 5th each year, the State Fairgrounds is a busy bargain spot. To keep tabs on their special sales, which change every year, phone 646-2200 during those months. They will inform you about upcoming events.

January

FRANK MURPHY'S GIVEAWAY SALE

PHONE: 291-8844

A Twin Cities sale that offers fun and savings on better women's designer clothes and accessories. It's usually held at the St. Paul Hotel during the first week of the St. Paul Winter Carnival.

DAYTON'S WHITE SALE

PHONE: 375-2200; 292-5222

CAROLE'S OF EDINA

PHONE: 926-6559

This "Giveaway Sale" cuts prices on the store's entire women's winter sportswear inventory. Sizes range from 2 to 14.

CHILDREN'S GENERAL STORE

PHONE: 925-2841

Designer and better children's clothing—the store gets packed with parents for this winter (and later spring) sale.

TRADITIONAL RETAIL SALES AND ITEMS

Winter coats and clothing
Jewelry
Home furnishings
White sales (linens, bathware)
Luggage
TV/radio/electronics
Cosmetics

February

JACKSON GRAVES GOLD ROOM SALE
PHONE: 331-1563 — A popular sale that slashes women's winter merchandise. It's held at a downtown Minneapolis hotel and requires competitive shopping strategies.

DAYTON'S ANNIVERSARY AND HOME SALE
PHONE: 375-2200;
292-5222

NATURALIZER SHOES AUDITORIUM SALE
PHONE: 338-6956 — If you're a Naturalizer fan, you'll walk away with winter shoe and boot bargains.

ANTHONIE'S HATCHET DAYS SALE
PHONE: 854-3370 — Great buys for men and women on good brand names and designers at this huge winter clear-out sale.

TRADITIONAL RETAIL SALES AND ITEMS

Washers/dryers
Men's suits
Furs
Home furnishings and carpeting
Housewares (dishes, glassware, silverware)
Final winter clothing clearances
Radio/TV/sound equipment
Washington's Birthday sales

March

J & S TEXTILES MILL-END FABRIC SALES

PHONE: 475-2154 — Truckloads of fabric remnants are brought in for this sale. Call and they will put you on their mailing list.

NORTHWEST RACQUET AND SWIM CLUB

PHONE: 546-9666 — This sale is held at the St. Louis Park club, but sportswear is collected from all their clubs for a year-round merchandise sale with prices cut 50% to 70%.

TRADITIONAL RETAIL SALES AND ITEMS

China/housewares
Drapes
Shoes
Mattresses
Pre-Easter clothing sales

April

MINNETONKA MILLS FABRIC SALE

PHONE: 935-2663 — This fabric wholesaler offers first quality fabrics for savings up to 75% off. A great sale—just call and they will send you the date and location directions.

ST. PAUL COLLEGE CLUB BOOK SALE

PHONE: 227-4477 — This annual sale is very popular with book collectors. Always a large supply of books with bargains available in many categories.

FRED G. ANDERSON'S WALLPAPER WAREHOUSE SALE

PHONE: 927-1800 — When Fred G. Anderson's opens up their warehouse to the public, the redecorating bargain hunters have a ball.

MT. SINAI HOSPITAL BOOK SALE

PHONE: 871-3700 — You'll see reasonable prices at this annual book sale, sometimes held in April, sometimes in May. Check with them for this year's date.

TRADITIONAL RETAIL SALES AND ITEMS

Tires
Garden items
Paint and wallpaper
Diamonds/fine jewelry
Air conditioners/vacuum cleaners
Fabrics
Kitchen appliances
Closet organizing accessories

May

PAPPAGALO SHOE SALE

PHONE: 333-2478

This annual sale is usually held at the Hopkins House. Pappagalo lovers really line up for this one! In season and out of season shoes and boots are sold at a savings.

SPRING WHOLESALING DAYS

PHONE: 333-3314

Several downtown Minneapolis wholesalers open their doors for a spring and summer sale.

WOODBURY 100-FAMILY GARAGE SALE

PHONE: 738-0041

This sale is sponsored by the Woodbury Township Lions Club. Many hunters have found good bargains at this giant sale.

BOYS' AND GIRLS' FRENCH ROOM BENEFIT SALE

PHONE: 522-3636

This annual sale gets a great selection of good used clothing, antiques and household items. Good savings for the second-hand shopper.

TRADITIONAL RETAIL SALES AND ITEMS

Auto tires and accessories
Outdoor furniture
Mother's Day sales
Sportswear sales

June

EAST CALHOUN COMMUNITY ORGANIZATION'S SUPER GARAGE SALE

Held the first Saturday in June, this is a 100-family garage sale held in the E. Lake Calhoun area of Minneapolis. Garage sale fans love it. Head for the area bounded by W. Lake Street, Hennepin Avenue, 36th Street, and the lake. You'll see signs everywhere.

CHILDREN'S GENERAL STORE

PHONE: 925-2841

Summer clearance sale of designer and better name brand children's clothing.

DAYTON'S DAISY SALE

PHONE: 375-2200; 292-5222

TRADITIONAL RETAIL SALES AND ITEMS

Men's and boy's clothing
Women's shoes
Sporting goods
Sportswear for men, women and children
Silverware
Father's Day specials
Bridal and graduation gift specials

July

FORMAL AFFAIR'S TUXEDO WAREHOUSE SALE
PHONE: 822-5132 Good place to pick up a black traditional style tux. Most on sale are used. If you miss this affair, it will be held again in October.

DAYTON'S JULY WHITE SALE
PHONE: 375-2200; 292-2200

TRADITIONAL RETAIL SALES AND ITEMS

Air conditioners/freezers
Tires and batteries
Lawn furniture
4th of July specials
Pre-season winter coat sales
Summer clothing clearance sales
White sales
Pre-fall fabric sales
Back-to-School clothing sales
Furniture and bedding sales

August

NATURALIZER SHOES AUDITORIUM SALE
PHONE: 338-6956 Spring, summer and year-round shoe savings for Naturalizer fans.

THERMO-SERV PUBLIC SALE
PHONE: 421-2224 This annual sale pulls in early Christmas shoppers. Look for the plastic Thermo-Serv tumblers and serving bowls.

DAYTON'S HOME SALE
PHONE: 375-2200; 292-5222

TRADITIONAL RETAIL SALES AND ITEMS

Stationery/school supplies
Camping supplies
Back-to-School clothing sales
Fur sales

September

LIFT SKI SALE AND SWAP

PHONE: 571-6850 This is a popular swap meet for ski bargain hunters. Some good savings on new equipment.

MINNETONKA MILLS FABRIC SALE

PHONE: 935-2663 First quality fall fabric bargains. (See April listing for more information.)

A.J. SALES

PHONE: 332-7150 You've probably heard of Arlene Cohen's special children's clothing sales at the Ambassador Hotel. Look for this one in September, but call to get on her mailing list for surprise sales.

CARVER ANTIQUE SHOW

PHONE: 474-6744 This sale is held in conjunction with Carver's Steamboat Jubilee, the first weekend after Labor Day. Lots of country antiques await collectors in the little town west of Chaska on Highway 212.

VASSAR SALE

PHONE: 935-6942 This two-day sale has been going on since 1944 and there are bargain hunters who won't miss it. Lots of goodies in the second-hand clothes, furniture, and housewares. The Vassar Scholarship Committee also has some influence in drumming up new merchandise from posh retailers. Call for the location—it changes every year—but the date of the sale is traditionally the last weekend in September. When you call, ask to be put on their mailing list.

TRADITIONAL RETAIL SALES AND ITEMS

China/glassware
Gourmet items
Dishwashers
Auto supplies
Energy/heating items
Children's shoes and outerware
New cars
Fall and winter clothing specials

October

COURAGE CENTER FUR SALE

PHONE: 588-0811, ext. 163

This sale only lasts half a day and the furs go fast—prices go from $1 for scraps to $2500 for top of the line furs. Furs are priced at 1/2 their appraised value.

CANCER SOCIETY GARAGE SALE

PHONE: 925-2772

A very popular annual sale. Lots of clothing bargains, but also furniture and miscellaneous goods. Most hunters go early for this one.

DAYTON'S JUBILEE SALE

PHONE: 375-2200; 292-5222

FORMAL AFFAIR'S TUXEDO WAREHOUSE SALE

PHONE: 822-5132

Another shot at formalwear on sale. (See July listing.)

TRADITIONAL RETAIL SALES AND ITEMS

Washers/dryers/ranges
Wool/fabrics
Outerwear
Radio/TV/electronics
Furniture

November

ST. PAUL COUNCIL OF JEWISH WOMEN'S DRESS FOR LESS SALE

PHONE: 698-0751

This annual sale offers great savings on men's, women's, and children's clothing. Be sure to check out the Designer section.

BANK'S TOY SALE

PHONE: 379-1222

Christmas shoppers wait for this sale each year. Give the store a call and find out when it's being held. You'll fight crowds, but the toy savings can be worth it.

ST. PAUL JUNIOR LEAGUE'S TOY AND RUMMAGE SALE

PHONE: 291-7377

This fun sale offers good deals on nearly new toys. Stuff the stockings with some good second-hand buys.

CHRISTMAS WHOLESALING DAYS

PHONE: 333-3314

The downtown Minneapolis warehouse area opens up several spots for Christmas shopping at a savings.

LAKESIDE GAMES

PHONE: 835-3000

This sale has traditionally been held on Friday of the first week in November. You can get up to 50% off on various games—discontinued ones, seconds, and overruns. Although it has been a very popular sale, it may be discontinued, so do call to confirm the facts.

CALHOUN COLLECTOR'S SOCIETY

PHONE: 941-0250

This sale is planned just in time for Christmas shopping, with one-of-a-kind new collectable plates, coins, stamps, and sculptures.

PGA WAREHOUSE SALE

PHONE: 454-5681

This annual sale combines the inventories of 20 metro area golf pro shops. Save on clubs, shoes, bags, and clothing. All are priced at cost or below. The sale starts the day after Thanksgiving and is held at the Lost Spur Country Club.

TRADITIONAL RETAIL SALES AND ITEMS

Toys and games
China/glass
Lamps
Gourmet foods
Menswear
Day after Thanksgiving sales

December

LIFT SKI SALE

PHONE: 571-6850

If you're outfitting the family with ski equipment, this sale may help ease the Christmas budget. Held at the Minneapolis Auditorium.

TRADITIONAL RETAIL SALES AND ITEMS

Sporting goods
China/glassware/silver
Fine jewelry
Housewares
Infants'/children's clothing
Holiday dresses
Cameras/electronics
Luggage
Post-Christmas clearances

PART IV

MISCELLANEOUS BARGAINS

CHAPTER 13

FOOD AND PARTY GOODS

If your entertaining obligations are growing but your party budget is getting slimmer, you'll savor these food bargains. The bakery thrift stores will supply plenty of grain for holiday celebrations or help multiply the loaves when company's coming. The question is—is it worth the gas and travel? Only you can decide.

Here's one bargain hunter's story. "Do you know what I purchased for just $7.04 at the Pepperidge Farm Bakery Thrift Store? One package each of croutons and cornbread stuffing, two bags of parmesan Goldfish crackers, two raisin croissants, two dozen sandwich buns, one loaf of raisin bread, one loaf of whole wheat bread and three loaves of white bread." Not bad for one stop. The other sources of food and party items are fun to visit, and seem especially interesting to children. I suggest you give each store a call before you shop to make sure they have the items you need.

Baked Goods

DUNWOODY INDUSTRIAL INSTITUTE BAKERY

818 Wayzata Blvd.
Minneapolis
PHONE: 374-5800
HOURS: Mon.-Fri., 1:45 p.m.-4:30 p.m.; closed mid-June to mid-September

POLICIES: No checks; no phone orders.

If your bargain hunting tastes go for sweet surprises and variety, drop by Dunwoody's Baking School. Students bake every day and often experiment with a new goodie that makes its way into the Bakery. You can always count on bread for $.65 a loaf, two-layer cakes for $1.00, and some type of sweet roll and bun. Before holidays, it's jammed here.

Savvy baked goods shoppers stop at 11:00 a.m. to pick up numbers and then come back when the bakery opens. At Christmas a bargain bonus is the regular fruitcake at $6.50 or the candied fruitcakes (little dough here) for $7.75.

MIDDLE EAST BAKERY

555 N. Snelling
St. Paul
PHONE: 644-4409
HOURS: Mon.-Fri., 9 a.m.-6 p.m.; Sat., 9 a.m.-4 p.m.
POLICIES: Checks accepted.

Go directly to the Twin Cities pocket bread source and save 20% to 50% on whole wheat or white flour pita. If you're planning an exotic party, you'll find other middle Eastern specialties here.

MINNESOTA BEST MAID COOKIE CO.

3830 Dight Ave.
Minneapolis
(1 block east of 38th & Hiawatha)
PHONE: 722-7234
HOURS: Mon.-Fri., 7:30 a.m.-4:30 p.m.; Sat., 8 a.m.-noon
POLICIES: Checks accepted.

If your kids run to the cookie jar when they get home from school, here's a cheap way to keep that jar filled. Stop at this warehouse for a varied assortment of imperfect cookies (chocolate chip, oatmeal, butterscotch chip)—three one-pound bags for $2.50. When you get to Best Maid, you enter a door that goes right into their warehouse. There's a small retail set-up inside with bags and bags of cookies.

BALDINGER BAKING CO.

215 Eva St.
St. Paul
PHONE: 224-5761
HOURS: Mon.-Sat., 8 a.m.-5 p.m.
POLICIES: Checks accepted.

You can buy delicatessen rye bread here for less than a dollar a pound. Use one bakery bargain hunter's strategy. "Baldinger will send a price list on request. I have learned to be ready with my exact order when I call because their order takers are very busy (though polite). Call the day before, pick up fresh goods the next day. Now, the pick-up is not convenient—you need to park in the factory lot, walk around the building and upstairs, where you pay—then go back downstairs, just inside the factory, and find your bread order. It's a hike, but it's worth it."

BROWNBERRY NATURAL BREADS THRIFT STORES

9412 Lyndale Ave.
Bloomington
PHONE: 884-6836

6200 Bass Lake Rd.
Crystal
PHONE: 537-2225

HOURS: Mon., 9 a.m.-6 p.m.; Tues., 9 a.m.-7:30 p.m.; Wed.-Fri., 9 a.m.-6 p.m.; Sat., 9 a.m.-5 p.m.; Sun., 11 a.m.-5 p.m.
POLICIES: Checks accepted; senior citizen discount card available.

Catherine Clark's bakery goodies are sold here, as well as Entenmann's sweets and low sodium Health Valley products. If you go for the whole grain, you'll love their bread prices at $.89, or four loaves of Healthnut bread for $3.29.

Get an extra 10% off on Tuesdays.

PEPPERIDGE FARM BAKERY THRIFT STORES

4503 France Ave. S.
Minneapolis
PHONE: 927-9111
HOURS: Mon.-Fri., 9:30 a.m.-6 p.m.; Sat., 9 a.m.-5 p.m.

POLICIES: Checks accepted; senior citizen discount days Wednesday and Thursday.

All the familiar Pepperidge Farm products, perfect and imperfect, are sold here. But somebody's mistake is your good fortune—you'll save 20% to 60% when there is a minor flaw. French bread, two loaves for $1.39.

Get an extra 10% off on Mondays.

EGEKVIST THRIFT STORE

922 E. 24th St.
Minneapolis
PHONE: 871-2961
HOURS: Mon.-Sat., 9 a.m.-6:30 p.m.
POLICIES: Checks accepted; senior citizen discount days Monday and Tuesday.

Five loaves of white bread for $1.99 may be worth the trip. You'll also find imperfect frozen pies for $1.99. The everyday discount is 50%.

Get an extra 10% off on Wednesdays.

MASTER BREAD THRIFT STORES

2911 Oakland Ave.
Minneapolis
PHONE: 823-7263
HOURS: Mon.-Sat., 9 a.m.-5 p.m.

1134 S. Robert St.
St. Paul
PHONE: 451-6117
HOURS: Mon.-Fri., 9 a.m.-6 p.m.; Sat., 8 a.m.-5 p.m.

3510 Winnetka Ave.
New Hope
PHONE: 544-4195
HOURS: Mon.-Fri., 9 a.m.-6 p.m.; Sat., 8 a.m.-5 p.m.

121 Miller Rd.
Champlin
PHONE: 427-4810
HOURS: Mon.-Fri., 9 a.m.-7 p.m.; Sat., 8 a.m.-6 p.m.; Sun., 11 a.m.-5

15704 Wayzata Blvd.
Wayzata
PHONE: 473-7671
HOURS: Mon.-Fri., 9 a.m.-6 p.m.; Sat., 9 a.m.-5 p.m.

3207 Sibley Memorial Hwy.
Eagan
PHONE: 454-7998
HOURS: Mon.-Fri., 9:30 a.m.-6 p.m.; Sat., 8:30 a.m.-5 p.m.

1190 Prosperity Ave.
St. Paul
PHONE: 771-4137
HOURS: Mon.-Fri., 9 a.m.-6 p.m.; Sat., 8 a.m.-5 p.m.

POLICIES: Checks accepted; ask for Bonus Bread Club Card at first $5.00 purchase.

You'll save 40% to 60% off Master's day-old Roman Meal, Hollywood, Nature's Harvest, and wheat bread. There are Jumbo doughnuts for $.89 a dozen. Plenty of stuffing, too.

WONDER BREAD THRIFT STORES

2404 Rice St.
St. Paul
PHONE: 484-6020
HOURS: Mon.-Fri., 9 a.m.-7 p.m.; Sat., 9 a.m.-5 p.m.

5130 Winnetka Ave. N.
New Hope
PHONE: 533-2268
HOURS: Mon.-Fri., 9 a.m.-6 p.m.; Sat., 9 a.m.-5 p.m.

1213 Cliff Rd.
Burnsville
PHONE: 890-7335
HOURS: Mon.-Fri., 9 a.m.-5:30 p.m.; Sat., 9 a.m.-4:30 p.m.

1200 Third Ave. S.
Minneapolis
This store connected to main plant. (Smells great!)
PHONE: 332-3326
HOURS: Mon.-Fri., 9 a.m.-5:30 p.m.; Sat., 9 a.m.-4 p.m.

POLICIES: Checks accepted.

Here's where to get day-old goods on Wonder's specialties: Home Pride and Wonder breads and Hostess Cakes. Wheat bread is $.60 a loaf; a bag of stuffing is $.89. Pack the kids' lunches with Ding Dongs, Snowballs or Twinkies at five packages for $1.00.

Bargain days are Wednesday and Saturday.

HOLSUM COUNTRY HEARTH BAKERY THRIFT STORES

3100 N. Ranchview Lane
Plymouth
PHONE: 559-1515
HOURS: Mon.-Fri., 9 a.m.-5:30 p.m.; Sat., 9 a.m.-2 p.m.

7365 E. River Rd.
Fridley
PHONE: 571-8630
HOURS: Mon.-Sat., 8:30 a.m.-6 p.m.

5306 Minnehaha Ave. S.
Minneapolis
PHONE: 721-2586
HOURS: Mon.-Fri., 8:30 a.m.-6 p.m.; Sat., 8:30 a.m.-4 p.m.

641 Broadway Ave.
Minneapolis
PHONE: 379-3047
HOURS: Mon.-Fri., 8:30 a.m.-6 p.m.; Sat., 8:30 a.m.-5 p.m.; Sun., 10 a.m.-4 p.m.

1608 Como Ave.
St. Paul
PHONE: 646-7048
HOURS: Mon.-Sat., 8:30 a.m.-6 p.m.

POLICIES: Checks accepted.

Breads and sweets abound here. No loaf is higher than $.99. Everything is a day old and there are good buys on Entenmann's products and the Country Hearth brand.

Get an extra 10% off on Wednesdays and Saturdays.

TAYSTEE BREAD BAKERY THRIFT STORES

Twelfth & Robert
St. Paul
PHONE: 224-3891

69th & Brooklyn Blvd.
Brooklyn Center
PHONE: 566-4310

6328 Penn Ave. S.
Richfield
PHONE: 861-1646

221 Concord Blvd.
South St. Paul
PHONE: 455-2035

HOURS: Mon.-Fri., 9 a.m.-5 p.m.; Sat., 8 a.m.-4 p.m.
POLICIES: No checks.

The bakery goods here are sometimes more than just one day old. White bread is 5 loaves for $1.99; wheat bread is 3 loaves for $1.99; and buns are 3 packages for $1.39.

Get an extra 10% off on Wednesdays and Saturdays, except for the Brooklyn Center store, whose bargain days are Wednesdays and Fridays.

MCGLYNN'S BAKERY OUTLET

Mitchell Rd. & Hwy. 5
Eden Prairie
PHONE: 937-9404
HOURS: Mon.-Fri., 6:30 a.m.-6 p.m.; Sat., 7 a.m.-3:30 p.m.; Sun., 9 a.m.-1 p.m.

2007 E. 24th St.
Minneapolis
PHONE: 724-3683
HOURS: Mon.-Fri., 7 a.m.-6 p.m.; Sat., 8:30 a.m.-4 p.m.
POLICIES: Checks accepted; no senior citizen discount.

I'm sure you've sampled McGlynn's bakery products from one supermarket or another. Well, the outlets offer the same breads and sweet goods in both fresh and day-old goods. The bargain, of course, is on the day-old items, which are marked down 50% from McGlynn's regular price. From day to day, you'll find even bigger discounts on targeted bakery products. The day I shopped most recently, hot dog buns and hamburger buns were $.20 a package. The average price on day-old bread is $.55.

Tuesday is bargain day at the Minneapolis outlet: they offer $1.00 off on a $5.00 purchase. The Eden Prairie store changes their bargain day each week.

Groceries

H. BROOKS & CO.

2521 E. Hennepin Ave.
Minneapolis
PHONE: 331-8413
HOURS: Mon.-Fri. 8 a.m.-5 p.m.; Sat. 8 a.m.-noon
POLICIES: Accept checks, money orders, or cash; delivery available with minimum $200 order.

Here's a money-saving grocery shopping alternative good for large families or for times when you're entertaining a crowd. H. Brooks Company is a produce and grocery distributor for large supermarkets. So you can bypass some middle-man costs by ordering directly from them. You can order produce, meat, milk, butter, and a variety of other food items. Some of the goods must be bought in bulk or full lots, but the majority can be broken down to fit a family's needs.

Here's how it works. The first time you order from them, you will have to stop at their customer service office and pick up a grocery price list. Then you can just give them a call and order by phone. The next day you go to their warehouse. They will load your groceries into your car. If you want home delivery service, you must place a minimum $200 order.

Shopping this way, you can avoid those tempting impulse buys located around the supermarket checkout counter.

NEW YORK TEA CO. CASH & CARRY STORE

818 Vandalia St.
St. Paul
PHONE: 645-0282
HOURS: Mon.-Fri., 8 a.m.-5 p.m.; Sat., 8 a.m.-1 p.m.
POLICIES: Checks accepted.

New York Tea Company has been peddling coffee, tea and spices for over a century. Their Cash & Carry store is packed with party food. In fact, many caterers shop here. Some of the best value items are a five-pound tray of frozen lasagne for $8.12, a ten-pound case of hors d'oeuvre meatballs (320 of them) without the sauce for $12.55. Five-ounce Chicken Kievs cost $33.47 for a case of 24 (that's $1.39 each). Fresh roasted coffee, the house blend, is $2.64 a pound; decaffeinated is $3.41 a pound. And, of course, they have tea and spices—a one pound bag of cinnamon is $2.09.

The food quality is excellent. If you entertain a lot, you're in for some delectable discoveries. Some families shop here together and split the cases. The items are frozen with a quick-freeze method that prevents icing and allows portions to be repacked in smaller portions.

New York Tea also has all the paper goods to go with the treats. You'll get 125 plates for $7.40 and good quality plastic silverware (100 knives, forks, or spoons) for $2.45. Sign their mailing list and watch for notices of special holiday sales.

CAPTAIN KEN'S FIREHOUSE BEANS

344 S. Robert St.
St. Paul
PHONE: 298-0071
HOURS: Mon.-Fri., 8 a.m.-5 p.m.; Sat., 8 a.m.-noon.
POLICIES: Checks accepted.

Next time you're feeding a bunch Dallas-style, rustle up the chili or beans at Captain Ken's. You'll get up to 50% off on beans purchased in 6-pound to 48-pound tins. You can order fresh or frozen, but give them a call first. An 8 1/2-pound bag of chili is $11.50, a 6-pound tin of beans is $5.25.

G & L SWISS FOODS

1124 Hwy. 13 E.
Burnsville
PHONE: 894-4530
HOURS: Mon.-Fri., 8:30 a.m.-5 p.m.
POLICIES: Checks accepted; discounts to churches and groups

If real men really don't eat quiche, they can always try the cheesecake or soup. Your best deal here is on the imperfects, but if there are none in stock the day you're there, G & L will sell you perfects at the imperfect (actually, the most perfect!) price. A 16-slice imperfect cheesecake is about $6.00, 4-inch quiche is $.80 (they do have bigger sizes). Select from broccoli and spinach, seafood, or the old standby, quiche Lorraine.

Wednesday is an even bigger bargain day.

NELSON CHEESE FACTORY

1562 Como Ave.
St. Paul
PHONE: 647-1288
HOURS: Mon.-Sat., 10 a.m.-7 p.m.; Sun. 10 a.m.-6 p.m.
POLICIES: Checks accepted.

This is a great place for cheese. As one bargain hunter put it, "The cheese is very fresh and on some items they have the best prices I've found anywhere in town." Two big sellers are the Montery Jack at $1.59 a pound or the Wisconsin Cheddar at $1.69 a pound. Call them and they will send you a complete price list.

They also sell party trays, gift boxes, big tasty deli sandwiches. One of the items I love is the wooden cheese boxes, all sizes for $3.99 each. These are great for crafts. I've even dyed mine with Rit in pastel colors and put scarves and jewelry inside. They would also make nice stenciled gift boxes.

Produce

MINNEAPOLIS FARMERS' MARKET

East Lyndale Ave. North,
between Glenwood Ave. & Olson Memorial Hwy.
PHONE: 333-1718
HOURS: Mon.-Sat. 5:30 a.m.-1 p.m.; Sun. 8 a.m.-2 p.m.; April to December

See description under St. Paul Farmers' Market.

ST. PAUL FARMERS' MARKET

Downtown St. Paul between
Fifth & Wall St.
PHONE: 227-8101 (Phone to get information about other smaller markets around St. Paul.)
HOURS: Sat. 6 a.m.-1 p.m.; Sun. 9 a.m.-1 p.m.; May 1st to October 31st; weeknight hours added mid-July to October; in December a Christmas tree lot.

Both these markets and the outlying ones in St. Paul beat grocery shopping any day. They are entertaining and the farm-fresh produce can be 25% down from supermarket prices. At the Minneapolis and St. Paul Markets you'll also find eggs, chickens, turkeys, trout, honey, maple syrup, and plants or cut flowers. Best selection and prices are always during the peak of a growing season. At the St. Paul Market you can pick up a brochure with information about the peaks.

LAFAYETTE PRODUCE MARKET

524 Lafayette
St. Paul
PHONE: 228-9351
HOURS: Mon.-Fri., 8 a.m.-5:30 p.m.; Sat., 7 a.m.-5 p.m., year round.
POLICIES: Checks accepted.

This small market has a real down-home atmosphere. The prices on produce overstocks and closeouts are appealing, and they also carry new fresh items which are competitive with most places in town. Call first to comparison shop before making the trip. Last time I shopped there, strawberries were $.89 a quart, watermelon was $.15 a pound, and baking bananas were $.10 a pound. They stock cheese, eggs, butter, and you'll save some pennies on a gallon of milk.

EISENBERG FRUIT CO.

170 E. Tenth St.
Downtown St. Paul
PHONE: 227-0634
HOURS: Mon.-Fri., 8 a.m.-6 p.m.; Sat., 7 a.m.-5 p.m.
POLICIES: Checks accepted.

Eisenberg stocks plenty of produce, mostly overstocks, distressed goods, and closeouts. Some prices can be so close to your supermarket's that it may not be worth the trip. But when they have a large overstock the price will be low.

Call ahead first and see what's available—supply will fluctuate, but bananas always seem to abound.

Salvage Foods

STEVE'S WAREHOUSE SALVAGE

651 S. Smith
St. Paul
PHONE: 224-8855
HOURS: Mon.-Wed., 8 a.m.-6 p.m.; Thurs.-Fri., 8 a.m.-8 p.m.; Sat., 8 a.m.-6 p.m.
POLICIES: Checks accepted.

Steve's is a fun, crazy place to shop. It's loaded with damaged canned goods, crushed cereal boxes—all kinds of overstocks, closeouts and warehouse damaged items. The supply varies, but owner Steve Godes says you'll always find a good deal on canned vegetables (one-pound cans of corn sell at 3 for $.89). Prices are low; with probing you'll find some stuff you need. A few enterprising neighborhood kids buy up the candy here and turn it into playground profits.

If it's dented cans you're worried about, let me give you a tip. Make sure there are no sharp dents on the top or bottom *rims* of cans, and watch for bulges. Rest assured, however, that all damaged packages are checked by an inspector before they get sold to the public.

HELLER'S SALVAGE FOOD MARKET

1521 E. Franklin Ave.
Minneapolis
PHONE: 870-9661
HOURS: Mon.-Wed., 9 a.m.-7 p.m.; Thurs.-Fri., 9 a.m.-8 p.m.; Sat., 9 a.m.-6 p.m.; Sun., 10 a.m.-4 p.m.
POLICIES: Checks accepted.

If you're still in pursuit of cheap canned goods, check out Heller's. They maintain one long aisle of dented cans, selling them all at four for $1.00. The rest of the store has basic grocery items; some are closeouts and overstocks, but all are marked reasonably. If the larder is low, it may be worth the trip.

Nuts and Sweets

S. R. CO.

1423 Lowry Ave. N.
Minneapolis
PHONE: 522-3407
HOURS: Mon.-Fri., 10 a.m.-2 p.m.; November 1-December 31, 9 a.m.-2 p.m. Call about special summer hours.
POLICIES: Checks accepted.

S. R. Co. specializes in roasting and selling nuts. A one-pound bag of roasted salted peanuts is $1.25; large, whole cashews are $5.65; and Deluxe Mixed Nuts are $5.25. You can buy your nut pieces for baking here or order gift tins (order two days ahead—a one-pound tin is $6.50). But this place is also soup to nuts. They have a salvage grocery section, plus hardware and cleaning supplies. The nuts you can rely on; the salvage inventory changes all the time.

NATIONAL NUT COMPANY

414 Third Ave. N.
Downtown Minneapolis
PHONE: 333-6496
HOURS: Mon.-Fri., 8 a.m.-4:30 p.m.

Hwy. 12 & Willow Dr.
Long Lake
PHONE: 475-2067
HOURS: Mon.-Fri., noon to 9 p.m.; Sat., 9 a.m.-9 p.m.; Sun., noon-6 p.m.

1123 Riverwood Dr.
Burnsville
(between Cliff Rd. & Hwy. 13, 1 block W. of Burnsville Post Office)
PHONE: 890-0676
HOURS: Mon.-Fri., 9 a.m.-3:30 p.m.

POLICIES: Checks accepted.

All the nuts hang out here. The prices are very competitive with S. R. Co. Roasted Fancy Deluxe Mix at $5.25 a pound, super large whole cashews at $5.95 a pound, and a pound of Spanish peanuts at $1.50. Health nuts will find good prices on dried fruit, yogurt and carob-coated items, and all the assorted trail mixes.

MIDWEST NORTHERN NUT CO.

3105 Columbia Ave. N.E.
Minneapolis
PHONE: 781-6596
HOURS: Mon.-Fri., 8 a.m.-5 p.m.; Sat., 8 a.m.-1 p.m.
POLICIES: Checks accepted.

By now it is pretty obvious that you should never have to pay full retail prices for nuts again. Roasted Spanish peanuts are $1.45 a pound, Deluxe Fancy mix $6.00 a pound.

During the holiday season, all these stores are hopping.

ABDALLAH CANDIES MFG.

12220 12th Ave. S.
Burnsville
PHONE: 890-4770
HOURS: Mon.-Fri., 8 a.m.-5 p.m.; Sat., 9 a.m.-1 p.m.

3805 Cedar Ave.
Minneapolis
PHONE: 722-1312
HOURS: Tues.-Fri., 10 a.m.-4:30 p.m.; Sat., 10 a.m.-2 p.m.

POLICIES: Checks accepted.

Chocolate lovers will blissfully overlook the imperfections in the candy at $3.25 a pound, and if they buy five pounds, the savings are even greater. Abdallah also sells perfect chocolates and at the Burnsville store, there is a small gift shop.

Watch for the fudge sale the first two weeks in November.

GOGGINS CANDY CO.

902 S. Fourth St.
Stillwater
PHONE: 439-1516
HOURS: Mon.-Fri., 9 a.m.-9 p.m.; Sat., 8 a.m.-noon
POLICIES: Checks accepted.

On your next outing to Stillwater, stop at Goggins and get up to 50% off on candy bar specials. Other store specials are frequently marked down 25%.

JACOB SCHMIDT BREWERY (A DIVISION OF G. HEILEMAN BREWING CO.)

882 W. Seventh St.
St. Paul
PHONE: 228-9173
HOURS: Free tours Mon.-Fri., 10 a.m., 2 p.m., and 3 p.m.
POLICIES: Large groups should call for tour reservations; must wear hard-toe shoes—no open toes or sandals.

At just about any time of the day or night you'll see someone armed with containers filling them up with the free well water in front of the Schmidt Brewery. You can stop here 24 hours a day, seven days a week. Often there's a line. But the water is so pure—it comes from a *deep* 1130-foot well. Be sure to bring your own containers.

Schmidt's gives free tours of the brewery three times a day during the week, and they always let in stragglers. Plus you'll get a couple of free beers!

STROH'S BREWERY

707 E. Minnehaha
St. Paul
(between Payne Ave. & Arcade St.)
PHONE: 778-3100
HOURS: Free tours Mon.-Fri. from 1 p.m.-4 p.m.
POLICIES: Large groups must make reservations.

Bring your own containers and fill up with Stroh's free artesian well water, which is so pure, it's worth the trip. You can stock up as much as you want, 24 hours a day, seven days a week. The well is located outside, near the parking lot.

If you arrive between 1 p.m. and 4 p.m., Monday through Friday, you can join one of their free tours and sample some beer.

SURDYK'S LIQUOR STORE

303 E. Hennepin Ave.
Minneapolis
PHONE: 379-9757
HOURS: Mon.-Thurs., 8 a.m.-8 p.m.; Fri.-Sat., 8 a.m.-10 p.m.
POLICIES: Checks accepted.

Surdyk's boasts the lowest liquor prices in town for a store of their size, and they are not just blowing hot air. This is a discount liquor store the size of a supermarket, one with a lot of savings as well as class. They sell lots of spirits and every imported beer manufactured. The staff includes five wine and three liquor consultants. So if you're giving a party and need help, all you need to do is ask.

In the cheese and gourmet shop you'll see many unusual and hard-to-find imports. During the winter months you'll even find fresh truffles.

Fridays and Saturdays are crowded in the store, so if you can, go early in the week. You can also call Surdyk's and get on their mailing list to peruse their extensive wine catalog.

In May they have a special beer sale that coincides with the opening of the fishing season.

Party Goods

LITIN PAPER CO.

701 N. Washington
Minneapolis
PHONE: 333-4331
HOURS: Mon.-Fri., 8 a.m.-5 p.m.; Sat., 9 a.m.-2 p.m.

Litin has a huge selection of disposable entertainment supplies. The stock is high grade with high quality name brand items (Solo, Georgia Pacific, Hoffmaster Paper) sold at wholesale prices. This is a fun, family-owned store and everyone is more than helpful. But it is not the type of place you just run into and buy a package of napkins. Plan to spend some time. It is a huge general store atmosphere and on your first visit, you'll want to look and look.

When you walk in the front door, you're met with cases of paper towels and toilet paper, which give way to typing paper, notebooks, legal pads and scratch paper. If you're planning a party, just keep walking toward the back until you come across tables and tables of paper plates, cups (all different sizes), napkins, and paper tablecloths. The plastic silverware is located in front by the cash registers. You're bound to find everything you need to set your table, all under this warehouse roof. The stock changes to fit the holiday (Christmas, Easter, Valentine's Day, etc.), but keep this place in mind, as well, if you're planning a wedding.

ACADIAN CANDLES, INC.

689 N. Dale St.
St. Paul
PHONE: 227-7465
HOURS: Mon.-Fri., 9:30 a.m.-4:30 p.m. (will extend to Saturday hours during Christmas season).
POLICIES: Credit cards—Master, VISA and Shoppers; returns: exchange only.

Acadian manufactures candles for retail stores, but you will find their factory outlet a blessing to your budget. This store is stocked with their factory seconds; often the only problem is uneven color on the candle. You can put a glow on the party table and save at least 50% off the regular retail price of candles. Candle holders and accessories are available at regular retail prices.

CHAPTER 14

MISCELLANEOUS

In writing this guide book I kept running into square peg stores and bargains that wouldn't fit the round holes of the chapters. Some stores just don't fit a category neatly. Other categories won't fill a chapter. But bargains do come in an abundant variety. So this section gathers up all the square pegs and makes them into a category of their own—good old miscellaneous.

Cars

JOHN PETERSON MOTORS

114 N. Lakeshore Dr.
Lake City
(65 miles south of the Twin Cities)
PHONE: Toll free number for the Twin Cities 1-800-292-9261; toll free number for Rochester area 1-800-288-1864; outlying areas 1-612-345-3366
HOURS: Mon.-Thurs., 9 a.m.-9 p.m.; Fri.-Sat., 9 a.m.-6 p.m.
POLICIES: Financing available; take used car trade-ins, will honor all new car warranties; full deposit refunds on new car orders if the car has not gone into production at time of order cancellation, full deposit refund when new car is delivered to the dealer if defective or dealer makes ordering mistake; mechanical repair service available; VISA, Master, certified checks and bank cashier checks accepted for repair charges; all car protection services offered (rustproofing, extended warranties).

Located 65 miles south of the Twin Cities, there is a car dealership that will sell you a new General Motors car or truck for just $49 over the dealer's invoice. That's a heck of a deal, especially when you consider that anywhere you shop in the Twin Cities area you will pay from $150 to $1,000 over the dealer's invoice. So what's the catch? Of course there is one, but it just may be one that you can live with. There are some new GM cars that John Peterson may not be able to order. He can't get GMC trucks. Buick and Oldsmobile have placed some limitations on his ordering, but Chevrolets and Pontiacs are no problem. Still, if you have a particular make and style in mind, just give John a call and he will let you know right away if he can order the car you want.

This $49-over-dealer-invoice price does not include state and local taxes or license and filing fees. But if General Motors offers a rebate or incentive program after you've ordered your car, and it comes to a better price than John Peterson's, you'll be given the benefit of the rebate. He also sells used cars, and you can bring your old car in for trade.

If you're just naturally suspicious of car dealers, it may ease your mind a little to know that John Peterson has been around the car business all his life. His father owned Downtown Chevytown in Minneapolis and his grandfather before that owned a car dealership.

John recommends ordering next year's model in June, July, or August for fall or winter delivery. And, he warns, don't buy a leftover model unless you can purchase it for an unbelievably low price, because the depreciation on a new car is so great the first year.

Many Twin Cities car bargain hunters also recommend buying a new car through Jack L. Rubenstein (see p. 108).

If you abide by the old saying that you get the best service on your new car from the dealer you bought it from, you may find it a drag driving down to Lake City to get your car checked or fixed. However, if you don't care about getting service from your dealer, remember that it is stated in all General Motors franchise dealers' contracts that GM new vehicle warranties are good for servicing by any authorized dealer.

Outdoor Gear, Tools, and Equipment

BLACK & DECKER (U.S.) INC.

9712 Garfield Ave.
Bloomington
PHONE: 884-9191
HOURS: Mon.-Fri., 8 a.m.-5 p.m.; Sat., 9 a.m.-4 p.m.
POLICIES: Credit cards—Master and VISA; checks accepted.

You'll get reconditioned power tools here at a real savings. They also sell blemished and discontinued Black & Decker tools. Pick up a respectable brand name tool here for a Christmas present, or select blue-ribbon gardening gear. All warranties apply.

If you already own Black & Decker tools, you may want to use their repair service. If you have a discontinued tool, you may still be able to get parts here. They backlog for about 7 to 20 years. You'll pay wholesale prices for the parts.

OTT'S DISTRIBUTING

1919 Central Ave. N.E.
Minneapolis
PHONE: 788-7014
HOURS: Mon.-Fri., 9 a.m.-5:30 p.m.; Sat., 9 a.m.-2 p.m.
POLICIES: Local checks only; lay-by 2 weeks to 30 days; no returns.

Ott's is a small liquidation store, but Gil Ott, the owner, has many private leads for buying closeouts on automotive accessories. So at his shop, you'll get good deals on seat covers (they range from $3.49 to $9.95), floor mats, oil, filters, antifreeze and more. He also carries general merchandise.

Everything in the store is priced 30% to 50% below regular retail. But as it often happens with liquidated items, you'll find a catch. Gil had some beautiful Rafelli golf shirts one day, selling for $4.95. I grabbed them fast, then noticed when I looked closely at the symbol embroidered on the shirts that they had been customized by a local realty company. But that first moment of discovery felt great.

SMALL ENGINE CITY

2612 Lyndale Ave.
Minneapolis
PHONE: 872-4288
HOURS: Mon. & Thurs., 9 a.m.-8 p.m.; Tues.-Wed., Fri., 9 a.m.-6 p.m.; Sat., 9 a.m.-5 p.m.
POLICIES: Checks accepted.

You can expect good discounts on new power mowers here, but even better ones on the used ones, and there's a nice large selection. Owner Warren Jensen won't let anyone get away with a bad mower. If there's a problem, you'll get your money back. Some of the remanufactured mowers even have warranties.

ACME ELECTRONICS

224 Washington Ave. N.
Minneapolis
PHONE: 338-4754
HOURS: Mon.-Fri., 8 a.m.-6 p.m.; Sat., 9 a.m.-5 p.m.
POLICIES: Credit cards—Master and VISA; checks accepted; returns: policy varies with type of product purchased.

Don't even come near this place unless you have some do-it-yourself electrical wiring talent. This store is great for the hobbyist, because the electronic parts are discounted. One of the most popular bargains awaits anyone who wants to build a set of stereo speakers. They'll give you a free set of speaker plans to go with the parts.

3M SURPLUS

1925 Case
St. Paul
PHONE: 733-1110
HOURS: Mon.-Fri., 9 a.m.-3 p.m.
POLICIES: Checks accepted; returns: exchange only.

This unusual place is where the 3M Company liquidates its electronic equipment and office furniture, all at a tremendous savings. You won't find any 3M products here. But if you're looking for a typewriter or computer disks, this is a good place to keep a constant eye on.

INSTANT OFFICE FURNITURE

119 N. Ninth St.
Minneapolis
PHONE: 333-2505
HOURS: Mon.-Fri., 8 a.m.-5 p.m.; Sat., 10 a.m.-3 p.m.
POLICIES: Credit cards—Master and VISA; checks accepted

Come here for a large selection of good quality used office furniture. Last time one shopper was here, he found office stock from the Burlington Northern Railroad. A 5-drawer file cabinet (made with heavy metal) was selling for about $120.

REI CO-OP

35W & 98th St.
Bloomington
PHONE: 884-4315
HOURS: Mon.-Fri., 10 a.m.-9 p.m.; Sat., 9:30 a.m.-5 p.m.; Sun., noon-5 p.m.
POLICIES: Credit cards—Master and VISA; checks accepted; lay-by: 30 days; returns: satisfaction guaranteed.

If you're the outdoorsy type, REI is worth checking out. A mere $5.00 will get you a lifetime membership in this co-op. REI has outdoor sporting equipment: skis; backpacking, hiking, and climbing gear—even bicycles. And, of course, clothes to fit the action for men, women, and children. You will get four free mail order catalogs a year, but you can also go directly to the Bloomington store to shop. Free clinics are set up for skiers, hikers, climbers, etc., in season.

You'll see competitive prices on rugged brand names, but if you order REI's Peak Value label goods, you'll save more. For example, if a Woolrich chamois shirt sells for $24.95, the Peak Value shirt of the same quality will sell for $17.95.

The bonus for joining this co-op is that at the end of the year, *you will get a check mailed to you!* The size of the check is based on how big REI's profits were and how much you spent on gear.

BULLSEYE GOLF CENTER

1658 Snelling Ave.
Falcon Heights
PHONE: 647-0233

8650 Lyndale Ave. S.
Bloomington
PHONE: 884-8206

5313 Excelsior Blvd.
St. Louis Park
PHONE: 926-1240

HOURS: Spring & Summer: Mon.-Fri., 9 a.m.-9 p.m.; Sat., 9 a.m.-6 p.m.; Sun., 11 a.m.-6 p.m.; Winter hours: Mon.-Fri., 10 a.m.-6 p.m.; Sat., 9 a.m.-6 p.m.; Spring & Summer hours are also in effect from the Friday after Thanksgiving until Christmas.
POLICIES: Credit cards—VISA, Master, American Express and Shoppers; checks accepted; lay-by: 90 days; returns: for exchange only.

Bullseye has good discounts (20% to 40% below suggested retail) on golf clothes, clubs, shoes, and accessories. The name brands are tops: Sounder, AMF Ben Hogan, Ping, PGA, Ram, Wilson. And half their stock of golf club sets is reduced 50%. They will match or beat any local competitor's prices. No irregulars are sold here except the X-Out golf balls. These are merely imperfectly stamped on the package or the paint-job is off on the balls. The confident golfer can buy these by the dozen for $8.99 to $9.99.

Watch for a clearance sale in August and March each year. A new branch should be opening soon in Fridley.

PRO GOLF DISCOUNT

617 W. 98th St.
Bloomington
PHONE: 881-0310

6249 N.E. Hwy. 65
Fridley
PHONE: 574-1262

HOURS: Spring & Summer: Mon.-Fri., 10 a.m.-8 p.m.; Sat., 10 a.m.-5 p.m.; Sun., noon-5 p.m.; Winter: Mon.-Fri., 10 a.m.-6 p.m.; Sat., 10 a.m.-5 p.m.; inquire about Christmas shopping hours.
POLICIES: Credit cards—Master, VISA, American Express and Shoppers; checks accepted; lay-by: 90 days; returns: flexible.

Put yourself on the green with X-Out golf balls from Pro Golf for $6.99 to $8.99 a dozen. Clothes, golf clubs, bags, shoes, and all the accessories are sold at 20% to 40% below retail prices. Name brands include Wilson, Lynx, MacGregor, Delta, Spaulding, and Titleist.

Toys

ANIMAL FAIR FACTORY OUTLET STORE

581 W. 78th St.
Chanhassen
PHONE: 934-0444
HOURS: Mon.-Fri., 9 a.m.-4:30 p.m.; Sat., 9 a.m.-1 p.m.
POLICIES: Checks accepted.

Animal Fair makes teddy bears, elephants—really a whole zoo of cuddly stuffed animals. At this outlet store they sell the discontinued styles. Some of the items are imported. But you're sure to find some child a good friend at a 60% discount, and sometimes more.

TRADER JACK'S

615 N. Third St.
Minneapolis
PHONE: 339-1998
HOURS: Mon.-Fri., 9 a.m.-5 p.m.
POLICIES: Credit cards—VISA and Master; checks accepted.

Trader Jack's is a liquidation store, so you'll find housewares, sporting goods, odds and ends, and a fairly consistent stock of toys. But from the Friday after Thanksgiving until Christmas Eve, this place turns into a wonderland. It is packed with toys, gift wrapping, games, and many gift items. Be a good comparison shopper and know your Target and K-Mart prices before you get here.

At any time during the year it is best to call ahead and see if they have what you're looking for.

A-Z WHOLESALE

2617 E. Franklin Ave.
Minneapolis
PHONE: 338-7759
HOURS: Mon.-Fri., 9 a.m.-6:30 p.m.; Sat., 9 a.m.-7 p.m.

POLICIES: Credit cards—VISA and Master; checks accepted.

This funny little toy store is piled with imported toys that "do something." Many are battery operated (you're encouraged to play). When I shopped there last, there was a made-in-China U.S. helicopter that not only had a whirring propeller, complete with sound effects, but then a cargo hold opened and an Army jeep was lowered out of the back. A-Z's price was $10.95.

This spot is loved not only by kids, but by adults, too. Starting in October, A-Z is well stocked for Christmas shoppers. The prices are great. An atomic Robot is $10.95, space guns (with all that noise) $3.95, and police cars with three sirens and a microphone $12.95. Crying and laughing baby dolls go for $10.95.

Really Miscellaneous Goods and Services

FITNESS WORKS

PHONE: 474-1549 or 544-5243
POLICIES: Call for a free brochure and information. Various sessions held throughout the year at Lyman Lodge in Minnetonka; for women only.

The cost might seem like a fat price to some: $385 for 5 days of sweat. But it includes meals; lodging; exercise classes; and seminars on health, beauty and fitness. I guess it depends on how much your shape is worth. Women from 20 years to 75 years have participated in this program. The bargain here is in the eye of the beholder—perhaps the one staring back at you in the mirror. By comparison to other health and fitness spa costs, Fitness Works wins the race.

50% OFF STORE

8942 Hwy. 7
St. Louis Park
(Next to Rainbow Foods)
PHONE: 935-2399
HOURS: Mon.-Fri., 10 a.m.-9 p.m.; Sat., 10 a.m.-6 p.m.; Sun., noon-6 p.m.

POLICIES: Credit cards—Master and VISA; checks accepted; returns: exchange only.

Kids love this place—it really has that old-time dimestore atmosphere. Most of the items are imports...they have quite a variety of toys, stickers, posters, candles, jewelry, tape, tools, ashtrays, magazine racks, and always, an assortment of stationery and greeting cards. Everything is liquidations, closeouts or overstocks, but nothing is damaged. You'll save at least 50% (of course), and sometimes more.

MENDOTA HEIGHTS ANIMAL HOSPITAL

1938 Dodd Rd.
Mendota Heights
PHONE: 454-3558
HOURS: By appointment, Mon.-Fri., 8 a.m.-5 p.m.;
other hours by arrangement.
POLICIES: Cash only.

This animal hospital specializes in spaying and neutering only. They are one of the clinics referred by Zero Pet Population Growth for quality work and low prices. For this work, their prices are some of the best in town. To spay a female cat, the cost is $29.50; a male cat is $17.50. To neuter any weight male dog the cost is $23.50, and to spay a female dog, it is $45.

TENNANT CO.

701 N. Lilac Dr.
Golden Valley
(Drive through the Tennant Company parking lot
to the back fence at Zane Avenue)
PHONE: 540-1200
HOURS: Anytime.
POLICIES: Take what you need.

You're settling for scrap wood, but the price is unbeatable—it's *free*. The Tennant Company breaks up pallets and piles the free wood near the fence in back of the company parking lot on Zane Avenue. The size of the woodpile varies from day to day. It's not first quality wood, but it is great for fireplace kindling and craft projects.

HORST INTERNATIONAL EDUCATION CENTER FOR COSMETOLOGY

1900 LaSalle Ave.
Minneapolis
PHONE: 871-3444
HOURS: Tues.-Sat., 8:30 a.m.-5 p.m.
POLICIES: Cash only for haircuts and services; checks accepted on hair care products. Appointments recommended.

Pamper yourself with a $3.50 pedicure, a $6.50 facial or haircut, or an $18 perm. All the services are performed by students.

PICTURE FRAME SUPPLY CO.

2828 University Ave.
Minneapolis
PHONE: 379-0552
HOURS: Mon.-Fri., 10 a.m.-6 p.m.; Sat., 10 a.m.-5 p.m.
POLICIES: Credit cards—VISA and Master; checks accepted.

This store is geared to people who enjoy framing art for themselves. Everything is pre-cut for you, and the staff leads you through the simple process. You'll save up to 50%.

UNIVERSITY OF MINNESOTA DENTAL CLINICS

School of Dentistry
515 Delaware St. S.E.
Minneapolis
PHONE: Adult Clinic, 373-3277;
Children's Clinic, 373-3262
HOURS: Mon.-Fri., 9 a.m.-4 p.m. for phoning; clinic hours vary.
POLICIES: Checks and dental insurance plans accepted.

You can save 30% to 50% compared to regular dental rates by going to this clinic. You'll be worked on by third- and fourth-year dental students, but there's a staff dentist watching over at all times. Appointments are necessary.

If you've never been here before, you'll have to get a screening checkup first. The cost is $27, including x-rays. Children must have a screening checkup first, for $9.00. This does not include x-rays.

INDEX

A

B

N

O

P

T